MW00816575

BISON BOOKS

Mrs. Cook and the Klan

Booze, Bloodshed, and Bigotry in America's Heartland

Tom Chorneau

University of Nebraska Press
Lincoln

© 2024 by the Board of Regents of the University of Nebraska. All rights reserved.
Manufactured in the United States of America.

The University of Nebraska Press is part of a land-grant institution with campuses and programs on the past, present, and future homelands of the Pawnee, Ponca, Otoe-Missouria, Omaha, Dakota, Lakota, Kaw, Cheyenne, and Arapaho Peoples, as well as those of the relocated Ho-Chunk, Sac and Fox, and Iowa Peoples.

♾

Library of Congress Control Number: 2024038710

Set in ITC New Baskerville by A. Shahan.

For Leo, Margot, Peter, and a
shortstop to be named later

Contents

Illustrations

Acknowledgments

No one succeeds at much of anything without the help of others, and I have been blessed with a long list of people who have taken time away from other duties and interests to assist me. At the top of that list are my brother Peter and my good friend Paul Ingalls. Both men have spent countless hours providing encouragement, line-by-line guidance, and whiskey-laced wisdom all to improve my work. Thank you. And I need to also recognize their wives, who allowed them that time to perform those miracles on my behalf: to my sister-in-law Nancy and Pam Ingalls.

Chris Mazzia, Jim and Laura Wasserman, Linda Rapattoni, and John Rofe have all spent too much time reading and rereading something I have written. Each has gently provided insight, which I always tried to follow.

My daughters, Charlotte and Alice, and their families need to be acknowledged, if only for listening to me ramble on about this part of the book or another.

I want to thank Hang Nguyen of the State Historical Society of Iowa for her research and assistance. I very much want to thank Leo Landis, curator of the State Historical Society of Iowa, who spent part of the summer editing my manuscript with honesty and thoroughness. Thanks to Christy Webb for her expertise in photo editing, and Anne and Rachel Leedom for marketing and web support.

That leaves W. Clark Whitehorn, executive editor at Bison Books and the University of Nebraska Press. Thank you, sir, for believing in this book and shepherding it along.

Introduction

THE MURDER

Over Labor Day weekend in September 1925, two big stories made national news: the crash of the U.S. Navy's first military dirigible in Ohio, which killed fourteen; and the kidnapping of the six-year-old daughter of a wealthy New Jersey banker.[1] A third story appeared on the front page of the *New York Times* just as the city was getting back to work. It carried an unsettling headline: "Woman Dry Worker Murdered in Iowa."

The term *dry worker* made more sense in 1925 than today. The country was five years into the grand prohibition experiment. Someone who was *dry* was opposed to drinking. On the opposite side were the *wets*, who were either unabashed drinkers or tolerant of those who were. As a reader of the *New York Times* in 1925, you were almost certainly wet. Thus, the story spoke to you, and you read.

The victim was the fifty-one-year-old leader of the Woman's Christian Temperance Union in a stand-still town about halfway between Cedar Rapids and Waterloo, Iowa, on the banks of the Cedar River. Her name was Myrtle Underwood Cook, and she was shot once, right through the heart. Authorities were calling it an assassination—at least according to the *Times*. The paper breathlessly reported that gangsters from Chicago were responsible.

"Vinton has long been known as one of the wettest spots in Eastern Iowa," the *Times* said of the town where the murder took place. "It is halfway between Chicago and Omaha and is said to be used as a cache for alcohol run from Chicago and kept there until the Western rum-runners can get it."

The victim's home was adjacent to the Rock Island Railway station, and her parlor window had a clear view of the platform and the seedy café where the illicit liquor trade operated. The *Times* noted that Cook had been instrumental in the prosecution of bootleggers several times in recent months and implied she had been killed because of her activism.[2] "A prohibition official said tonight that the assassination had all the earmarks of a Chicago gunman's work," the *Times* reported. "And he believes that whoever sponsored the crime imported a Chicago gunman to do it."[3]

The mention of Chicago was not incidental. The bloody beer wars had become daily fodder for New York's ravenous news industry. Chicago crime boss Dion O'Banion had been gunned down in his North Side flower shop a year before. An unsuccessful reprisal hit on Johnny Torrio, leader of the South Side gang, took place a few weeks later, which led Torrio to hand the reins over to his top lieutenant, Al Capone, in early 1925.

The Cook murder appeared to be an escalation of Chicago lawlessness, and like the *Times* editor who flagged the story for page one the moment he ripped it off the wire, you too wanted more.

Two days later, you got more. This time it was Myrtle Cook's funeral, made noteworthy by the sudden appearance of two dozen members of the Ku Klux Klan. In full regalia, they assembled at the town square in advance of the service. Then, when the time came, they escorted the hearse from the undertaker to the church and then from the church to the cemetery. Myrtle Cook was one of theirs.

"The fiery cross of the Klan is burning tonight on the grave of Mrs. Myrtle Cook, where this afternoon the hooded order laid her to rest after one of the most dramatic funerals this town ever witnessed," read the lead of the *Times*'s second-day story.[4]

The Klan added another layer of curiosity, and you watched the paper for further coverage. The *Times* stayed with the story for only another week or so, long enough to report that authorities had floundered in their efforts to identify the killer. Within another month the case died out, even in Iowa, when investigators fingered the husband and the case became just another murder.

But it wasn't the husband, and after nearly a hundred years, the identity of the real killer remained unknown. Until now.

THE FLOOD

Winter storms came from the northwest out of Canada and the Dakotas in early December 2007. Ice and freezing rain spread across much of central Iowa, downing power lines and snarling traffic. Almost five thousand homes lost electricity in Iowa City and Coralville, many for more than a day.[5]

Another big storm hit on December 13, causing more outages in Cedar Rapids as tree limbs and power lines became coated with ice a half-inch thick.[6] There was a lull until Christmas, when heavy weather returned: four inches of snow fell in Des Moines on the twenty-fourth, six inches in Linn County, and ten more in Iowa's northeast corner.[7] January was cold but dry. Cities hit hard by the ice storms of December petitioned state and federal agencies for disaster aid. There was some optimism that the worst of the winter was behind them.[8]

It was not.

Over the weekend of February 2 more than a foot of snow fell in and around Des Moines. By Wednesday of that week there came another foot. Iowa City got eight inches, followed by wet sleet and rain. The next morning, a dense fog rose and froze among the tree limbs, casting an eerie white glow that resembled the sprouts of spring foliage.[9] Before February ended, measurable snowfall had fallen somewhere in Iowa on all but eight days.

State authorities viewed the historic snowpack with growing alarm. The Upper Mississippi River basin, which stretches across much of central and eastern Iowa, is always prone to spring floods, even after modest winters. The drifts of 2008 were mountainous—not just in Iowa but up-valley in Minnesota and Wisconsin too. A sudden spring thaw would unleash a tide of epic proportions.

And that's exactly what happened.

Warm rain, sometimes heavy, beat down day after day between May 29 and June 12. Near the town of Austin in southern Minnesota, where the headwaters of the Cedar River collect, there was an almost continuous downpour for twenty-four hours, ending Sunday morning, June 8. Rain gauges recorded 5.64 inches over that period. During the night of June 9, the Cedar River rose more than eleven feet at Charles City, Iowa, about fifty miles south of Austin.[10] At Waterloo, another hundred miles further south, the river flowed nearly 50 percent higher than had ever been recorded.[11]

Vinton, where Myrtle Cook had been murdered more than eighty years before, was 140 miles south of Austin. The people of Vinton were keeping a wary eye on the rising Cedar. The center of town was low and flat, and there were no natural or man-made barriers to stem the surging waters. The rain poured down relentlessly all day Monday, June 9. Police closed the highway to Cedar Rapids at nightfall, just after a fleet of big trucks from the Iowa National Guard arrived to help with sandbagging and evacuations. By Wednesday the skies had cleared, but the Cedar had yet to crest. It was expected to peak in the afternoon at twenty feet—four feet higher than any previous recording.

The Benton County supervisors held an emergency meeting that morning in the parking lot of the Sheriff's Department, which was just a block from the river. Before the supervisors could finish, word arrived that the drains in the basement of the town's historic courthouse were backing up and water was starting to seep in. Workers were dispatched to try to seal the drains and isolate, if they could, the computer servers. The file cabinets and the boxes of court documents piled in stacks on the floor of the basement became the next priority. Sheriff's deputies, judges, attorneys, and court staff formed a line and began passing out as many of the most critical records as possible. However, there were not enough hands to carry all the documents to safety, and some were left behind.[12]

Among the items believed lost in the flood of 2008 were all the official records related to the murder of Myrtle Cook. Everything. The autopsy report. The transcripts of the coroner's inquest. The investigator's files. The prosecutor's notes. Official correspondence. The arrest records.

All of them were gone.

"Over the years, we've been asked about this case," said David Thompson, Benton County Attorney from 1999 to 2022. "And we just don't know what happened. I've asked the sheriff. I've looked around at the courthouse. All I can say is, we don't have anything. It could have been something that was lost because of the flood. We just don't know."[13]

THE STORY

There is an old newspaper adage used to describe the dilemma a reporter faces when tantalized by a string of intriguing facts that don't seem to lead anywhere: *What do you say in the second graph?* The Cook murder would have been such a story. Any editor with a lick of sense would have waved it off with a hiss. *Pass. What else are you working on?*

After more than thirty years in the business, I'm reminded that there are at least two other newspaper truisms: *Reporters believe; editors challenge.* And: *Editors are not always right.*

Sometimes you keep kicking a story. You walk around it, looking for a crevasse, enough space to get a hand or foothold. You keep digging. You keep believing.

And sometimes you get rewarded. It may not be the story that you thought you would be writing, but it is a story nonetheless. And sometimes it turns out to be a really good story.

That is what happened here. Even without a full investigative record, history still needs to explain what happened to Myrtle Cook. What was it that brought a street-hardened assassin into the corn-fed town of Vinton on a stormy night in 1925? What social, economic, and political forces created a head-on collision between a gunman, the temperance movement, and the Ku Klux Klan? To answer these questions, big historical boulders, long settled in place, needed to be dislodged and examined.

As you will note going forward, this story is not a classic cold case. It would be wrong for bookstore owners to place it among the other true crime offerings. And yet, at the same time, it would be wrong not to.

To tell this story is to tell the story of Iowa and its painful history of intolerance, its jarring relationship with liquor, and its many heroes and felons. In the end, there is the murder of Myrtle Cook to examine. The list of possible killers is analyzed and, from among them, the likely prime suspect is pointed out.

Mrs. Cook and the Klan

1

The Hawkeyes from Dixie

There is an engraving of Robert Lucas, the first territorial governor of Iowa, that suggests a striking resemblance to the Wizard of Oz. Not the softhearted sorcerer who gave away medals and diplomas and promised to carry Dorothy back to Kansas in a hot air balloon. No, here Lucas looks more like the wizard's avatar, which floated in the ether above the flame-throwing pedestal within the inner sanctum of the Emerald City. This was the intimidating wizard who behaved so contemptuously that the Cowardly Lion fled from his presence, down a hallway and out a random window.

Lucas apparently conducted himself in a similar fashion around the new capital. Barely a year into the governor's only term, a delegation from Iowa's territorial assembly was dispatched to Washington DC, hoping to obtain an audience with President Martin Van Buren. They wanted the president to fire Lucas and find someone else. Instead, the president called upon Congress to pass legislation that trimmed some of the powers of the territorial governors while increasing the authority of the assemblies. Congress agreed, giving the lawmakers the right to override an executive veto.[1]

This congressional action helped but did not resolve the conflict between Lucas and the leaders of Iowa's new assembly. The governor had reason to be scornful of the lot surrounding him. He was fifty-seven years old when Van Buren appointed him, and his résumé already displayed an impressive list of accomplishments. He had been a brigadier general in the Ohio militia and fought as a captain in the U.S. infantry during the War of 1812. He spent more than a decade in the Ohio Legislature before being elected governor twice. He owned and successfully oversaw a 437-acre farm, where he and his wife raised seven children. These were credentials no one in the Iowa statehouse could begin to match.[2]

The newly elected lawmakers whom voters sent to the territorial capital were a ragtag bunch. Most were farmers. A third were under age thirty. They were so rough and untamed that one of the more educated and refined among them got himself shot to death in a duel just days before the legislature convened. This victim, Cyrus S. Jacobs, came from Pennsylvania. He was enough of a player in early Iowa politics that he won appointment as the territory's first prosecuting attorney. His rival was another attorney, named David Rorer, who hailed from Virginia. Rorer would later become a prominent railroad lawyer and legal scholar and receive credit for coining Iowans' iconic moniker, "the Hawkeyes."

Both men were candidates for office in 1838. Jacobs ran for a seat in the legislature, while Rorer wanted to represent Iowa in the U.S. Congress. There were frequent interactions between them out on the stump, but no signs of trouble. After the election, however, in which Jacobs won and Rorer lost, hard feelings emerged. Exactly how this enmity began remains unclear, although the growing North-South rivalry between each man's home state is suspected of playing some part.

The Mississippi River town of Burlington was then the state capital. Both men were there for the start of the legislative session and crossed paths near the waterfront on October 29, 1838. They exchanged harsh words. Jacobs charged, swinging a leaded cane, and struck Rorer several times in the head. Both men then pulled pistols. Jacobs missed; Rorer didn't.[3]

Lucas knew both well enough that he made mention of the unfortunate business in his inaugural address to the newly sworn class of lawmakers a week later. "The recent transaction in this city that deprived the Legislative Assembly of one of its members elect, as well as all other transactions of a similar character, should meet with the indignant frown of every friend of morality and good order," Lucas said in his speech on November 12, 1838. "And the practice of wearing concealed about the person—dirks, pistols, or other deadly weapons, should not only be considered disreputable, but criminal and should be punished accordingly."[4]

The governor went on to lay out what he expected during the first legislative session. The organization of townships and the election of local officials were of primary importance. Schools were next, followed by courts and law enforcement, criminal codes, and prison terms. Finally came the construction of roads, river navigation, and bridges. Lucas wanted something else too. He passionately urged the assemblymen to consider a ban on what he called the twin "fashionable" evils of liquor and gambling. "These two vices may be considered the fountains from which almost every other crime proceeds," he preached. "They have produced more murders, robberies, and individual distress than any other crimes put together."

The governor did not get all that he had requested. Lawmakers passed legislation largely prohibiting gambling in its many forms, although they were careful to include a provision giving those who won a bet the right to sue those who lost for recovery of the winnings. On the question of liquor, however, a far less adequate effort was made. The only bills to regulate alcohol approved by the assembly in that first session were measures that banned liquor sales to "Indians" and one that established jail terms for anyone selling "unwholesome" booze. Of greater concern was the threat posed by Native American tribes who still inhabited much of western and northern parts of Iowa. The territorial assembly formally petitioned Congress for the delivery of three six-pound brass cannons, one thousand carbine rifles, two thousand pistols, and one thousand short swords—all expressly for the purpose of "Indian fighting."[5]

Another group viewed as an outlander also drew the attention of Iowa's first legislative assembly, the Free Blacks of America.

By the late 1830s there were pockets of Black families living in Iowa's river towns of Burlington, Muscatine, Davenport, and Keokuk. They found work where they could, as farm hands and domestic servants, many on the riverboats.[6] Their numbers could not have exceeded a couple hundred, but their presence fostered unease among the majority whites, who were predisposed to racial intolerance.

The vast majority of the early settlers of Iowa came from Kentucky, Tennessee, and the Virginias. They were poor themselves. Some had worked as sharecroppers and even as servants to wealthier neighbors. There were fears of having to compete economically with Black people. Iowa's white majority sent representatives to the capital, who shared those worries. Twenty of the thirty-eight members of the first territorial assembly were born below the Mason-Dixon Line. Thus it was considered imperative that among the first acts of the session was legislation discouraging Black people from coming into Iowa and restricting their activities upon arrival.[7]

Titled the "Act to Regulate Negros and Mulattos," Iowa's race laws were known as the "Black Codes" and were intended to be as oppressive as any adopted in a free state. Interracial marriage was outlawed. Public schools were for white children only. Black people could not use the court system for any cases involving white people. A free Black person wishing to reside in Iowa was required to register with the local authorities and to post a hefty bond, which could be forfeited at the discretion of law enforcement. A Black man who failed to provide the bond could be arrested and hired out to the highest bidder. A $100 fine was established to punish anyone who harbored a "fugitive slave" (an enslaved person who had fled, seeking freedom), and judges were authorized to order the safe return of runaways. "Slave owners," the enslavers of these refugees, were granted the right to pass through Iowa Territory.[8]

Slavery had existed in Iowa well before Iowa was recognized by Congress as a free territory, first as part of the District of Louisiana in 1804 and then as part of the Missouri Territory after 1812. Even after the modern boundaries were established and Iowa became a territory, some townships with majority southern populations disregarded federal law and adopted municipal codes embracing slavery.[9] Governor Lucas, an abolitionist, was a Virginia native whose father owned slaves.[10] John Chambers, who succeeded Robert Lucas as Iowa's second territorial governor, brought his slaves with him from Kentucky in 1841. Between 1835 and 1859, three members of Congress who represented Iowa were also slave owners.[11]

Iowans living closest to the Missouri border were probably the most tolerant of—or sympathetic to—the slave trade. As late as 1855 the editor of the *Daily Gate* in Keokuk—in Iowa's southernmost corner—published the auction prices paid for recent human purchases in Lexington, Missouri: "negro man aged 57, $295; woman aged 26, $735; woman aged 20 and child, $870; boy aged 10, $596."[12]

At the same time, there was a significant abolitionist movement in Iowa. Scores of Iowans served as agents and conductors in the Underground Railroad well before 1850. That list included Josiah Bushnell

Grinnell, who would later become a congressman and founder of Grinnell University.[13] More striking, however, were events that led to the landmark ruling of the territorial supreme court, in January 1839, that solidified Black freedom in Iowa.

At issue was a slave named Ralph Montgomery, who came to Iowa after striking a deal with his owner, promising to pay $550 within two years in exchange for being allowed to move to Dubuque and work in the mines. Some of the white workers in the camp where Montgomery was living were aware of the bargain this Black man had made, and they were also aware that Montgomery barely scratched out enough ore to feed himself, let alone pay off the significant debt. One of the white miners contacted Montgomery's owner back in St. Louis and offered to send the Black man back for a fee of $100. The St. Louis slave owner agreed. Next, the sheriff was alerted that a runaway slave was in their midst, and Montgomery was arrested. A white farmer named Alexander Butterworth witnessed the arrest, but to him it appeared to be more of an abduction. As the sheriff was taking Montgomery to the docks for transport to St. Louis, Butterworth hurried to town in search of the local judge, a man named Thomas Wilson. When he heard what Butterworth had to say, Wilson issued an order holding Montgomery in Dubuque until the facts could be sorted out. Wilson, it turned out, was also a member of the territorial supreme court, which agreed to take up the matter.[14]

The high court was a three-member body led by a New York native named Charles Mason. Mason was an alumnus of West Point who had graduated first in the same class as Robert E. Lee and ten other cadets, who would later become generals fighting on both sides of the Civil War.[15]

The Montgomery case came before the court in July 1839—six months before the legislature adopted the Black Codes. Attorneys representing the slave owner argued that Ralph was a fugitive and that, under Article IV of the U.S. Constitution, the white owner had the right to regain control of his property.[16] Representing Ralph Montgomery was David Rorer, the same attorney who, later that year, would kill a political rival in a duel on the streets of Burlington.[17] Rorer argued that the slave owner had no standing in Iowa. He pointed out that the Missouri Compromise of 1820 banned slavery in the territory of Iowa.

Thus, Ralph Montgomery was free and not a slave and therefore he could not be a fugitive. All three justices ruled in favor of Montgomery, with Mason writing the opinion.[18] In a case with many similarities, the U.S. Supreme Court eighteen years later came to exactly the opposite conclusion in making the *Dred Scott* decision.[19]

As consequential as the Montgomery ruling might look from today's perspective, it did little to change the attitude of the white southern majority that was in control of Iowa's government. Not only did the territorial assembly move ahead with adoption of the Black Codes the same year that the court issued the Montgomery ruling, but lawmakers continued to enhance the restraints through the end of the 1850s and did not fully dismantle them until 1880.[20] Iowa's reputation nationally was of being "to all intents and purposes, a Slave State," said poet John Greenleaf Whittier, who was both a Quaker and an ardent abolitionist.[21] Horace Greeley, editor of the *New York Tribune*, mocked the sophistry of Iowa's status as an antislavery state: "What gain had freedom in the admission of Iowa to the Union?"[22]

The laws governing liquor in the territory of Iowa, inherited from the state of Michigan, were a confused mix of restraint and indifference. Tavern owners, for instance, could sell spirits only after being granted a license from the county and as long as the business was not conducted within a mile of the nearest church. The Code of Iowa, adopted in 1851, contained an entire chapter on "the sale of intoxicating liquors." In one section the law declared that the sale of liquor was "not prohibited." Yet in another, lawmakers ordered that liquor sold "by the glass or by the dram" was prohibited.[23]

Chapters of the Sons of Temperance sprang up in Burlington, Muscatine, and Davenport not long after Iowa achieved statehood in 1846.[24] The first push to turn Iowa from wet to dry began with a well-attended temperance convention held in Iowa City in December 1853. The next year, prohibition emerged as a key issue in the gubernatorial campaign, in which James Grimes, a member of the Whig Party, narrowly defeated the Democratic candidate. Although slavery was the dominant theme in the election, Grimes pledged to support a statewide liquor ban and was himself a dedicated nondrinker. Both attributes worked to gain the temperance vote, which proved big enough to swing the election his way.[25]

By then, enthusiasm had swelled nationally in favor of a voter-approved prohibitory law following the adoption of the novel "Maine Law" in 1851. The notion that the law could be used as a method of regulating personal drinking habits was first employed in Massachusetts during the 1830s. Candidates for office in some towns were screened out based on their drinking habits. In 1838 the Massachusetts Legislature banned liquor sales of less than fifteen gallons, except for medical reasons. The people of Maine took the concept a step or two further. Led by Portland's prohibitionist mayor, Neal Dow, the state of Maine became the first in the nation to adopt a constitutional amendment banning the manufacture, sale, and consumption of liquor, while providing a license to sell it for medicinal or industrial purposes; heavy fines were imposed on violators. By 1855 twelve other states and territories had adopted similar amendments.[26]

That same year, Iowa lawmakers agreed to place a constitutional amendment banning the manufacture and sale of liquor before voters. On April 2, 1855, the amendment passed, with 53 percent of some forty-eight thousand votes supporting it. Of the sixty-five counties participating in the election, prohibition was approved in thirty-three and rejected in thirty-two.[27] The law took effect on July 1, 1855; almost immediately, it was widely ignored.

"In Dubuque, no regard whatever is paid to the law," the *Muscatine Evening Journal* reported on January 15, 1856. "In Muscatine, several persons have been indicted for selling liquor, but the right state of feeling does not exist in the public mind to render the law as efficient as it should be. When the law went into effect, its warmest friends hoped the magistrates would fulfill their oaths of office by seeing it was enforced. But the officials, with rare exceptions, have proved recreant to their trusts and at present the law is violated with impunity."[28]

Only a year after the liquor ban was imposed, members of the general assembly concluded that the law could not be enforced and settled on a compromise: they left the constitutional amendment unaltered but adopted a local licensing option that allowed alcohol to be manufactured and sold in those counties where voters were tolerant. The local option came with an odd condition that restricted saloon sales to beer, wine, and ale made from fruit or grains grown in Iowa. That provision was also widely ignored.[29]

Among those who voted against the local license option was Senator George McCoy, a Republican and zealous temperance advocate from Kentucky. McCoy, best known as the author of legislation establishing the Iowa Institution for the Blind at Vinton, represented Benton County between 1855 and 1860, where Myrtle Cook was murdered sixty-five years later.[30]

Before there was a university, there was a prison. The first inmate admitted to Iowa's Fort Madison Penitentiary stepped into a cell on September 22, 1839; the legislature didn't establish the University of Iowa until February 1847.[31]

The first legal hanging in Iowa took place in Burlington on July 15, 1845. The accused were two brothers, Stephen and William Hodges, who lived in a Mormon community at Nauvoo, Illinois. It was in Nauvoo where Joseph Smith had first sought refuge for the Latter-day Saints a decade earlier and where Smith had been murdered just the year before by a mob whipped up in an anti-Mormon frenzy. The Hodges brothers were accused of killing two local farmers, both non-Mormons. An estimated crowd of ten thousand people gathered to watch the event, which took some ten minutes, as William Hodges kicked and struggled before dying.[32]

A leading critic of Iowa's use of capital punishment was Charles Mason, the state's first chief justice, who wrote the majority opinion on the Montgomery slavery case. Mason served on the territorial supreme court from 1838 until 1847 and was instrumental in the codification of Iowa law while imprinting the state's early jurisprudence with many of his own socially advanced beliefs. He was way ahead of his contemporaries in his support of women's suffrage and had recommended to the legislature that they enact laws to provide for the property rights of a wife, separate from her husband, and for the protection of that right.[33]

A year after the hanging of the Hodges brothers, Mason founded the Iowa Anti-Capital Punishment and Prison Discipline Society, joining a movement that had begun in Britain to make the incarceration system safer and more just. Pennsylvania did away with public executions in 1834, and Michigan became the first state to abolish capital punishment altogether in 1844. By 1850 there were active lobby groups against the death penalty in Tennessee, Ohio, Massachusetts, New York, Alabama, Louisiana, and Indiana, as well as the group in Iowa founded by Judge Mason.[34]

2

The Bridge at Davenport

As early as 1835 it was generally recognized that Iowa's future depended on unlocking the vast fertile lands of the interior. Yet, because of its unique topography, there were few navigable waterways that could support the easy transport of families, farm animals, food, seed, and whatever else might be needed to establish new farms. The one exception was the Des Moines River, which was also the only one that fully traversed the state, flowing south from Minnesota and then east, where it joins the Mississippi at Keokuk.

A unit from the First U.S. Dragoons was ordered in the summer of 1835 to travel to the Des Moines River and evaluate its potential for navigation. Just to undertake such an operation, the calvary would have needed to come north from their headquarters at the Jefferson Barracks, near present day St. Louis, probably to Fort Snelling, near what is now Minneapolis. The leader of the exploration team, Lt. Albert M. Lea, returned with nothing but good news.[1] Iowans would spend much of the next two decades unsuccessfully chasing the fulfillment of Lea's vision for the Des Moines River.

Just ahead of Iowa's admission into the union, Congress authorized the territorial government to offer land grants along the Des Moines to anyone willing to invest in building the locks and dams needed to make the river more manageable. However, the value of the land grants never kept pace with the expense of making the improvements. Still, some progress was made, and steamboats operated between Keosauqua and Des Moines by 1855, at least from spring until early fall. But adding mileage to the water route came in fits and starts. One contractor would begin only to run out of money within months. Another would pick up but then become mired down by floods or ice. The state agency charged with overseeing the project was rife with mismanagement and graft, which brought lawsuits and political division.[2]

The other option for settling the interior of Iowa was roads. There was hope, for a time, that a network could be built using long timber boards to tame the heavy black soil, which became glue-like during rainy periods. The concept had been introduced to the New World when, in the late 1830s, an English diplomat had been sent to Canada after a long posting in Russia, where he had seen plank roads in operation.

As the name would suggest, the plank road utilized boards laid at right angles to the direction of the traveler. They were spiked into heavy logs called "stringers," which were embedded firmly into the ground. The first plank road in North America is thought to have linked Toronto to a neighboring village. The first in the United States came in 1846 and connected Syracuse, New York, with Oneida Lake, fourteen miles away. To pay for the construction and provide a profit, the developers planned to charge a toll. The cost of building the road proved much lower than expected, and enthusiasm among investors was much greater. "So favorable were all these circumstances that the company have never extracted more than about three-quarters of the tolls they were entitled to by law," noted the *New York Evening Post.*[3]

Not much later, Iowa lawmakers gave approval to a group of investors to connect Muscatine to the unlikely destination of Vinton, Iowa—the Benton County seat and the location where Myrtle Cook would be murdered in 1925. Lawmakers gave the developers twenty years to complete the project, which would have covered a distance of ninety-four miles. Vinton was a curious choice for the western terminus, given that it had a population of just over three hundred. That fact, as well as the rough terrain the road would need to traverse, led to the plan's demise. Not a mile of that first road was ever completed. Between 1849 and 1853 the Iowa Legislature approved fourteen partnerships to construct some six hundred miles of plank roads, of which perhaps fifty miles were ever actually put into use.[4] Even if more of the roads had been completed, there was something new and exciting on the horizon, literally, that ended up drawing all the attention, the railroad.

With the exception of New Orleans, no transportation hub in the western United States during the first half of the nineteenth century was as dominant as St. Louis. Advantaged by its location at the confluence of the Mississippi and Missouri Rivers, St. Louis had begun as a fur trading camp around 1764 and emerged as a city after the Louisiana Purchase in 1803. The first steamboats arrived around 1815, and for the next fifty years St. Louis had no real rival as the commercial capital of the American interior.[5]

The decline of St. Louis and the rise of Chicago were not hard to see coming. There was little doubt by the early 1850s that the railroad would one day dominate the nation's transportation system—the only question was when. In St. Louis, weighed down by its deeply rooted investment in the steamboat and the river traffic, the feeling was that it might take decades. Unrestrained by the biases of the past, there were men in Chicago who were free to risk and to dream.

The Illinois and Michigan Canal opened in 1848, giving steamboats access to the Illinois River through the Great Lakes. With that came instant cost advantages for moving freight from Chicago to New York using the Illinois and Hudson Rivers. Two years later, a rail line was built from Chicago to the dusty town of Elgin, forty-two miles to the west, marking a turning point in the new race for commercial dominance. William Butler Ogden, a land speculator and brewery owner, as well as Chicago's first mayor, is credited with envisioning the boom that a rail link to the Mississippi River would bring to the city. The idea was not popular with all the businessmen in Chicago, however, as some were reluctant to create competition for their very successful canal trade. Therefore, to raise the money Ogden needed, he and his partners peddled shares in the new company to the farmers and merchants living along the proposed route. It was an overnight success. In 1851 lawmakers in Springfield also saw the potential and chartered the Illinois Central Railroad. Their mandate was to lay the tracks from Cairo, in the southernmost corner of the state at the intersection of Illinois, Kentucky, and Missouri, all the way north to Dunleith, which sits across the Mississippi from Dubuque, Iowa.[6] A rival company, the Chicago Rock Island & Pacific, began operating between Chicago and Joliet in October 1852 and reached the banks of the Mississippi at Rock Island in February 1854.[7]

Construction of the bridge at Davenport, perhaps better known in the history books as the Rock Island Bridge, represented much more than the first railroad to cross the Mississippi. The bridge would play a small but consequential role in two of the country's titanic historical events of the nineteenth century—the looming war between the states and the construction of the transcontinental railroad.[8]

Jefferson Davis, later president of the Confederate States of America, was the secretary of war under President Franklin Pierce. As the railroad tracks reached the Mississippi across from Davenport, Davis was doing everything he could to encourage his boss to designate a southern route for the transcontinental railroad. Davis and the rest of the South's congressional contingent wanted the line to begin in New Orleans, go west through Texas and the territories of New Mexico and Arizona, and arrive at the Pacific Ocean in San Diego. Davis recognized the threat the Rock Island Bridge posed because, once completed, it would all but ensure that the cross-country rail route would be built through the northern free states and territories.

Work was already underway when officials from the Rock Island Bridge Company submitted an application to Davis for use of the federally owned island. As expected, he denied permission and ordered them to stop working. Confident that they had the political support needed, the bridge managers ignored Davis's order and finished in time to welcome the first locomotive to cross the Mississippi, on April 22, 1856.[9] Meanwhile, many of the same investors in the Chicago–Rock Island line incorporated the Mississippi and Missouri Railroad Company in Iowa and began laying track west to Council Bluffs.[10]

Despite the frantic pace of railroad construction, resistance to its dominance continued to fester. One of the last great gasps to halt the railroads' advance came in May 1856, only a few weeks after the Rock Island Bridge opened. The steamer *Effie Afton*, christened in Cincinnati a year before, was on its way to St. Paul when it collided with the mid-span of the bridge. The ship caught fire and sank; the bridge suffered substantial damage but remained functional. A year after the accident, the steamer's owner filed suit in the U.S. District Court in Chicago, claiming that the bridge created unsafe currents and eddies, and demanded $50,000 (about $1.6 million today) in damages. The railroad countersued for $200,000 ($6.5 million today).[11] "It will be recalled that the new steamer *Effie Afton* was sunk a year or more ago by coming into collision with that detestable nuisance, Rock Island bridge," the *Nashville Republican Banner* sneered.[12]

Hired by the defense was an experienced railroad attorney and former member of Congress from Illinois, Abraham Lincoln. The trial ended in a hung jury: nine for the railroad and three for the steamboat owner.[13]

Lincoln would again play a prominent role in the development of the railroads of Iowa as well as those of the country. While campaigning for president in 1859, he was invited to speak to a full house in Council Bluffs. Among those in the audience was Grenville Dodge, only twenty-eight years old but already a veteran railroad surveyor and one of the few experts on the topography between Nebraska and Salt Lake City. After Lincoln's speech, one of his hosts introduced the two men. Dodge and Lincoln spent much of the rest of that afternoon sitting on a cliff overlooking the Missouri River, talking mostly about the Platte Valley. Dodge was adamant that the best route to the Pacific was the northern route and that the eastern terminus of the transcontinental line had to be Council Bluffs. Six years later President Lincoln, although fully consumed by the ravages of the Civil War, issued the order just as Dodge had suggested.[14]

The population of Iowa advanced steadily from 43,112 in 1840 to nearly 200,000 in 1850 and then to 675,000 by 1860. Unlike the earliest settlers, who came from the South, the later waves of newcomers were from the northern states, including New England. There was also a burgeoning immigrant presence from Scandinavia, Ireland, and western Europe. Germans comprised the most influential group of new foreign settlers in Iowa; they were also the largest, numbering close to 40,000 by 1860, representing about 7 percent of the state population.[15]

Unlike many other European immigrant groups, the Germans arrived ready to contribute to the economy. Many of them were skilled craftsmen, professionals, and experienced farmers. Their numbers in the river towns of Dubuque, Davenport, and Burlington swelled during the late 1840s and early 1850s. Many of them had been forced into exile because of failed uprisings against the monarchies of western Europe during that decade.[16]

The stirrings of unrest could be found in Belgium, Spain, and certainly in France—but conditions were desperate in the German states in the mid-nineteenth century. Battered by crop failures, banking scandals, and high unemployment, Germany languished far behind the rest of Europe. Anyone who could get out of Germany did. Paris was a popular choice and became the sixth-largest German-speaking city in the world.

The Revolution of 1848 came close to unseating the Habsburgs. At one point, an unlikely collection of students, unemployed workers, and intellectuals controlled most of Vienna and pressed the emperor and his court to flee. The rebellion wasn't put down until the Prussian army was sent brutally into the fray.[17] Some disillusioned participants made their way to America by choice; others agreed to follow when given an ultimatum: banishment or the gallows.

Iowa became a popular destination for this wave of German émigrés. Some fellow countrymen had already arrived and would have written home about the pleasant cities along the Mississippi and the endless prairie to the west. Germany and Iowa are situated at roughly the same latitude and thus have similar climates and growing seasons. The second big swell of Germans that came to Iowa thus had high expectations.[18]

This group, known as the "48ers" because of the year of their arrival, were distinct in many ways from those Germans who had come a decade before. The 48ers were better educated, more worldly, and more politically experienced. They would have been proud of a heritage that produced Mozart, Beethoven, Luther, and Goethe. They would have been aware that this new country, the United States, had nothing similar.[19]

This confidence of the 48ers led almost immediately to a confrontation with their native-born neighbors over the Germans' fondness for a fine *Schwarzbier* on a Sunday afternoon in the company of friends and family. The biergarten was an essential piece of German culture they brought to America, and one they had absolutely no intention of giving up. Suppression of the Sunday *Lagerbier* was unthinkable.[20]

The first anti-temperance meeting in Iowa took place in Davenport on February 18, 1852. It was organized by the leaders of the town's German community. Among them was Hans Remer Claussen, an attorney and former member of the German Parliament. He was exiled for his role in leading an uprising in Schleswig-Holstein, now Germany's northernmost state but then a part of the Danish Empire. Claussen would later become one of the first German immigrants elected to the Iowa State Senate.[21]

The gathering in Davenport in support of liquor freedom came a year after voters in Maine had adopted their prohibition amendment. By the early 1850s political temperance groups flourished in New York, Pennsylvania, Vermont, and Iowa as well. In response, the Germans of Scott County (where Davenport was the seat) turned out by the hundreds on that bone-cold February afternoon in 1852. They adopted a resolution declaring that the consumption of alcohol produced from the "fruits of the earth" was a "natural right" and that the Maine Law had "the same tyrannical character as the suppression of the freedom of the press."

To the editor of the *Davenport Democrat Banner*, who was most likely native born, there was an unruly tone to the meeting that demanded pushback. "Laws on the subject of temperance are equally binding with other laws, and while they are on statute book, they must be enforced," the editor advised the Germans. "If too stringent, let them be repealed; but no citizen will violate the laws or see them violated with impunity."[22]

With the temperance question still looming, the 48ers looked to flex their political muscle elsewhere as soon as they could. Under Iowa law, it took five years to meet a residency requirement before a male newcomer was given the right to vote. As a result, the first major campaign in which the 48ers had an influence was the gubernatorial election of 1854. The 48ers carefully weighed their options and interests before aligning with any political party. It didn't take them long to decide. The threat perceived as the most dangerous to them was the rise of the nativism movement during the mid-1850s, characterized by the Know Nothing Party. As much as anything, links between Stephen A. Douglas, the leading Democrat of the Midwest, and the nativists made it an easy decision for the Germans to join up with the Whigs, some of whom would help establish Lincoln's Republican Party. With the backing of many Germans, the Whigs narrowly defeated the Democrats in 1854. It was the first time the Democrats had been defeated in Iowa. A Whig candidate, James Wilson Grimes, was elected governor, also a first.[23]

There was some evidence that the 48ers played a role in the selection of Lincoln as the Republican presidential candidate in 1860. The delegates to the national convention were split between William Seward of New York, Salmon P. Chase of Ohio, and Edward Bates of Missouri. Lincoln emerged on the third ballot as Seward's main challenger and won the nomination. Among the reasons that the Germans backed

Lincoln was his opposition to a national residency proposal that would have banned any naturalized citizen from voting or holding office until a four-year probationary period had been served. Lincoln denounced the idea, while Seward didn't take a position.[24]

Iowa achieved statehood in December 1846 but couldn't fill either of its two U.S. senatorial seats until two years later because of capital politics. In Iowa, as in most states, only members of the legislature could participate in the election of a U.S. senator, and it took until December 1848 for the Democratic leaders in Des Moines to corral the votes. When they did, their first choice was Augustus Caesar Dodge (no relation to Grenville Dodge, the railroad engineer). Dodge was already a seasoned Washington lawmaker, having served as a congressman, representing the territory of Iowa, for six years.[25] He was the son of Henry Dodge, a famous frontier warrior and the first governor of the territory of Wisconsin. The younger Dodge had spent his childhood in Missouri, a slave state, where his political views on race relations were imprinted. The family moved to northwest Illinois in the 1830s when the elder Dodge was given command of a post there. During the Black Hawk War of 1832, the senior Dodge served as a colonel in the Michigan Territorial Militia, and Augustus fought alongside his father as a lieutenant and aide-de-camp. When Henry Dodge was appointed governor of the Wisconsin Territory, Augustus was a brigadier general in the Iowa militia. Augustus Dodge also won election as an alderman in the city of Burlington and was selected as a territorial delegate to Congress representing Iowa. When Augustus Dodge was sworn in as a U.S. senator, he joined Henry, who was representing Wisconsin in the upper house, making them the nation's first father-son members of the Senate.[26]

The Iowa senator's arrival in Washington came at a precarious time in American history. Tensions were escalating between the North and the South, between the slave and free states. Iowa's admission into the union was balanced with the simultaneous acceptance of Florida: one free, one slave. However, during the 1854 congressional session, debate grew tense over the disposition of some 450,000 square miles that encompassed the present states of Kansas, Nebraska, the Dakotas, and Montana. The question that bedeviled Congress was in which of those future states slavery would be allowed.

A bill crafted by Illinois senator Stephen A. Douglas would tear up the Missouri Compromise of 1820 and admit two more states: Kansas and Nebraska. The enabling legislation would give the voters in each new state the authority to decide the slavery question for themselves.

Senator Augustus Dodge supported the Kansas-Nebraska Act of 1854, just as he had strongly backed the Fugitive Slave Act four years earlier as a territorial representative to Congress. He had clearly articulated at the time that both votes came from a pragmatic perspective. Returning runaway slaves to their owners was a constitutionally protected property right, he said. Turning the slavery question over to voters living in those states was simply the democratic thing to do. Speaking from the floor of the Senate in August 1852, Dodge lashed out at "political abolitionists," who he said harbored one of two objectives:

"Either an overthrow of our government by revolution and bloodshed or the establishment of an absolute equality between the white and black races." Dodge continued, "The accomplishment of the latter object is their cherished and darling hope. They would introduce black-skinned, flat-nosed, and woolly-headed senators and representatives. They seek to break down and destroy all distinctions between the whites and blacks in respect to suffrage, office, marriage, and every other relation of life."[27]

The majority of voters in Iowa had been, at the time, most certainly pro-slavery, and Dodge was reflecting that position. By 1854 attitudes in Iowa were changing. In the gubernatorial election that year, the anti-slavery Whigs overcame decades of dominance by the Southern Democrats. Meanwhile, the notion that Congress might allow another slave state on the Iowa border was troubling to a majority of voters, and that Dodge backed such a plan spelled the end of his time as a U.S. senator. By the following spring, when Dodge's term expired, he faced a crowded field of challengers, most of whom were abolitionists. He was not returned to the Senate and would spend the next twenty-seven years trying unsuccessfully to recapture political relevancy in a state that had become fully anti-slavery.[28]

In October 1856 John Brown limped into the town of Tabor, Iowa, weary and weak with fever after a vicious summer of fighting in Bleeding Kansas. He was welcomed as a hero by the citizenry of a town comprised mostly of Congregationalists. Although Tabor was nearly fifty miles from the Missouri border, it was nonetheless a well-known stop on Iowa's Underground Railroad. Most freedom seekers who traveled through Iowa on the Underground Railroad had begun their journey in Appanoose and Davis Counties and then traveled northeast to Burlington or Muscatine and from there to Chicago.[29]

Brown's arrival came only a few months after his notorious Pottawatomie Massacre, in which he and his sons savagely murdered five unarmed slavery sympathizers. Brown stayed a week in Tabor, and when he was well enough he headed east on a fundraising trip, first to Chicago and then Upstate New York. He wanted to bring volunteers to Iowa, where they would be trained and made ready for the anti-slavery war he would bring to Kansas.[30]

Brown was not the only one in Iowa willing to risk bloodshed over slavery. Governor James W. Grimes, a Whig, was concerned enough about Kansas becoming a slave state that he secretly allowed guns and ammunition to be taken from the state armory for use by militia groups.[31] Iowa City welcomed "Jim Lane's Army," a loosely organized band of about two thousand armed abolitionists who invaded Kansas in 1856.[32]

A year later, Brown and his sons returned to the town of Tabor, where they began plotting their reckless guerrilla attack on a military installation at Harpers Ferry, Virginia. Four Iowans participated in the Harpers Ferry raid. Two were killed during the fighting. One, named Edwin Coppoc, was captured by federal troops and executed along with Brown. Coppoc's younger brother, Barclay, escaped and made his way home on foot. A Virginia official was sent to Des Moines to take the young man into custody, but Governor Kirkwood was intentionally slow in carrying out the extradition request, allowing Coppoc to flee to Kansas. He was killed in 1861 in a train accident.[33]

Iowa sent close to seventy-six thousand men into the Civil War; thirteen thousand never returned.[34]

One of the most successful Black businessmen in Iowa, both before and after the Civil War, was Alexander Clark. A resident of Muscatine since coming north from Cincinnati in 1841, he began by selling firewood to steamboat skippers and used his profits to buy a barbershop.

As his reputation for a steady hand with the ever-dangerous single-edge razor grew, more and more of Clark's customers were among the white business elite of the city, some of whom happily passed on investment advice that often centered around real estate. Unable to buy property in town yet, Clark bought up tracts of swampy "river bottom" parcels to feed his firewood business and, later, to rent out to farmers. Soon, he was trading up to bargain commercial property in town as well. While still in his twenties, he was already one of the most affluent Black men in Muscatine. He helped found the Muscatine African Methodist Episcopal Church and, in 1857, organized one of the first political campaigns aimed at repealing the Black Codes. He was instrumental in bringing together Iowa's all-Black Sixtieth Infantry Regiment and led the fight after the war to convince the state assembly to grant suffrage to Black men.[35]

In 1867, against the backdrop of the North's victory in the war, Clark and his wife decided to send their twelve-year-old daughter to the local public school, well aware that the child would be turned away. Iowa law mandated that the education of Black children be separate from that of white families. The Clarks found the school offered them by the Muscatine School Board woefully inadequate, and after his daughter was refused admission to the white school, Clark went to court.[36]

"My personal object is that my children attend where they can receive the largest and best advantages of learning," Clark wrote to the *Muscatine Journal*.[37]

The case was heard by the Iowa Supreme Court in 1868, which ruled in favor of Clark's daughter. Nearly ninety years before the U.S. Supreme Court would find segregation in public schools unconstitutional, the Iowa high court ruled that the Iowa Constitution required "the education of all youths of the state" and that school boards could not "deny a youth admission to any particular school because of his or her nationality, religion, color, clothing, or the like."[38]

Susan Clark would graduate from Muscatine High School in 1871, followed by her younger brother Alexander Jr., who went on to be the first Black graduate of the University of Iowa's College of Law. Alexander Sr., at age fifty-six, became the law school's second Black graduate in 1884.[39]

In 1868, Iowa became the first state outside of New England to grant Black men the right to vote, ahead of the adoption of the Fifteenth Amendment by Congress in February 1869.[40]

The Civil War interrupted the expansion of railways all over the United States, Iowa included. But after Appomattox, transportation companies fiercely competed to reach unserved markets. The first lines in Iowa fed into the Mississippi & Missouri system, connecting the river cities of Dubuque, Clinton, Davenport, and Burlington. By 1870 the state was crisscrossed with rail lines, all with Chicago at the center. The railroads offered the farmers of Iowa—as well as the rest of the Midwest—access to markets that could have only been imagined before. Yet, no sooner had the rails arrived than the harsh economic realities of the new transportation system took hold. The owners of the Chicago-based railroads were uninterested in promoting any market other than their own. Road agents were directed to offer only shipping rates that benefited Chicago. It became cheaper to send Iowa corn and hogs all the way to the Windy City than to send them to closer markets on the Mississippi River. Thus arrived the dreaded concept of "long and short haul" discrimination.

"On Monday morning, Messrs. Adams Bros. shipped a load of rags to Dubuque by team, rather than pay the exorbitant rates charged by the railroads," the *Manchester Press* observed in February 1874. "They say they have a large amount of freight to ship both ways and shall transport it with teams as long as the railroad rates are so outrageously high."[41]

The farmers found themselves no match for the rail monopolies. Many communities that beckoned the rails with offers of free land and other subsidies found the rail operators unforgiving and tyrannical upon arrival. As frustrations mounted, efforts to organize the rural vote took root. A key rallying point was the Grange societies. Formally known as the Patrons of Husbandry, the Grange was founded in the mid-1860s to promote new and better agricultural practices and to serve as rare social outlets for isolated farm families. The Grange also became a natural focal point for rural dissatisfaction with the rails. The first successful use of the ballot box by Grange members took place in Illinois and Minnesota during the early 1870s, when farmers united with town merchants to force their state lawmakers to pass the first restrictions on rail rates. By 1874 there were more than two thousand Grange organizations in Iowa, representing more than one hundred thousand members. That same year, Iowa lawmakers agreed to impose rate restrictions that fixed the maximum the railroads could charge for freight and passengers.[42] That law, however, used a complex formula that ended up benefiting the railroads and had to be repealed in 1878. By then, attention had turned to Washington and Congress in hopes of national railroad reform, something that wouldn't jell for another ten years.[43]

One lasting provision of the 1878 rail reform legislation, however, was the establishment of one of the nation's first regulatory commissions to oversee railroad activities. The board was made up of three members, all appointed by the governor, with three-year terms. The Iowa Railroad Commission had limited authority over rail companies, but the board did have the power to investigate the safety conditions of the roads and any significant accidents.[44]

The safety provision, which for many years was rarely invoked, would prove a bellwether nationally and indirectly help launch a far wider rebellion years later against the monopolistic hold the rails had on America.

3

The Witches of Temperance

The attack should not have been a surprise. Tensions in the town of Clinton had been building for months. The saloonkeepers, the brothel owners, and the gambling interests had run their businesses for years without interference. Now, suddenly, they were getting new scrutiny. The town's vice trade, considered by city leaders as a necessary evil for attracting all the single young men needed to work in the town's lumber mills and on the wharf, was under attack. By 1874 there were hundreds, if not thousands, of newcomers. Families. Children. The fathers and husbands worked as merchants, doctors, and lawyers. The wives went to the markets and to church, trailed by children with clean faces and neat clothes. These were people who wanted better schools and safer streets. They wanted the city council to clean things up: to eliminate the liquor trade, the prostitution, and the gambling.

Change would not come that easily in Clinton. Although it had been chartered in 1857 and the county seat since 1869, the town clung to its frontier roots even as its importance to the regional economy grew. Located about halfway between Minneapolis and St. Louis, the town was, by the end of the Civil War, one of the biggest suppliers of milled lumber anywhere in the United States. Millions of logs were sent down the Mississippi, in spring and summer, from the forests of Minnesota and Wisconsin on huge rafts. The timber was off-loaded at Clinton and the adjacent city of Lyons. The twin towns boasted five major sawmills, including one that employed nearly four hundred men. There were also dozens of cabinet shops, box makers, a match factory, and a paper manufacturer.[1] Clinton was booming, and thriving right alongside all the success of Main Street was the depravity of not just the saloons and the gambling halls but also brothels, opium dens, and dead-end flop houses.

J. Ellen Foster was one of the newcomers. She arrived in Clinton around 1870 on the arm of her second husband, Elijah Caleb Foster, an attorney. She was the daughter of a righteous Wesleyan Methodist minister from Massachusetts. Young and attractive, Foster would become one of the first female practicing attorneys in Iowa. She would, by the mid-1880s, also become the unrivaled leader of the temperance movement in her adopted home state and would use that influence to harness the powerful force of Iowa's dominant Republican Party to challenge the liquor threat. A skilled writer and public speaker, she would become known to the nation and later advise U.S. senators and presidents.[2]

But on the night of September 26, 1874, she was likely barefoot and dressed in a nightgown, standing disheveled and disoriented as she watched their rented home in Clinton burn to the ground. She, her two young sons, and her husband got out uninjured. Officials believed that the fire had been intentionally lit, but there was no investigation nor any arrests. "Undoubtedly the work of malice," the *Des Moines Register* (known as the *Iowa State Leader* from 1870 until 1902) speculated a few days after the incident.[3]

The Fosters had no doubt either. Although E. C. Foster's law practice mostly revolved around the lumber industry and Clinton's other commercial activities, he was increasingly drawn into the liquor debate. He was, like his wife, a devout Methodist and staunch prohibitionist; news accounts at the time captured him occasionally taking on cases that put him at odds with the whiskey trade. Iowa law provided a local option for the legal sale of liquor—a path that voters in Clinton had long before endorsed. Still, there were several legal avenues available to an activist attorney intent on making war with the saloon owners. For instance, a civil case could be raised against a barkeeper who stayed open on Sundays, which was a violation of state law. Liquor sales to a minor could also be prosecuted in civil court. Taking up the plight of the wife of a chronic alcoholic was a third option. One exasperated housewife, Sarah Esher Collard of Wales, Michigan, placed an ad in her local paper threatening to sue anyone who offered drink to her wayward man:

> You and your clerks and servants are hereby requested and notified not to sell or give any intoxicating drinks or liquors to my husband,

Edward Collard, or permit him to be treated by others in your house or saloon. I shall prosecute anyone who permits him to drink any intoxicating liquors in his house. This notice is given under legal advice.[4]

Most cities also had laws forbidding any ill-defined "public nuisance," a ban that local marshals could almost whimsically put into use to shut down anything that didn't meet with community acceptance. Applying the public nuisance codes to the legal operation of a saloon was a novel legal strategy that was just beginning to be explored. A sharp-eyed editor at the *Burlington Vermont Weekly Free Press* noticed the legal concept being employed in several cases in his town and quickly understood its threat to the status quo. The *Free Press* reported on July 4, 1877:

That plan is to use the law, not for the absolute and entire suppression of the liquor traffic, but for the suppression of the nuisance in the shape of rum holes and open bars and to do this by the application of the lesser rather than the larger penalties of the law. Some of our most sagacious temperance men have always maintained that the most effective method of repressing the liquor saloon is to prosecute frequently and persistently for "first offense." Under a daily prosecution and fine of ten dollars and costs, the business soon becomes unprofitable.[5]

One of the first references to J. Ellen Foster in the local press came in May 1874—four months before the arson attack. She led a petition drive by the Ladies' Temperance Aide Society. They delivered more than twelve hundred signatures, which accounted for nearly 10 percent of the adult male population, to the city council.[6]

That petition was probably not, by itself, enough for the saloon owners of Clinton to hire an arsonist, but another recent event probably was. Two days before the attack, Mrs. Foster had been admitted to the Iowa bar.[7] As she stood watching the roaring flames and the chaotic efforts of the volunteer firemen, she no doubt reflected on the terrorist message being sent to her by the saloon owners. The attempt to intimidate her would fall well short, and if anything the fire would only strengthen her resolve.

Iowa's liquor laws were, at the time, both conflicting and convoluted. The language in the state constitution imposed a ban on the manufacture and sale of intoxicating liquor. But an exemption had been carved out in statute during the late 1850s to allow the making and selling of beer, wine, and ale where local voters supported the endeavor.[8] Foster found the incongruity as serious and as appalling as the prewar compromise over slavery. "Is not our house divided against itself? Is not the spirit of harmony in our governmental dualism woefully violated?" Foster would write in 1888: "We said in the old slavery days, the nation cannot live half free and half slave. Neither can a nation live half drunk and half sober."

Which side should prevail was without question: "When we consider the liquor crime, from a moral standpoint, when we try its character and fruits by the light of philanthropy or of revelation, its condemnation is sure and final," she said. "The destruction of health, of happiness, of the home, of the glory of manhood, the beauty of womanhood, the innocence of childhood, the blasting of individual character, the blighting of society relationships; and the poisoning of even the Church of God."[9]

Foster concluded that the Iowa Legislature lacked the political resolve to move against the liquor interests. The Republicans, led by pious Methodists, had nonetheless done little to suppress intemperance in the decade since taking power after the Civil War. The men of Iowa simply could not be counted on to take up this fight. "I pray that God may hasten the day when woman may not only go to the polls to bolster up our weak-kneed, limber back and on top of the fence sort of men to do their duty," an exasperated female temperance leader said. "But when she can go as a God-given right to the polls and say by her vote that wine and libertines shall no longer have authority over us."[10]

In November 1874 the Iowa Chapter of the Woman's Christian Temperance Union (WCTU) was incorporated at a convention in Cedar Rapids. Foster was in attendance and was elected secretary. Later that year, she would attend the WCTU's national meeting in Cleveland, where she would come to the attention of Frances E. Willard, who would become president of the organization in 1879. Willard recognized Foster's talents as both a savvy political operative and an effective public speaker and quickly brought the young attorney into the union's inner circle. Soon Foster was traveling all over the Midwest, helping to build a temperance network, making speaking appearances, meeting with newspaper editors, and, indeed, lobbying lawmakers.[11]

In the fall of 1878 Foster sensed a political opportunity and proposed at the annual meeting of the Iowa WCTU the adoption of a constitutional amendment outlawing alcohol in all forms. "I recommend to this convention that a form of petition be issued by our State Union praying the next Legislature to pass a bill, submitting to the vote of the people an amendment to the constitution, forever prohibiting the manufacture and sale of intoxicating liquors," Foster said.[12]

Although the WCTU convention was open to the public, none of Iowa's major newspapers covered the event, and they only later learned what Foster had proposed. She may have intended that to happen. She would have known how controversial a liquor amendment would be, and she might have wanted to leave the ladies of the WCTU free to react to the idea without the presence of male reporters. For her plan to succeed, it would require widespread buy-in. She knew that efforts to curb the liquor trade in the past had failed for the same reason: the lack of enforcement. For prohibition to work this time, there had to be a consensus broad and strong enough to convince the river towns that there could be no exceptions.

"We know the traditional love of the Irishman for whiskey, the German for beer, the Frenchman for wine, the Englishman for ale," she said. "But we also [know] by sight, not by tradition, that the *American drinks everything*, and we fear that the charge upon the foreign population covers like a fact nearer home."[13]

There is little doubt that among those who did know of Foster's prohibitory speech—probably within hours—was Colonel Joseph Eiboeck, editor of one of the best-known German-language newspapers in the Midwest. A feisty defender of German culture and immigrant rights, the Austro-Hungarian Eiboeck had arrived in Dubuque from Vienna in 1849 at age eleven. He bought his flagship paper, the *Iowa Staats-Anzeiger*, in 1874, and had, by 1895, a weekly circulation of sixty-four hundred.[14]

While history is oddly silent on Eiboeck's claim to a military title, the record overflows with evidence of his personal crusade against what he called "Iowa's prohibition plague." He found the temperance movement both baffling and infuriating, and it sent him to the writing desk, where he produced some of the most colorful and brash editorials of his day. He once compared the uneven enforcement of Iowa's liquor laws to the wild persecutions meted out by the Spanish Inquisition. He called the Republicans in the capital xenophobic because of their lack of respect for other cultures. He called women like Foster "the witches of temperance." When a zealous prohibitionist pastor was murdered on the streets of Sioux City by a brewer, he casually dismissed the crime, saying that the victim had only himself to blame.

"There's a joke," Eiboeck wrote in 1900, recalling the rough-and-tumble politics over drinking in Iowa. "If a Swabian turns 40 without having gotten some sense into his head, then he'll never be sensible. One might apply this proverb to a class of Anglo-Americans in Iowa, for in 40 years they have not yet come to their senses nor realized that, in the long run, a law prohibiting the consumption and production of spirits cannot be enforced."[15]

Eiboeck's family was part of the mass immigration of Germans into Iowa between 1850 and 1856. Eiboeck's father was shot to death in a duel, and his stepfather was one of the "48ers" who had been arrested in the failed uprising against the Habsburg monarchy and sent into exile.[16]

After apprenticing with a local printer, Eiboeck bought his first newspaper at age twenty-seven. The *Clayton County Journal* was a Republican organ written in English, both of which Eiboeck respected and didn't change. His deep interest in politics, however, led him to move to Des Moines, where his *Staats-Anzeiger* aggressively followed action in and around the capitol. He allowed his politics to evolve freely. He allied himself at times with both Republicans and Democrats; he backed Horace Greeley's radical run for president in 1872 and aggressively favored the progressives and the Anti-Monopoly Party of the 1880s. Eiboeck's commitment to immigrant rights, however, never wavered, and he often gave voice to a form of German nationalism that sometimes exasperated even his American friends. One of them was John P. Irish, an anti-temperance leader and once editor of the *Iowa City Journal*, which was one of the leading Democratic papers in the state. "We [non-German Americans] didn't understand anything of personal liberty," Irish said after listening to one of Eiboeck's speeches. "We were as ignorant as the cattle among which we have grown up; that the majority of us were but raised in log huts, where a pig sty was on one side, a cow stable on the other side, we in the middle."[17]

What most offended Eiboeck and his German readers was the tinge of jingoism attached to any and all temperance laws. Eiboeck boldly pointed out the hypocrisy of Iowans "whose forefathers had left their home country once their freedom of conscience was infringed upon, only to become equally if not more intolerant and oppressive."[18]

Prohibition leaders like Foster would have liked to believe that their campaign was unblemished by such ethnic tensions, but that was not the case. Drunken stereotypes—the Irish with their whiskey, the Italians with their wine, and the Germans with beer—were all too frequently on display. In an attempt at humor, the *Des Moines Register* published an imaginary interview with a German brewer from Millersburgh, Iowa, in 1874. "Ven I goes to mine bet I sleps not good," the make-believe brewer began. "I dreams in mine head dat I hears dem vemens brayin' and singin' in mine ears do Jesus loves me. Dot bother me so I got right straight up and walk on de floor and take anudder glass of beer."[19]

There's no record of Eiboeck and Foster facing off in a debate or even having a private discussion. Had that happened, each might have been impressed with the logic of the other's position. Eiboeck, for instance, advocated moderation. "Alcoholism is a great evil; it creates much misery and woe," he said. "Nonetheless, prohibition has created the worst form of inebriety and the greatest of all evils—clandestine drunkenness. 'Der heimliche suff'—the tenet that it is immodest and immoral to consume alcoholic beverages in public and that it is better to keep them private and behind the curtains."[20]

Foster, no doubt, knew upstanding men who shared Eiboeck's perspective—men who drank, but not to excess. And she would also have to agree that the honest and hardworking German enjoying a Sunday *Lagerbier* could never be mistaken for the destitute alcoholic of the city slums. Where they would part company, however, was Foster's insistence on a law demanding total abstinence. "That intemperance is a most prolific source of pauperism, insanity, and crime need but be stated," she said. "Does not wise political economy then as well as Christian philanthropy demand that the cause of this wanton profligacy, this outrageous waste of men and money be stopped?"[21]

Foster and Eiboeck would soon confront each other in the greatest political battle ever waged in Iowa over liquor, a confrontation that would lead to riots, mayhem, and murder.

Two of Iowa's worst highwaymen of the late 1870s and early 1880s were brothers Ike and Bill Barber, who were thought to have killed as many as five men in connection with numerous robberies in Iowa and Illinois. One of their most vicious assaults took place in August 1882, when they robbed and murdered a wealthy farmer named Charles McMahon in central Illinois. Two of the farmer's hired men interrupted the crime, and they were murdered too. The bodies were not discovered for several days. McMahon's head was crushed and mutilated; the other two victims were nearly decapitated. A posse was organized, rewards posted, and the Barber brothers went on the lam.[22]

There were repeated false reports of their capture, many around Fayette County in northern Iowa, where the brothers had been raised and still had family. And, indeed, just a few weeks after the McMahon murders, a sheriff's deputy did come across the outlaws near their home base in the town of Wadena. There was a gunfight, and the deputy was killed. Nine months later, the Barbers were spotted in Fayette County again, and a phalanx of police and armed citizens surrounded them. Once again, the brothers shot their way free, although this time on foot.

Days later, the brothers, famished and exhausted, knocked on the door of a farmhouse and asked for food and a place to rest. The owner recognized them but gave them shelter and food while quietly sending word to a neighbor and to the sheriff. Before the law arrived, however, the farmer and his friends got the jump on the Barber brothers, rendering them harmless and putting them in chains. The sheriff took them into custody and brought them to the Buchanan County jail at Independence. News of the brothers' arrest spread, and a mob soon assembled, led by a brother of the deputy slain by the Barbers in September. Using crowbars and sledgehammers, the vigilantes broke into the jail and then into the cells. The Barbers were seized and walked a half mile to a grove of trees on the edge of town, where they were hanged.

"Boys, I am willing and ready to die," Ike Barber reportedly said in his last words. "But don't jerk a fellow to pieces. Hang me high, hang me well, and hang me dead."[23]

A surprising number of illegal executions took place in Iowa between 1878 and 1899. The lynchings were more common in rural, sparsely populated areas. Here, where the men worked long hours, often in fields far from their wives and children. Here, too, the anxiety of isolation and the vulnerability of life on the farm sometimes gave way to the temptations of mob rule. This exposure was a universal threat, and when a crime against a family did take place, the farmers rallied, just as they might to help a neighbor whose home had been damaged by a tornado or ice storm.[24]

Law enforcement as an institution was well established in Iowa by 1860, but there remained a legacy of vigilantism. Organized cattle and horse thieves were rampant on the frontier. The lack of standardized currency and a badly organized banking system attracted bandits and counterfeiters of all stripes. Even when an offender was arrested and brought to trial, the outcome was often unsatisfactory. A vigilante wave crested in 1857 in eastern Iowa and ended with the lynching of sixteen men—all white and all accused of murder, horse theft, or counterfeiting.[25]

In some cases, the local sheriff would join the mob and help with the administration of justice sans court or trial. A report in the *St. Charles City Republican* noted the lynching of two brothers in Tama County in January 1860. The men were suspected of stealing a pair of horses in Des Moines. They were arrested in Independence and were being brought back to Polk County when the captors changed their minds. "For some reason, not yet made apparent, the sheriff, Mr. Seaman, and the owner of the horses, Mr. Small, both of Des Moines, together took it into their heads to administer summary punishment to the prisoners by hanging them and thus save the trouble of taking them to Des Moines," the *City Republican* reported.

It was three days later that the bodies were discovered. A coroner's jury was convened, which ruled that the brothers' deaths were murder. The sheriff and the horse trader were arrested, although they were never tried.[26]

In the summer of 1887, near the southern Iowa town of Leon, not far from the border with Missouri, an accusation of rape by a farmer's wife prompted more than three hundred men to chase the alleged assailant for two days before capturing him near Decatur City. Although the victim claimed to have evidence of his innocence, he was lynched on the spot.[27]

Iowa became one of four states to abolish state-sanctioned capital punishment in 1872. Sympathy for a railroad worker, whose conviction for first-degree murder appeared to come despite strong extenuating circumstances, galvanized public opinion. His execution would have been the first in twelve years, sparking an outcry in favor of mercy and the condemnation of capital punishment. "If an individual kills his fellow man, shall the State of Iowa commit a greater outrage by deliberately killing him?" questioned Marvin Bovee, a nationally known death penalty opponent, in a speech before the Iowa General Assembly in April 1872. Only a few days later and on the eve of the scheduled execution, Iowa lawmakers removed the death penalty as an option for sentencing.[28]

A distinct shift in mood began two years later in Des Moines following the discovery of a body dumped under the Court Avenue Bridge on June 14, 1874. The victim, John Johnson, was a downtrodden resident of one of the city's flophouses who spent his nights in any number of Des Moines's worst gin joints. His murder became a source of civic tension because it was the latest of four unsolved killings committed in the red-light district of the city in three years. The editors of the *Register* demanded justice. "Here have been four murders, of the foulest and most mysterious manner, of which absolutely nothing has ever been discovered," decried the paper as it denounced the police for failing to find the killers. "If authorities cannot do it, or will not, have we not the mettle and the decency as citizens to do it ourselves?" the *Register* threatened.[29]

The jab was enough to set investigators in motion. Within a few weeks, a gaggle of unholy witnesses and potential suspects were rounded up as charges were filed against those responsible for the murder. The ringleader was a part-time bartender named Charley Howard, who was married to an aging courtesan who ran a notoriously mangy brothel. Gradually, the facts began to emerge. Johnson's murder was the result of drunken jealousy, the theft of ten dollars, and a cheap watch. The jury convicted Howard, who stood before the judge at sentencing defiant and grinning at the spectators in the packed courtroom. A life sentence was all that the law would allow.

In the dead of night, however, the crowd struck back. A well-organized band of about twenty-five masked vigilantes broke into the jail and overpowered the guards. The intruders tore Howard out of his cell, marched him outside the courthouse, threw a rope over the nearest lamppost, and hanged him.[30]

Outrage at the lawlessness in Des Moines resonated throughout the state for weeks. There was a consensus, however, that had the judge been able to apply capital punishment to Howard, the lynching would not have happened. Crime statistics were circulated that showed a clear uptick in violent crime since the death penalty had been abolished. When lawmakers came back into session only weeks after the Howard lynching, in January 1876, several bills were introduced to restore capital punishment. It wasn't until 1878, however, that a pro-gallows majority would finally prevail.[31]

That action did not by any means curtail mob violence in Iowa. Between 1878 and 1899, there were twenty-one lynchings and forty-five near-lynchings. All but one of the victims was white, nearly all were poorly educated, and most straddled the lowest rungs of the economy. Much of the violence took place in the southern half of the state, where tolerance for "rough justice" had stronger historical roots. But some of the incidents happened in cities with far more established judicial institutions, including Des Moines, Winterset, and Burlington. That said, the number of incidents in Iowa was not high when compared to other states during the same period. Louisiana, for example, over the same twenty-year period, had 254 documented lynchings.[32]

After lawmakers restored capital punishment in 1878, only four legal executions took place through 1899. That was seen as justification for some people to take the law into their own hands. "Are mobs wholly and entirely to blame?" an editor in Ringgold County asked in April 1887. "We think not. They are encouraged and cultivated by a lax and feeble magistracy."[33]

By 1868 Governor W. M. Stone was already worried about prison overcrowding and noted in his January address to the legislature that Fort Madison had 160 inmates and 162 cells. "It will be observed that the number of convicts has nearly doubled within the last two years, and with progress of the population, it is but reasonable to anticipate a continued increase of crime, requiring additional facilities," he told lawmakers. "Unless the State is prepared to adopt the vicious and discarded system of doubling the convicts in cells."[34]

The tiny eastern Iowa town of Anamosa was chosen as the location for the new prison, largely because of its proximity to a large deposit of high-grade limestone. In early summer 1873 the first inmates were transferred to the worksite from Fort Madison and given jobs in the quarry. The first limestone blocks for the prison were moved into place by a prisoner named Ed Sheridan. He had been sentenced to prison in the spring of 1873 for breaking into a farmer's home brandishing a big butcher knife and making off with $26 in cash before being arrested two days later.[35] The operation had barely begun when three prisoners dropped their hammers and disarmed a guard before making a clean getaway. Although a posse was quickly organized and a $300 reward posted (about $7,000 today), only one of the three was recaptured.[36]

Designed by architect L. W. Foster of Des Moines, the penitentiary at Anamosa created a stir when the first buildings were finished in 1875. Nicknamed the "White Palace of the West," the prison was adorned with stunning Gothic Revival features and crenelated towers, along with lush landscaping. It is still in operation today, and the original prison buildings are protected by the national register of historic places.[37]

Connecticut's Wethersfield State Prison set the standard for progressive inmate administration. Prisoners slept individually in single cells and were given some choice in the work they did during the day. Hospital units and chapels were included as part of the prison campus. There were libraries and, later, educational opportunities. A system for classifying and separating prisoners based on their crimes and conduct had been imported from Ireland. Reform, instead of punishment, began to emerge as the greater goal of the American correctional system after the Civil War. That did not mean that life for a prisoner in the mid-nineteenth century wasn't harsh. Transgression of prison rules brought floggings and sometimes the ball and chain. Inmates were forbidden to speak under almost all circumstances. Prisoners were expected to perform hard work during the day, and the food provided was never enough and rarely well prepared.[38]

One of the first women to serve time at Anamosa was Betsy Smith, who also came close to becoming the first woman in Iowa to be hanged. As described in various news accounts, she was in an unhappy marriage and schemed with one of her adult daughters to kill her husband and take possession of his savings, estimated at $600 ($18,000 today). In April 1893 her husband, Michael Smith, withdrew his money from a Des Moines area bank and was shot in the face at close range that night. He survived but was blinded by the shooting. The rest of his family swore to the police that he had been attacked by a burglar. An insurance payout of $3,000 ($93,000 today) was issued to him as a result of losing both eyes. A year later, Mr. Smith was found dead in his bed, poisoned.

"The Smith woman is thoroughly tough," reported the *Cedar Rapids Gazette* as her murder trial opened in June 1894. "According to her own story, she took rat poison and put it in her husband's tea and in lemon pies she made for him."[39]

Perhaps the most famous inmate in Anamosa during the late nineteenth century was John Wesley Elkins, known in the Dubuque area as the "boy murderer."[40]

Elkins's mother was still pregnant with him when she went to court to divorce his father. She remarried but died when he was seven, and his stepfather abandoned him in Waterloo. The newspapers claimed young Elkins then walked the nearly seventy-five miles to the town of Elkader, where his father and stepmother lived—people he had never met before. "The elder Elkins was a severe man and of primitive ideas," the *Ottumwa Tri-Weekly* reported in 1902. "He was sturdy and believed thoroughly that the rod should play a definite and conspicuous part in the training of children. He used it unsparingly. The strange lad was whipped with great severity and often. The stepmother was also severe."[41]

Even as an adult, John Elkins was slight and just over five feet tall, and when the murders took place he would have needed a chair to get his father's rifle down from above the front door. They made him sleep in the barn, on a bed of hay. He told the authorities later that he woke in the middle of the night with a splitting headache and concluded that he needed to kill both his father and his stepmother. He shot his father in the head and then bludgeoned his stepmother with a threshing flail that he had brought in from the barn. He struck them both again and again with the flail until the walls and floor of the bedroom were covered in blood. His half sister, just two years old, was in the parents' bed too, but Elkins didn't attack her. When he was sure both parents were dead, he scooped up the little girl and fled the house. He woke the neighbors next door, making up a story that robbers broke in and committed the murders.[42]

Investigators doubted the boy's story and finally wrangled a confession out of him. He was charged and convicted of first-degree murder. He entered the men's reformatory at Anamosa on January 14, 1890. He was eleven years old.[43]

4

A Schoolhouse on Every Hilltop and No Saloon in the Valley

Petitions that could be measured by the foot arrived at the capitol ahead of lawmakers in January 1880. Almost all the signatures gathered were in support of J. Ellen Foster's prohibitory amendment. The playbook being used by the prohibitionists put a premium on getting the Republicans organized early in the legislative session. Iowa law required that a constitutional amendment could not go before voters until it had been approved by lawmakers twice, in consecutive general assembly sessions. If the temperance leaders could successfully take the first of those two steps in 1880, then the earliest that the prohibitory measure could go on the ballot would be 1882.[1] The language of the proposed law was both direct and sweeping: "No person shall manufacture for sale, or sell or keep for sale as a beverage, any intoxicating liquor whatever, including ale, wine, and beer." It was approved by both houses in March 1880 and quickly received the governor's signature. The liquor-tolerant legislators could do little but watch as the GOP steamrolled ahead. The Democrats were outnumbered in the senate, 41 to 7, and in the house, 81 to 15.[2] Two other liquor bills were adopted at the same time: one barred druggists and pharmacists from giving away alcoholic beverages; the other outlawed free drinks offered to voters while they waited in line at the polls on election day.[3]

The pro-liquor camp organized early too, although the coalition was fractured. The Irish and the Scots, for instance, still harbored a deep resentment that state law tolerated the beer of the Germans, but not their whiskey. Liquor distillers were also resentful that they could not sell their product within state borders, whereas brewers and winemakers had been free to conduct their business unimpeded for decades. Eiboeck took it upon himself to bring the troops together.

"The time in which brewers and liquor dealers regarded each other with enmity must end," Eiboeck warned in an editorial in the summer of 1879. "For the experience of the last years teaches us that the temperance fanatics are determined to prohibit the manufacture and sale of beer just as strictly as they have already forbidden liquor."[4]

Shortly after the amendment was ratified the first time, Eiboeck helped incorporate the State Protective Association and began raising money from brewers and distillers. The money didn't come from producers just in Iowa but also in Chicago, St. Louis, and Milwaukee. Some of the money was used to rouse economic fears about what the loss of the liquor industry might bring. The Iowa State Brewers' Association issued a widely circulated report on the jobs and tax income that would disappear overnight if the amendment were adopted. In 1881 there were 120 active beer manufacturers, which directly employed over a thousand men and indirectly provided paychecks to another five hundred. Collectively, the liquor trade paid $252,000 in taxes (about $7 million today).[5]

A more manipulative scheme from the wets sent operatives all over the state armed with plans to build new breweries and distillery factories, which might or might not have had any real money behind them. "The object is to get up a manufacturing sentiment against the prohibitory amendment," a report in the *Sioux City Journal* declared in May 1881. "It is a very thin device. If whisky [*sic*] manufacturing is the only sort of manufacturing enterprise looking toward Iowa, we want none of it. Iowa wants the enterprises that feed and clothe and educate and enrich and make people happier and better—not those that curse and impoverish."[6]

A better and more substantive argument questioned the fairness of the liquor ban. Over the years, the owners of breweries and distilleries had invested hundreds of thousands of dollars to improve their facilities, expand operations, and develop new equipment and transportation networks. All of that money was spent on a legal enterprise, which the proposed prohibitory amendment completely ignored. Even the most ardent prohibitionists conceded the inequity. "If it can be shown that the business is inimical to the public welfare, the State undoubtedly has the police power to control it and prohibit it, but no one can claim it has the power to confiscate the property," the editor of the

Muscatine Weekly Journal reasoned in September 1881. "Confiscation is permissible only where there is a violation of law. But in this case, there is no violation of law."[7]

There were some dry sympathizers in the capitol who suggested that the injured business owners should be reimbursed with tax money. Nonsense, the tight-fisted majority answered. J. Ellen Foster clarified that the prohibitionists would consider reimbursements with public funds if the liquor interests agreed to pay back to the state all the expenses that their business had cost the public in terms of crime and social welfare. "When every poor woman beggared by the drunkenness of her husband has been furnished her the barest, plainest home in which to gather children, when these children have wholesome food, and decent clothing, when the long list of losses to the state from the traffic has been covered, then it will be time to consider how much shall be paid this presumptuous pleader," she said.[8]

Yet, the economic uncertainty that the prohibitory measure posed could not be so easily dispelled, even for some backers of the ban. James S. Clarkson, the GOP kingmaker and editor of the *Des Moines Register*, had been a champion of the temperance movement but threatened to withdraw his support unless an exemption could be worked out for a major distillery that had just opened in Des Moines. The International Distillery began operations in January 1880, and within a year it was turning 600 bushels of Iowa corn into 2,400 gallons of alcohol every day. Later, after substantial expansion, the output grew to 25,000 gallons a day, valued at $3.4 million in the early 1880s ($144 million today). The plant, purported to be the largest distillery in the world, provided employment to about a hundred men, while hundreds of farmers also depended financially on the factory.[9]

Clarkson and the Des Moines business leaders argued that since most of the alcohol produced at the distillery was shipped out of state, it should be granted special status. Most of the state's smaller rival papers—including some that were also run by prohibitionists—took delight in pointing out the *Register's* two-faced somersault. "It seems that the Register wants the big gin mills at Desmoines [*sic*] and at Iowa City to have [the] opportunity to continue to manufacture high wines to be sent abroad," noted the *Muscatine Journal* in March 1882. "And if this cannot be done, it is willing to see the saloon curse continue in

Iowa."[10] With Clarkson unmoved, senate leaders acquiesced and added a line clarifying that the amendment was "intended to prohibit the sale and manufacture" of alcohol within the state of Iowa.[11]

A few days before the Iowa General Assembly was called into session in January 1882, Representative G. L. Johnson from Maquoketa stopped off in Davenport on his way to Des Moines. He was spotted by a reporter in a hotel lobby and agreed to give a quick interview about whether the coming term would be a busy one.

"No, I think not," Johnson answered. "At least not if what Mrs. J. Ellen Foster predicts comes to pass."

"Mrs. J. Ellen Foster?" the reporter asked. "What has she to do with it?"

"Why, everything to do with it," Johnson answered. "She is the general of the temperance forces, which control the Republicans in the state and are in the majority in the [General] Assembly. Mrs. Foster told me that the legislative matters had all been arranged."

Johnson counted them off on his fingers. The prohibition amendment would pass out of both houses, the governor would sign it and then call for a special election in the spring, and the voters would approve it.

"Mrs. Foster is a most interesting lady," the reporter said.

"She is, truly, and fine-looking too," Johnson agreed. "She can win almost anyone to her side."[12]

When the Nineteenth Iowa General Assembly convened on January 9, 1882, the Democrats immediately introduced a series of resolutions aimed at delaying or derailing prohibition's path toward the ballot. One questioned the governor's authority to call a "special election" for the purpose of adopting enforcement legislation unrelated to a state emergency. They also forced a lengthy debate on what exactly the legislature was voting on: were lawmakers being asked their personal positions on liquor or merely whether the question should go to the voters? Finally, they demanded more time to study the legislation and threatened to go to court if their request was denied. The stall tactics were unsuccessful. The amendment was overwhelmingly approved for the second time on March 9, 1882, and the governor signed the bill four days later. The special election was set for June 27, 1882.[13]

As Election Day approached, the campaign intensified. The temperance coalition held mass prayer meetings and blocks-long parades led by marching bands. "Vote for mother and me" was a favored slogan. Another was "A schoolhouse on every hilltop and no saloons in the valley."[14] Those opposed to the amendment worked just as hard, but mostly out of view. "The antis will not spend any money for coffee, they will not give their time to prayer, they will not bother with getting the children into a parade, but they will know every voter in every voter precinct and if he can be influenced to cast a ballot against the amendment they will have him to the polls and his help with the count," the *Sioux City Journal* warned on the morning of Election Day.[15]

Pro-liquor editors even took a poke at Foster. "Some of the saloon organs are heaping abuse upon Mrs. Foster of Clinton, calling her 'John Ellen Foster,'" noted the *Muscatine Weekly Journal*, "because she is spending time at Demoines [*sic*] endeavoring to secure the passage of the prohibitory constitutional amendment."[16]

When the ballots were finalized, the amendment had passed narrowly.[17] Even Mark Twain was impressed, remarking in his beloved travelogue, *Life on the Mississippi* (written between 1881 and 1882 and published in 1883), that voters in Iowa endorsed a law that prohibited "the manufacture, exportation, importation, purchase, sale, borrowing, lending, stealing, drinking, smelling, or possession by conquest, inheritance, intent, accident, or otherwise, in the state of Iowa, of each and every deleterious beverage known to the human race, except water."[18]

J. J. Barrett, a physician in the small Kansas town of Humboldt, was also very likely militantly anti-temperance. Voters in his home state agreed, in November 1880, to adopt a constitutional amendment outlawing the manufacture and sale of liquor, as well as its excessive consumption. Months after the Kansas prohibition law went into effect, Barrett allowed himself to drink until intoxicated in public and was arrested. It was all part of a plan.

Barrett and his drinking supporters were aware that Kansas law required that the title of a measure and its content be of a single subject. The title of the measure that had passed from the legislature to the voters didn't mention the drunkenness clause. Thus, when Barrett was taken before a district judge, his attorneys argued that the liquor ban was unconstitutional, and the judge agreed.

Most observers, however, believed that the ruling would be quickly overturned. "Judge Talbott of the Humboldt District Court has decided that the law punishing a man for drunkenness is unconstitutional," the *Anthony Journal* reported in November 1881. "He should be awarded a leather medal for stupidity."[19]

However, in February 1882, the Kansas Supreme Court agreed with Talbott and struck down the part of the amendment dealing with intoxication. Or, as the *Leavenworth Standard* phrased it in a headline, the high court established "The Right of a Citizen of Kansas to Get Drunk."[20]

It would be hard to imagine that Eiboeck and his cabal of liquor allies would not have been made aware of Barrett's challenge and would not have begun immediately to scour the legislative record in their own state, looking for similar inconsistencies in how the Iowa prohibitory law had been prepared for the ballot. Most likely, they found what they were looking for right away. More than two months before the landmark June 1882 election, in which the liquor ban was adopted by Iowa voters, a well-informed reporter from the *Burlington Weekly Hawk-Eye* laid out with precision the measure's fatal flaw. Iowa law required that before a proposed amendment to the state constitution could go before voters, both houses of the general assembly had to ratify the same measure twice and in consecutive sessions. The language of the amendment had to be exactly the same both times—which was where the error occurred.

"That this provision of the constitution has not been complied with becomes evident upon an investigation of the history of the pending amendment," the *Hawk-Eye* noted. "In this case there is no ambiguity."[21]

The very next day, Senator John Carver Bills, a wet Republican from Davenport, sent a letter to the *Quad-City Times* (then known as the *Davenport Morning Democrat*) backing up the *Hawk-Eye*'s contention that Republicans had failed to follow the law. "The question of submission will never be voted on here or anywhere; such a proceeding would be unconstitutional," he said.[22] Then, in May, with little more than three weeks before the election, the *Quad-City Times Democrat* added another letter that appeared to come from former state senator Nathaniel A. Merrell, a Democrat from Clinton. Merrell called the proposed prohibitory amendment's passage by two successive general assemblies a "miserable deception."[23]

As the election approached, Foster and the Republicans were oddly silent and left the unconstitutionality charge unaddressed. There can be no question that the temperance leaders fully appreciated the implications of the opposition's claims and knew that a legal challenge on a technical violation would certainly follow if the liquor ban were adopted by the voters. Someone in the prohibition camp must have researched the issue. If so, as the *Hawk-Eye* indicated, the analysis would have revealed a small but glaring variation in the language of the bills approved by lawmakers the first and second times. It seems very unlikely that Foster and the Republican leaders would not have convened a high-level meeting to consider what they should do about it. There were just two choices: either concede the error, call off the election, and start the process over when the next general assembly convened in two years or simply ignore the oversight and trust that no judge in Iowa would dare overturn the will of the people.

Fatefully, the temperance leaders chose obfuscation, which played right into the hands of their opponents, who absolutely knew of a judge who would indeed overturn the liquor prohibition.

The Honorable William I. Hayes was born in Michigan and received his law degree in 1863 from what was then called the University of Ann Arbor. By 1866 he had arrived in Clinton, Iowa, and started his practice. An ambitious man who would later serve four terms representing Clinton County in Congress, Hayes was elected city attorney three times before being appointed a district court judge by the governor in 1875. During his entire forty-year career in the law and politics, he never wavered from his position as a solid Democrat vehemently opposed to prohibition.[24]

"The principle of prohibition is detestable," Hayes said in a speech before a largely German audience in Davenport in 1886. "More than all other laws put together, it is a breeder of contempt of law in general, and warms into life more fanatics, hypocrites, visionary, zealots, and intolerant bigots than all other laws."[25]

The Seventh Judicial District, where Hayes served as judge, included the counties of Muscatine, Clinton, and Scott—all bastions of the wets. By design, just after the June election, a pair of well-known Davenport brewers sold $113 worth of beer to a local bar owner and demanded payment. The bar owner refused to pay, and they went to court.

The brewers, Rudolph Lange and his brother-in-law, Henry Koehler, were good friends with the saloonkeeper, a man named John Hill, who owned the bar within Davenport's largest German social club, Turner Hall. In papers filed before Judge Hayes, Hill said the debt was unenforceable because intoxicating beverages were no longer legal in Iowa. Attorneys representing Koehler and Lange pointed to the wording variations in the prohibitory measures that went before the legislature and argued that the amendment was unconstitutional. Thus, Hill must pay his beer tab.[26]

Not surprisingly, Judge Hayes agreed. What was very surprising, however, was that the Iowa Supreme Court upheld Hayes's ruling. The vote, announced in early January 1883, was 3 to 1.[27]

An epic round of indignation and finger pointing soon followed.

"What is this temperance defeat and what the saloon's victory?" the *Des Moines Register* asked upon hearing the unsettling news. "Not that prohibition is not right, not that a majority of the people of Iowa are not in favor of it . . . but that the Supreme Court over two quibbles raised by a controversy between a saloon keeper and a brewer, has decided that two clerical errors in the legislative part of the movement must weigh against and temporarily defeat the sovereign will of the people."[28]

Embarrassed Republicans even tried to deflect the blame onto legislative staff. A reader of the *Des Moines Register* called them on it: "Will the *Cedar Rapids Republican*, the *Newton Journal*, Mrs. Foster, and sundry other faultfinders please arise and explain which one of the ten stupid clerks of the 18th General Assembly is to assume the overwhelming burden of having thwarted the good intention of 155,000 of Iowa's best people?" an anonymous insider wrote in a letter to the editor. He or she went on:

Will these wise editors, lawyers, philosophers, and statesmen please analyze or otherwise demonstrate the astounding proposition they so constantly proclaim from the housetops? Surely, if such an unprecedented piece of gross carelessness is chargeable to one frail mortal, it should be an easy matter to define the offense and point out the offender. . . . Mrs. Foster states from the platform that the committee appointed by the temperance convention to closely watch the proceedings of both Houses of the Legislature, and see that the resolution was properly and lawfully carried through, did their duty. The writer would like to know where the temperance committee were during the informal proceeds of the Senate relative to erasing the words.

The letter was signed: "One of the Clerks."[29]

The high court's ruling was celebrated along the river. "Vive La Gambrinus," the *Davenport Gazette* rejoiced, which was interpreted to mean in Italian, "Long Live Beer." The *Dubuque Times* was perhaps better understood: "Prohibition is as dead as last year's mackerel."[30]

Ellen Foster, on her way through Davenport a week or so following the court ruling, told a reporter that the Koehler and Lang case should never have been allowed to go forward. "It was a put-up job from the beginning," she said. "No sir, no individual would consent to be robbed by adherence to mere technicalities. The reasoning of the Supreme Court is weak." Joseph Eiboeck gave the event a slight but pointed mention in his newspaper: "They laugh best who laugh last."[31]

Because both Judge Hayes and Ellen Foster were longtime residents of Clinton, it would be hard to imagine that they had not met, either in a courtroom or elsewhere, but there is no record of it. The closest they came, as far as newspaper records are concerned, took place in January 1878, when Ellen Foster became probably the first woman ever to argue a case before the Iowa Supreme Court. At issue was the seizure of some $2,500 worth of liquor by local authorities (about $80,000 today). A liquor dealer claimed the booze was his and won an injunction giving him possession until the whole matter could be sorted out by the district court. Judge Hayes was assigned the case and promptly ruled against the liquor dealer, ordering that the whiskey be given back to the county. The liquor dealer appealed the ruling to the Iowa Supreme Court and then faced off against Foster, who represented the prohibition officers. She won. This was perhaps the one and only time she and Judge Hayes agreed on anything having to do with liquor.[32]

Three years after the landmark Hayes ruling, Republicans sought their pound of flesh over the Koehler case, launching impeachment proceedings against him in the state's House of Representatives. As he prepared his defense, Hayes mused to a reporter that he intended to hire Foster as his defense attorney. He said that he had great "faith in the lady's legal ability." What a spectacle that would be, the reporter wrote, "Mrs. Foster, the leader of the temperance forces in Iowa and President of the WCTU in this state, the defending council of this noted judicial defender of saloons."[33]

5

The Martyr of Sioux City

The man most closely associated with Iowa's restrictive temperance laws of the late nineteenth century was a lawyer named Talton E. Clark. A meticulous lawmaker, Clark was hardnosed, serious, and the obvious choice for picking up the pieces after the courts threw out the prohibitory amendment. As chairman of the state senate's Committee on Suppression of Intemperance, it was left to him, more or less, to decide the path forward. His reading of the statewide political leaders was that no one wanted to bring the question back to the voters. Given that his Republican caucus still held a large majority in both houses, as well as the governor's office, it was Clark's view that the liquor trade should be rubbed out by statute, plain and simple.[1]

Clark was the son of a Presbyterian minister who, when not being hardnosed and serious, possessed a whimsical sense of humor that he used to sway juries, charm judges, and keep his rivals off balance. There was probably no better illustration of this wit than when, in the summer of 1877, Clark announced that he had decided not to run for the state senate. He was widely admired in the southwest corner of the state and thought by many to possess all that was needed to become a future governor, congressman, or U.S. senator. Aware that he would be disappointing some of his neighbors, Clark eased out of the race with flair.

"T. E. Clark of Clarinda, who was the leading candidate for State Senator in his district, has just done something which is beyond the comprehension of the average politician," the *Sioux City Journal* reported. "He has published a card in which he says he submitted the matter of his candidacy to God, and the decision was that he should not run, and therefore, he withdrew from the race."

Four years later, the leaders of the Republican Party in Page County nominated Clark before a second divine intervention could take place.[2]

Upon arriving in Des Moines, Clark was immediately appointed to the Judiciary Committee, where he learned a great deal about the inability of the state to enforce its liquor laws. Two years later, he was named chair of the temperance committee.[3] One of the first bills introduced when the January 1884 legislative session opened in Des Moines was the repeal of "the odious wine and beer clause from the prohibitory code of Iowa," as reported by *La Porte City Progress-Review*.[4] The failure of the prohibitory amendment the year before notwithstanding, the Iowa Constitution had been amended in 1855 to prohibit the manufacture and sale of alcoholic beverages. At issue before Clark's committee was the state law adopted in 1858 that allowed liquor in counties where voters would allow it. As for what couldn't be accomplished at the polls, the Republican majority needed only a few weeks to craft a set of prohibitory laws so extreme as to make it virtually impossible for anyone to manufacture or sell liquor in their state. The problem, of course, was enforcing it.[5]

The new laws became operative at 12:00 a.m. on July 4, 1884, but by noon holiday revelers were happily lapping up beer and whiskey all over the state. In Burlington, some twenty saloons were open and doing a brisk business all day long. Similar insubordination took place in Dubuque and other river towns.[6]

A far more serious insurgency took place a month later in Iowa City, home to three of the state's largest breweries. The city was badly divided over the temperance question, and some of the better-known prohibitionists had been threatened or had stones thrown through the windows of their homes. On August 13, 1884, two brewers were put on trial for violating the liquor ban, with the proceedings held at the home of the judge. A large crowd gathered in support of the brewers, threatening to burn the judge's home. The prosecutor was caught, tarred, and threatened with lynching. A witness against the brewers was also accosted and beaten by the liquor men. Order was not restored as much as it was ransomed. The county supervisors issued permits for six saloons to stay open, and the grand jury refused to indict any of the rioters.[7]

The Republicans huddled once again, more determined than ever to see the liquor ban fully carried out. Despite losing ground with voters in the election of 1885, GOP leaders agreed to make two key changes in their approach to dealing with liquor violators. One was to shift the crime's oversight to the police court. Secondly, they directed all fines paid by perpetrators into the municipal treasury. "Governments enforce laws for revenue better than they do for principle," noted the *Iowa City Daily Republican*.[8]

Clark, as chairman of the state senate's Committee on Suppression of Intemperance, took up the new mandate with zeal. In January 1886 he helped draft one bill that made it very clear that it was the duty of district attorneys and sheriffs to undertake abatement proceedings whenever illegal liquor operations were reported. Clark also hiked the penalty for a liquor conviction to not more than $1,000 and not less than $300.

Other provisions called for the closure of any building used in making illegal liquor; any furnishings or equipment used would also be confiscated. Confiscated properties of the bootleggers were to be sold at public auction, with a share of the proceeds going to prosecutors and judges. The ban on transporting liquor into Iowa from other states was enhanced with heavy penalties.

Finally, Iowa basically deputized the entire adult population to help carry out enforcement, by empowering all its citizens with the ability to bring a liquor trader to court, and then guaranteed a bounty of not less than $25 for any successful prosecution.[9]

The law had a profound and immediate impact on drinking in Iowa. Nearly half of the state's 111 breweries closed in the year after adoption of the "Clark laws"; the number fell to just 23 after two years.[10] The Clark Laws also fostered an army of "searchers," self-appointed and virtually unregulated. These were mostly men from the underbelly of the economy who found they could earn a decent living bringing in liquor violators—real or imagined. Constables and town marshals, who were meagerly compensated, gave up formal law enforcement to concentrate on finding underground booze operations.[11]

Joining this new segment of the economy were two enterprising attorneys from the town of Le Mars in northwest Iowa. One morning, only a few weeks after the passing of the Clark Laws, the men, identified in news reports only as Messieurs Ziak and Gosselin, set out by train for Sioux City, about twenty-five miles away. They planned to surprise the county auditor by demanding to see the activity reports for all licensed liquor sellers in town. Their assumption was that the auditor would have no such reports, given that Woodbury County was liquor friendly. If so, it would be just a matter of filing certain court papers and, just like that, a payday.

However, the assistant auditor on duty that morning grew suspicious of the visitors' motives and refused to comply. Ziak and Gosselin demanded that the sheriff be summoned, who arrived and listened to both sides. Sheriff Dan McDonald patted down both attorneys and found a pistol in one of Gosselin's pockets. He arrested Gosselin for carrying a concealed weapon and sent Ziak on his way. After some hours stewing in a cell, Gosselin was brought before a judge, who agreed to grant bail, which was set at $100—far more than Gosselin had in his pockets.

"The gentleman went to jail after telephoning to Le Mars for aid, which came not," the *Sioux City Journal* reported. "Later, by consent, the continuance was made sixty days, and the prisoner was released. It was generally understood outside that he would drop the matter and get out of town."

The same *Journal* story noted that Gosselin and Ziak had recently attempted to prosecute saloonkeepers and druggists in Orange City, forty miles north. They quoted from the *Orange City Herald*: "The next time these fellows come to Orange City they should be tarred and feathered and ridden out of town on a three-cornered rail."[12]

Iowa's efforts to stop liquor imports were also initially successful. Railroad managers and express shippers were reluctant to test the Iowa ban, but as time went on, liquor dealers in other states pressed for the courts to strike down the act, which many viewed as an overreach by Iowa of interstate commerce protections. The case went to the U.S. Supreme Court in 1890, and a majority of the justices ruled against the state, thus tearing yet another major hole in Iowa's absolute ban on liquor.[13]

Sioux City relished its legacy as Iowa's hard-driving outpost on the state's northwestern edge. Its people identified more with the frontiersmen and the cowboys of the Dakotas than the insurance men of Des Moines or the scholars in Iowa City. Its founding came in a land deal that today would reek of political corruption. John Cook, an Oxford-educated land speculator, put the deal together in 1854 after convincing seven seated members of Congress to become partners in the fledgling Sioux City syndicate. Among those who signed on were both of Iowa's U.S. senators, Augustus C. Dodge and George W. Jones.[14]

Writing about the dubious business venture eighty-five years later, D. Spence Lewis, a former Sioux City councilman and city finance director, said that such arrangements were not uncommon in those days. "As it was known that many favors of the national government would be needed, men of high political and business standing throughout the country were taken into the scheme," recalled Lewis, whose parents were among the earliest settlers of Sioux City. He noted that, along with the Iowa officeholders, company partners included two congressmen from Pennsylvania and one each from South Carolina and Alabama.

Once onboard, the company officials got Congress to designate Sioux City as one of four official end points for the proposed federally sponsored rail route across Iowa. Another favor was the appointment of Cook as a government surveyor so that he could earn a federal salary as he laid out the streets and property lines of the new city. Finally, the congressmen also maneuvered the opening of a district land office in town to help administer the coming land boom.[15]

Initially, the township succeeded far beyond expectations. With the stamp of legitimacy from Washington, Sioux City quickly attracted hundreds of new residents. Many were farmers looking to get a share of the fertile prairie soil. There were merchants and professional men as well. But most of all, the first settlers of Sioux City were, like Cook, land speculators. The first city lots were grabbed up, often for less than $50, but when the city was incorporated in 1857, the same properties were fetching as much as $1,200. Addison Oliver, who would later represent Monona County in the legislature, remarked that the land boom had quickly gone out of control. "When I came to Sioux City, I thought everyone was crazy," he said. "But after I had been here awhile, I got as crazy as the rest of them."[16]

The first steamboats arrived in 1856, and for a time the Union Pacific Railroad seriously considered naming Sioux City as the eastern terminus of the coming transcontinental railroad, but it later concluded that Council Bluffs, to the south, was the better choice. Nonetheless, the "Queen City of the Northwest" seemed destined to become the next great American city.

However, in the blink of an eye, everything changed.

The failure of the New York branch of the Ohio Life Insurance and Trust Company, in August 1857, set off a banking panic that ripped across the country, shuttering businesses and cutting off nearly all forms of investment. In Sioux City, where the local economy existed almost exclusively on credit extended from the East, the boom went to bust overnight. Millions of acres of land in Woodbury County were abandoned, much of it never having been tilled. The promise of the Queen City would have to wait.[17]

It was more than a decade later that the Sioux City and Pacific Railway Company finally arrived, and another fifteen years before Sioux City began to take shape as one of Iowa's most promising economic centers. Between 1880 and 1890 the population mushroomed from seventy-five hundred to nearly forty thousand, making Sioux City the second largest city in the state.[18] By then, the Union Stock Yards Company had been organized, prompted by the growth in hog farms. The discovery of gold in Montana made Sioux City a gateway destination through which thousands of tons of freight and supplies, worth millions of dollars, passed yearly. New grain elevators were built near the riverfront; factories sprang up for the making of farm tools, furniture, and household appliances. There were new hotels and boardinghouses, professional offices, churches, and schools.[19]

As much as prosperity brought some new respectability, Sioux City would not yet be tamed. As lawmakers in Des Moines put the finishing touches on the Clark Laws, there were still seventy-three saloons operating day and night along the riverfront in Sioux City. Between the bars were dozens of licensed brothels and gambling dens. The profits, derived from the folly of men, were an integral component of the local economy, as the taxes saloonkeepers paid underwrote most of the municipal services. The very worst of the debauchery, however, was relegated to a red-light district known as "the Soudan."[20]

"It is densely populated, and its inhabitants are a conglomeration of whites and blacks of both sexes living together without the sanction of human laws and in open defiance of the moral code," a reporter from the *Sioux City Journal* wrote, describing the Soudan in 1888. "White women consort with their colored paramours, and white men hold illicit intercourse with colored women. The legitimate offspring from such a reeking hotbed of vice is and can only be murder, robbery, drunkenness, and brawling. The very air is tainted with crime, and it is no wonder that the stench has grown to be unendurable."[21]

The ink on the Clark Laws had not yet dried when the city council of Sioux City openly rebelled. In May 1886 they adopted a new liquor licensing ordinance that gave the saloonkeepers another year to do business for the fee of $25 per month.[22] "They have a strange way of doing things in Iowa," the *Peoria Journal* remarked. "They passed a prohibitory law, then a constitutional amendment, then enabling law to assist in enforcing the other laws against liquor making and selling; they tell us that Iowa is a prohibition state and that a man cannot get anything to drink there and so forth. Right on the heels of that comes the report that the city council of Sioux City has passed a law licensing the saloons. We are at a loss to make these things dovetail. . . . It is very evident that there are saloons in Sioux City and that people there sometimes drink."[23]

All of this cast a sense of hopelessness over the prohibitionists of Woodbury County. Already, Reverend D. R. Watson of the First Baptist Church had given up and moved his family back to New York. Saloon toughs threatened to "pound" Representative Isaac Struble, a popular three-term congressman from Le Mars, for voting in favor of a temperance bill pending in Washington. A petition against enforcing the Clark Laws was signed by 136 of Sioux City's business owners—only some of them bar owners. "At this time, we are laboring under a heavy burden brought on by the increased necessities of the city in its change from a thriving village to an important business center and can ill afford to lose the revenues which may be had if the law is not enforced," the businessmen explained. An opposing petition was circulated and signed by women representing "not less than 460 husbands and 1,060 children."[24]

In July 1886 the people of Sioux City were on edge. There had been two murders and several violent skirmishes, all of which involved guns and alcohol. The first incident took place on Saturday night before the Fourth of July holiday, when a dispute over a faro game at Prescott's Gambling House ended with one player killing another and the perpetrator escaping into the night. Next was the unprovoked murder of a vagrant who happened to knock on the wrong door deep in the bowels of the Soudan slum. In reaction, the city council ordered gambling houses in Sioux City to close on Sundays. Such a weak response satisfied no one, certainly not Reverend George C. Haddock of the First Methodist Church.

Haddock hadn't been in Sioux City for more than a year when he began stirring passions over the outrages of the town's saloons. Originally from Upstate New York, he had spent most of his spiritual career in Wisconsin, where he had gained a reputation as a fearless prohibitionist. Above average in height with a muscular build, Haddock could present an intimidating presence and appeared to know it. He boomed from the pulpit, demanding that the good people of his church venture out into the community and stamp out intemperance where they found it. Following a similar performance while preaching in Sheboygan, Wisconsin, in 1874, a gang of men outraged by his words pulled him into a dark corner and attempted to rough him up. Haddock threw them off one by one until one of them drew a gun and took a shot at him. He missed.[25]

Haddock's fiery Sunday condemnations soon became well known around Sioux City. Embraced by many, he was also insulted and spat upon by those who feared his presence. In a biography of Haddock, written by his son, an incident was recalled where a half-soused bar tough called out as Haddock approached on the other side of the street. "Come over here and I'll cut your head off," the man threatened. Without delay or misstep, Haddock reportedly crossed the street and confronted his adversary, looking him in the eye as he passed. The other man never made a move.[26]

Two weeks after the July murders, Haddock stunned the city leaders by initiating liquor injunctions against twenty-seven of Sioux City's largest taverns. Within days, the first of the hearings was held, but a final ruling was delayed. Uncertain of the outcome, some of the saloon owners gathered on the night of August 3 to plot an answer to the potent threat posed by Haddock. They met at a saloon owned by John Holdenried, who was a target of one of Haddock's injunctions. One of the men who met with Holdenried that night was a Belgian immigrant named John Arensdorf, the foreman of the Franz Brewing Company. When Holdenried raised the idea of hiring someone willing to assault Haddock, Arensdorf said he knew of two "Dutchmen" who would do the deed. The conspirators agreed to use some $700 from the coffers of the Sioux City Saloonkeepers Union to pay for the hit.[27]

Haddock boldly went about his business that day, probably well aware that the liquor men might be plotting something. He spent most of the morning and much of the afternoon in court testifying against the saloon owners. In the evening, he rented a horse and buggy and ventured a few miles east of town with another minister to check on allegations of illegal liquor activities at a local roadhouse. Several of Holdenried's men stood outside the bar and watched as the two prohibitionists drove away.

What happened next was a matter of much dispute, with the exception that Reverend Haddock was shot to death around 10:15 p.m. Witnesses testified at two trials that the shooter was Arensdorf. But the defense produced others who said that Arensdorf was elsewhere. Both juries voted for acquittal. The only person convicted of anything was a bystander, who was given four years for "inciting deeds of violence." A headline in the *New York Times* fittingly captured the judicial dilemma: "Perjury Somewhere."[28]

Shortly after the second trial, a key prosecution witness—identified in reports only as Mrs. Josephson—was badly hurt after her wagon was struck by another team, in what was thought by some to be a deliberate attack carried out by a friend of Arensdorf. About a year later, bodies began turning up. The first was a former accountant who had worked at the same brewery as Arensdorf. He was found partially burned, with a bullet wound in the chest and a gun belonging to Arensdorf nearby. It was ruled a suicide. Another witness, who had disappeared, turned up about two months later, also on the grounds of the Arensdorf brewery. Nothing came of any of these grisly discoveries.[29]

Outrage over the Haddock murder resulted in some Iowa communities moving against the illegal liquor trade. However, they once again encountered the strong sentiment that prohibition simply could not be enforced in certain parts of the state. One widely acknowledged loophole was the exception in the prohibitory laws that allowed pharmacies to sell alcohol for medical purposes. "A great many druggists have the habit of allowing the purchaser to sign any name he chooses to the required certificate," noted Judge S. M. Ladd of Sheldon, in a letter to the governor, in December 1887. "I think a civil or criminal penalty ought to be attached to this practice."[30]

The general assembly agreed, imposing the requirement that pharmacists post a substantial bond as part of the licensing permit. The prescription forms were formalized, and blanks could be obtained only from the counties. The pharmacists, even the legitimate ones, protested the new laws, and once again enforcement became problematic.

"Isn't it well known that the most prosperous drug stores in Iowa are in the towns in which the prohibitory law is enforced?" a reader wrote to the *Quad-City Times* (then known as the *Davenport Morning Democrat*) in April 1886. "Calling a drug store a 'pharmacy' or a druggist a 'pharmacist' doesn't alter the case a particle."[31]

This medical exception remained a glaring problem decades later when the National Prohibition Act was adopted. In 1925, at the time of Myrtle Cook's murder, there were seven licensed pharmacies in her hometown of Vinton, serving a population of about twenty-five hundred.[32]

Three years after the Haddock murder, the Chicago Tribune sent a reporter back to Sioux City. He found that liquor, prostitution, and gambling had returned. "The law has been violated whenever possible, and the Law and Order League is kept busy ferreting out cases of illegal liquor sales," the *Tribune* reported. "Not a week passes in which from two to a dozen arrests are not made. Officers of this organization are subjected to all kinds of abuse, and lately, the rougher element has grown bolder." The reporter also found that while a large number of saloons in Sioux City had been closed, a similar number had opened across the river in Covington, Nebraska, including a wholesale liquor house partly owned by Arensdorf. Some enterprising investors acquired 185 flatboats and strung them together to form a pontoon bridge across the state line, charging a toll of five cents. The bridge, the reporter wrote, placed "thirst at one end and a beer saloon at the other."[33]

Despite being the state capital, Des Moines had its share of lawlessness caused by whiskey. Sarcastically known as "the largest city in the world without an open saloon," Des Moines supported dozens of underground dram shops and speakeasies, which in the 1890s were known as "blind pigs."[34] With all that liquor flowing came marauding liquor vigilantes who needed only to haul someone into court to be awarded the $25 bounty. Because the state allowed them to issue their own search warrants, there was nowhere they couldn't go and no one they couldn't threaten. Many of the searchers carried around thick rolls of blank warrants, ready to be issued at a moment's notice. In some courtrooms, a fee was paid on every warrant executed, whether liquor was found or not. Because judges and county prosecutors also received a share of the spoils, there was virtually no oversight of what some considered a raid on the civic treasury.[35]

In March 1887 a delivery man for a local pharmacist became aware that he was being followed while out on his route. A well-known constable named S. E. "Colorado" Logan was certain that a teamster, named Joe Row, was delivering illegal booze. He was indeed, and he was armed. Row confronted Logan. Both men drew pistols, and Logan was killed. Although Row claimed he fired in self-defense, he nevertheless jumped bail and fled to Missouri. He eventually went to a farm owned by a cousin of Jesse James, where he was finally arrested and brought back for trial. He was convicted and sentenced to five years in prison.[36]

An even more infamous "searcher" was Frank Pierce, a lawman of dubious credentials who ran a temperance gang in Des Moines. He was wiry and of average stature but quick-thinking and good enough in a scrap to have once bested a prizefighter hired by a brothel owner specifically to keep Pierce out of her place of business. He came from a prosperous farm in Maine and was raised vehemently Protestant and anti-liquor. He arrived in Des Moines about the time of the 1882 special election and was eking out a living as a drayman when lawmakers adopted the Clark Law. Pierce quickly realized the opportunity, and within a few months he got himself appointed constable for a village just outside the Des Moines city limits. Ignoring those boundaries, Pierce began dragging the backstreets and basement storefronts, hunting the new prey. Very quickly, Pierce acquired a reputation as the most aggressive prohibition agent in and around the capital city. Later, when he joined forces with two similar-minded men, George Washington and George Hamilton, they became perhaps the most enterprising enforcers of the liquor law in all of Iowa. In 1886 Pierce and his men raided both the city police station and the Fire Department. After finding kegs of beer at both agencies, he arrested the city marshal and the fire chief. The trial of the two officers took place on the lawn of the judge's house on Grand Avenue. Both men were found not guilty.[37]

As time went on, Pierce and his gang became more emboldened. His playbook came to include shakedowns, whereby he merely threatened affluent citizens with liquor charges to win big payouts. It was not uncommon for his gang to accept bribes from brewers or liquor dealers. He shot and wounded a bartender during a search in 1886, he was indicted for bribery and extortion in 1888, he killed an unarmed saloon owner in 1890, and he barely escaped being lynched by an angry mob a year later. None of these exploits ever led to a run-in with the law, but that changed in June 1891, when he tangled with a policeman manning the entrance to the city dump. A disagreement over the dump fee escalated until shots were fired. Pierce killed the officer and was convicted of manslaughter; he was given a four-year prison term at Fort Madison. Pierce received a pardon in 1896 from Republican governor Francis Drake—founder of Drake University in Des Moines—after serving all but eleven months of his term.[38]

A fitting finale to Iowa's turbulent 1880s is the story of Kinsey "Stormy" Jordan, owner of a notorious barroom in the center of Ottumwa called The Road to Hell. Jordan, famously a teetotaler who often counseled his customers on the evils of drink—even as he refilled their shot glasses—refused to submit to the state's prohibitory laws. He was repeatedly fined and jailed for continuing to sell liquor until he hired a creative attorney, who took his case to federal court. For more than a year, Jordan's bar was allowed to stay open while the Iowa liquor ban was being challenged as an unconstitutional infringement of civil liberty protections guaranteed under the Fourteenth Amendment. He lost the case and then his bar as a result of court costs in 1887. Jordan retired and lived quietly in Ottumwa until his death in 1905.[39]

6

Oily Tongued Sharpers and Swindlers

The drive well was an enormously important invention for the farmers on the prairie. Brilliantly simple but still stunningly innovative, it provided an efficient and inexpensive alternative to the backbreaking work of digging deep enough with shovels to find water. History credits Colonel Nelson Green of the Seventh Regiment of the New York Volunteers with envisioning a different approach. It was during training exercises near Syracuse in 1861 that a crew of Green's men were saddled with the responsibility of finding a better source of water for the unit. Rather than setting a crew to work digging as men had done for thousands of years, Green's genius spotted a pile of discarded pipes. A dart-shaped cone was fitted to one end of a pipe, and a team of soldiers were ordered to begin pounding the other end into the ground. As each section of pipe disappeared into the earth, another section was added. No need to worry about fortifying the well wall; the pipe's skinny diameter would maintain a vacuum-like seal as the dig proceeded. At some point, Colonel Green's men hit groundwater, and the pressure underground sent the water effortlessly to the surface.

The process was heralded worldwide as it could be successfully applied almost anywhere. The British Army was said to have used the technique during the Abyssinia Expedition into Ethiopia in the late 1860s. By the mid-1870s, there were close to a million wells developed using Green's idea operating all over the United States, many of them driven by farmers in Iowa and Minnesota. Royalties on such a popular process should have made Green a rich man, but unlike many other American inventors of the nineteenth century, Green didn't immediately move to protect his property. His distraction was caused by a shooting incident in which Green wounded a fellow officer for some unknown slight (probably just days after sinking the first successful drive well). The case resulted in charges against Green by a military court, and he was dismissed from the army. Other troubles followed, including litigation against the pastor who had banished Green from the church he was attending. So he didn't get around to submitting a patent application until 1865—long after imitators were everywhere. By then, there was a deeply held belief among the farmers of the Midwest that so many claimed ownership that no patent for the drive well was enforceable.[1]

"The drive-well is no new thing, or latter-day invention," B. J. Wardenburg of Minneapolis wrote in the *Chicago Tribune* in December 1878. "Twenty years ago I saw drive-wells put down in the high peatlands of the Netherlands during every summer for the benefit of large flocks of sheep."[2]

Farmers were wary of anyone claiming ownership of a patent and then demanding a royalty. The "oily tongued sharpers and swindlers" flooded the corn belt in the years after the Civil War, often waving fraudulent paperwork and pointing out anything and everything on the farm—from "clevis to a fence post"—and demanding immediate compensation. The number of patented farm tools in the United States jumped from four hundred in 1863 to more than eighteen hundred by 1866.[3]

Not only were new ideas being brought legitimately into the marketplace; there were scores and scores of patents being taken out on tools and equipment that had been in use for decades. Rather than investigate the legitimacy of any of the claims, patent administrators typically just approved everything that came through the door, leaving the question of actual ownership of an invention to the courts. In turn, the courts made no effort to sort things out either, typically ruling that any patent approved by the Patent Office was valid simply because of that designation. Rather than fight it out themselves for legal supremacy, the patent owners found it far easier and more financially rewarding to simply send their agents from farm to farm, threatening legal action unless royalties were paid. The cycle of fraud and incompetence gave the farmers no assurance of who could be trusted and which tools or applications were truly protected. "I believe there is not a farmer in this country today who is not liable to a score of suits or more for the infringement of patents on his farming implements," said Minnesota senator William Windom. "There is something about his plow, his harrow, his thrasher or his reaper, some little insignificant thing that nobody ever ought to have had a patent for and never would upon a properly administrated patent system."[4]

The drive well was one of the few that were finally sorted out by the courts. Colonel Green assembled a legal team and won an 1878 ruling, from the circuit court in Minneapolis, that he was the rightful inventor of the drive well process and was free to demand $10 from anyone using the system. The ruling was challenged, but nine years later the U.S. Supreme Court upheld the ruling that Green's patents were valid.

The fight didn't end there, however. The drive well dispute would come before the circuit courts in different states nine times, where it was sustained eight times, and on three occasions it was upheld by the U.S. Supreme Court. Then, in a fourth hearing in 1888, the court reversed itself, with the majority opinion declaring that the patent should never have been issued.[5]

Another invention of critical importance to the farmer on the treeless plains was barbed wire. Keeping livestock safe and away from vegetable gardens and neighbors' land was a real challenge, especially for farmers living in places where timber wasn't readily available. Beginning in the 1850s a hedge native to parts of the Southwest—the Osage orange—was brought to Iowa, among other northern states, and cultivated to act as a natural fence. Tough and quick growing, this shrub sprouted strong, flexible limbs that bristled with sharp thorns. The Osage orange seemed a perfect answer, except that it grew outward and its breadth at maturity could occupy as much as thirty feet of tillable land. Thus, it needed regular tending, which took time and energy away from other chores. Moreover, as it was indigenous to the warmer climate of northern Texas and Oklahoma, the Osage orange didn't always make it through the harsh Midwest winters.[6]

Another option was wire made of iron. It was costly and largely ineffective; farmers typically needed to string dozens of strands against fence posts to keep a determined cow from pushing through. By 1873 something better was coming. That fall, Joseph Glidden, a farmer in DeKalb County, Illinois, visited a local fair and came upon a merchant hawking a string of smooth wire with strips of wood attached, from which nail ends protruded. From there, Glidden wondered: Why not just incorporate a barb within the wire by twisting it?

Glidden brought his idea to a local hardware man named Isaac Ellwood. The first bales of barbed wire were barely off the production table before clones appeared. During the first decade after the invention of barbed wire, there were some 150 imitating corporations. Glidden sold his interest in the creation in 1876 to Ellwood, who, in turn, formed a partnership with one of the country's largest wire mills, the Moen Manufacturing Company of Worcester, Massachusetts. Charles F. Washburn, one of the company's vice presidents, was sent west to oversee the new operation. In time, under his leadership, the Moen company moved with dispatch to consolidate the market under its control. By the end of 1880 the Moen Manufacturing Company attained monopolistic status, and a federal judge upheld its patent claim.[7]

"There is scarcely a township in Iowa which does not contain farmers liable for royalty under this decision," the *Quad-City Times* (then known as the *Davenport Morning Democrat*) moaned in December 1880. "The drive-well patent is as nothing compared with it."[8]

Indeed, not long after the patent's validation, attorneys representing Washburn were dispatched all over the Midwest to enforce his company's property rights. Competitors were forced to sign expensive licensing agreements or face even more expensive legal action. As more licenses were issued, the price of barbed wire escalated by as much as 54 percent in only a few months.[9] As Moen tightened its grip on the entire barbed wire market of the United States, the farmers of Iowa mounted a challenge. The Farmers Protective Association was formed in July 1881 and established a manufacturing plant in Des Moines. W. L. Carpenter, superintendent of the new wire factory, claimed that he was using a milling method that fell outside the Moen patent. Within weeks, the factory was producing enough wire every day to fill an entire train car. To be safe, however, the members of the association agreed to build a legal defense fund. Some of that money was used to hire attorneys in Massachusetts. While the operation was still in its infancy, Moen attorneys went to federal court, in August 1882, filing an injunction to shut down the Des Moines operation.[10]

As litigation proceeded at a snail's pace, the farmers needed local attorneys to take control. They chose the firm of Wright and Cummins, led by Carroll Wright, a veteran railroad lawyer and the son of a former Iowa Supreme Court justice. It was quickly understood that

Wright's younger partner, Albert B. Cummins, would be assigned as the lead attorney on the barbed wire case.

Cummins would have been easy to spot. Even as a young and untested lawyer, there was an air of integrity, energy, and self-assurance about him that would have given his clients confidence. Born in Pennsylvania, he came west while still in his teens and worked as a clerk, a wire messenger, and a construction manager before joining a Chicago law firm, where he read for the bar. After obtaining his license, Cummins worked in Chicago for three years before moving to Des Moines in 1878, where his older brother was a partner at the Wright firm. His talents at making money and pleasing clients brought him quickly up the ranks, and in 1886, when turnovers at the top created new opportunities, Cummins became Wright's sole partner.[11]

The Moen case would prove a great boost to Cummins's career. The Massachusetts firm had seemingly unlimited resources to throw at the Polk County farmers, including access to some of the country's best legal talent. Cummins, however, was both relentless and creative. In preparation for the upcoming trial, he presented himself to the foreman of the Des Moines wire factory one morning, donning a pair of overalls and carrying a lunch pail. He politely asked to be put to work, telling the man that he wanted to learn all he could about the manufacture of barbed wire. By the time the trial opened in January 1881, the command Cummins held over the production of barbed wire was visible to everyone in attendance. In his opening argument, the *Des Moines Register* observed that he was "exceptionally strong and able, showing remarkable research in the intricacies of patent law and surprising the opposition with the power of his position. The friends of free wire were delighted with it, and the great monopolists much disturbed by it."[12]

But the slow grind of the legal process took a financial toll on the Iowa men, enough so that bolstering their case became a statewide point of honor. In early 1884 the legislature appropriated $5,000 (about $150,000 today) to help with litigation. Nearly all of that money went to pay the fees of the Wright and Cummins firm.[13] Although the farmers won key rulings in the lower courts, each was appealed and reversed. In January 1886 the farmers began running ads in newspapers across the state reminding everyone of their resolve: "We Are Still on Deck," the ad's headline declared, and then went on to promise prices that "never can be duplicated." They offered "galvanized hog or cattle wire at 5½ cents per pound; painted hog or cattle wire at 4½ cents per pound."[14]

Market forces, rather than the courts, ultimately delivered the farmers' victory. The price of barbed wire tumbled to under four cents per pound in 1889 from a high point of ten cents per pound eight years earlier. Public sentiment turned vehemently against monopolies and patent abuses, which sparked a number of imitators to resume operations. The Moen company found the cost of chasing down and prosecuting each and every violator a price too high, and by 1890 executives had generally given up; they allowed their underlying patent to expire a year later.[15]

Nowhere in the U.S. economy of the late nineteenth century were the tools of the monopolists more effectively employed than by the railroads. Iowans would play an important role in imposing new government control over the rails, led by a most unlikely rebel named William Larrabee.

Larrabee, arguably one of Iowa's most prominent—if not the most prominent—governors, sat on the back bench for eighteen years in the Iowa State Senate before getting his shot at running for chief executive. He was by then one of the wealthiest men in the Midwest, having made his first fortune milling flour and managing farmland. Land speculation and banking came later. His time in the legislature was spent quietly on the commerce and budget committees, where his work drew little attention. While he was a dependable Republican in every way, party leaders believed that he lacked the name recognition and voter appeal for higher office. Larrabee had also been ostracized for criticizing the railroads and their discriminatory rate schedules.

By the 1880s the Iowa Republican Party was something of a wholly owned subsidiary of the Chicago rail companies. Two of the more important lines in the Midwest had key executives living in Iowa: Joseph W. Blythe, general counsel for the Chicago, Burlington, and Quincy Railroad, and Nathaniel M. Hubbard, the lead attorney for the Chicago and Northwestern Railroad Company. Blythe, who lived in Burlington, and Hubbard, who lived in Cedar Rapids, were not just the most powerful lobbyists in Des Moines; they were so ingrained in party politics that no one would consider taking out nomination papers for any state office without first obtaining their blessing.[16]

Larrabee committed political suicide in 1874 simply by acknowledging the need to rein in rail rates. A decade later, he was still an unacceptable candidate, at least until he wasn't. In the presidential election of 1884, the Democrats, led by Grover Cleveland, had surprising success among the voters of Iowa. Cleveland's promise to curtail the "spoils" system and implement other reforms led Republican leaders in Iowa to look for a gubernatorial candidate who might appeal to some of those sentiments but not actually act on them. "He should be conservative enough to be safe and radical enough to be courageous, but never visionary nor impetuous." The editors of the *Des Moines Register* thus characterized Larrabee as the best option for the Republicans in the election of 1885.[17] He barely won, garnering just 50.76 percent of the vote, the narrowest Republican victory in nearly thirty years.[18]

Liquor was the dominant campaign issue, and although the voters were clearly divided, Larrabee announced in his swearing-in speech that the question was now "not between prohibition and license, but whether law or lawlessness shall rule."[19] Three months later, he signed the Clark Laws, thereby fulfilling one of his two campaign promises. The other promise was to bring order and efficiency to the state's finances.[20] It was his attention to the details of state spending that led Larrabee to make one of the most unexpected political turns in Iowa history.

Just a year into his first term, Larrabee made a habit of spot-checking incoming bills from various state suppliers and service providers. In December 1886 he came across an invoice from the Chicago, Burlington, and Quincy Railroad for the delivery of coal to a state school in western Iowa. He made enough inquiries to learn that the Chicago–Burlington line charged less for hauling the same amount of coal to private customers living in Council Bluffs, about twenty miles farther west of the mines in Lucas County. Larrabee sensed malfeasance, or at least an oversight, and dispatched an aide to complain to the railroad managers. When officials at the Chicago–Burlington rebuffed the governor's man, Larrabee became incensed and made plans to use the power of his office to get satisfaction.[21]

First, the governor ordered the Iowa Railroad Commission to investigate. A hearing held in April 1887 settled nothing as a railroad superintendent rattled off a confusing and convoluted explanation of how freight rates were set and why, in some cases, the rails might charge less to haul a delivery farther. Larrabee would later agree that he was no expert on rates and rebates, road conditions, and classes of freight, but nothing could change his core argument: Iowa law said railroads could only charge a rate that was "reasonable," which he demanded of the executives of the Chicago–Burlington line.

Charles E. Perkins, president of the company, arrogantly dismissed Larrabee's complaints. In a show of contempt, Perkins raised the rates charged to the private customers of Council Bluffs while leaving the state rates unchanged.[22]

It was a fateful move that started a war.

Larrabee spent part of 1886 recruiting legislative candidates who would back real railroad reform. He also spent time selling his anti-monopoly agenda to the voters as he ran for reelection. He was very successful at both endeavors. In his inaugural address to lawmakers at the opening of the 1888 legislative session, Larrabee outlined one of the most aggressive reform agendas ever proposed—not just in Iowa, but anywhere in the nation. He wanted the state to have the power to set maximum fare rates. He also proposed a ban on the practice of giving free rail passage to state and local officials. Moreover, he wanted the Railroad Commission to have real authority and be accountable to the people by becoming an elected board.[23] His speech was peppered with egalitarian language that many of his fellow Republicans found radical, if not unhinged.

"Railroad companies are public corporations, and the railways should be, by law, declared public highways," he said. "And their [railroad] officers should be required to take an oath to obey the constitution and the laws of this State and of the United States. The right of the State to control railroad companies has been confirmed by the highest judicial authority. While stringent means should be applied to the strong corporations, the weak ones should be protected and especially the new roads making efforts to do business at [a] lower rate. Combination should be prevented, and competition secured."[24]

The railroads, united in fear of a new regulatory threat, brought in their big political guns to take on the governor. Blythe of the Burlington line coordinated a campaign against the governor with Hubbard of Chicago Northwestern. They got rail-friendly newspapers, which also happened to be the biggest, to bitterly criticize Larrabee. "The governor is wild in his utterances," wrote the editors of the *Burlington Hawk-Eye*. "Many of his positions are wholly indefensible. There is a glamour of boldness, frankness, and directness that is well calculated to win popular attention if not popular applause, but the sober second thought of the people will produce the inevitable reaction." From the *Cedar Rapids Republican*: "The message contains much that raises the grave suspicion that our usually level-headed chief executive has lost his head on the transportation question."

James S. Clarkson, publisher of the *Des Moines Register* and GOP kingmaker, called the speech "exceedingly radical," one that "caters to that sentiment which, unfriendly to capital and invested interests of all forms, is giving Iowa the reputation of being unjust to capital and property."[25]

Larrabee knew better. Even as Blythe and Hubbard called in every debt they could and made promises to anyone who would listen—Larrabee outflanked them. His populist, radical plans for regulating the railroads were adopted by the general assembly in April 1888. The legislative package was ushered through by one of Larrabee's new lieutenants, Albert Cummins, the barbed wire attorney, who was serving his only term in the Iowa Legislature. The package survived legal challenges, taking effect a year later.[26]

One of Iowa's first railroad commissioners was Lorenzo S. Coffin, a farmer from Fort Dodge who had also worked as a journalist and schoolteacher. Almost immediately, Coffin discovered that the prior board had never carried out one of its key duties—to investigate and report back to the governor on any serious train accident. "It had not been the custom, nor the belief of the commission that it was required of it, to investigate the maiming or the killing of a trainman," Coffin would write in 1903. "These cases were of such everyday occurrence; it was taken as a matter of course that the men must of necessity be maimed and killed."[27]

Indeed, the toll on train employees was staggering: 1 in every 375 railroad workers were killed annually. Among the "running tradesmen"—the engineers, firemen, conductors, and brakemen—deadly accidents were even more frequent, killing 1 out of every 117 on the job. These numbers were considered to be vastly underreported because they came from the railroad companies themselves.[28]

Massachusetts congressman Henry Cabot Lodge (soon to be a U.S. senator) wrote in a nationally circulated magazine in 1892 that an estimated 22,000 rail employees were killed nationally in 1889, a number comparable to any of the world's bloodiest battles. "Wellington won Waterloo and Meade Gettysburg with a loss of 23,185 and 23,003, respectively, and the total loss on both sides at Shiloh in two days' murderous fighting did not reach 24,000," Lodge observed.[29]

Gruesome reports of brakemen falling off speeding trains or firemen crushed between rolling cars were a staple of the newspapers of the day. A single edition of the *Muscatine Weekly Journal*, in September 1890, contained nine separate articles detailing train collisions, accidents, and mishaps—all of them on the front page.[30] The *Waterloo Courier* devoted several stories to an accident that took place in November 1891, when engineer John Banton and fireman Joseph Docker were sent into the yard of the Illinois Central Railroad's Waterloo station to lead an engine and twenty-four heavily loaded freight cars to a sidetrack for later connection to another locomotive. They were in the yard and not traveling fast, but fast enough to cause harm. When both became distracted by a gauge malfunction, neither realized the cars had been inadvertently sent down the wrong track. Before either could react, their engine, pulling the enormous momentum of twenty-four cars, collided with a line of fourteen cars sitting idle in their way. The impact from the crash drove the tender into the cab where the men were stationed, crushing their legs. Just as quickly, the recoil ruptured engine pipes and scalded them badly with hot steam. Hours later, a surgeon amputated Bandon's left leg. Doctors were prepared to do the same with Docker, but he never rallied and died the next day.[31]

Coffin took it upon himself to visit accident sites like that of the Waterloo incident to memorialize what had happened. It was quickly apparent that there were two rail-related activities that caused, by far, most of the serious injuries—the coupling of cars and the application of brakes.

The job of joining cars was usually performed by a brakeman, often the least experienced and lowest paid of the "running men." The process required the worker to step between the cars, one of which was moving. Once the cars were close enough, he pulled a heavy pin from a link arm called a drawhead and then replaced the pin once the coupling had been completed. Hands, arms, legs, and feet were all threatened by the fifteen to twenty tons of pressure that a fully loaded freight car could apply, even when traveling at less than five miles per hour. Adding to the hazard was the fact that there was no standard coupling apparatus, which meant that an inexperienced brakeman had almost no chance to avoid injury. A report from 1884 found forty-two different systems for linking cars that were used by companies running just on the Erie Railroad.

Once the cars were joined and the run began, the brakeman's duties were no less perilous. The brake controls were located on top of the cars, typically at three points, which one man might be called upon to close on his own. Thus, it was his job to climb to the roof of a moving train as it bucked and bounced like an angry bull. Then he had to spin the brake wheel down before jumping from car to car until he reached the next brake station. At night or in bad weather, missteps were common; even under ideal conditions, any number of complications could send a man tumbling off a car roof and down into the wheels of the speeding train. According to a survey conducted by the *Railroad Gazette*, between 1878 and 1887 about 52 percent of all accidents involving railroad employees in Iowa were caused by coupling and braking actions.[32]

"As likely as not, the brakeman emerges from between the crashing cars unhurt and unruffled, ready to go in again when the occasion requires," the *Atchison Daily Globe* reported in May 1890. "Day after day this continues, and the man naturally grows daring and self-confident. He forgets the danger because, a hundred times a day, his agility and skill bring him out of danger unscathed. The next time he goes in, perhaps, the engineer awaits in vain his reappearance and the signal to go ahead or back up. The train men run back to see what the matter is, and they find a man with a white face and a bloody, mangled arm, the latter held fast in the bumpers as in a vise."[33]

As Coffin dug deeper into the crisis, he realized that the technology existed to make the trains safer. Automatic coupling devices had been invented and were in use on some rail lines as early as 1867. The air brake, which was applied from the locomotive cockpit, was patented by George Westinghouse that same year and would be widely in use on passenger trains within ten years. Railroad executives were not completely callous to the loss of life and limb, but they resisted for a whole host of reasons, the expense being biggest: the installation of air brakes and automatic coupling systems would cost $50 million industrywide.[34] Some executives argued that the railroads were already transitioning to the safer technology and that interference from lawmakers would only interrupt that process. Some companies, the Burlington, Cedar Rapids, and Northern Railroad, for instance, had already installed automatic couplers and air brakes but wanted any legislative mandate to exclude all other versions of the devices they had bought.[35]

Another unexpected barrier to providing a safer workplace for railroad employees was the reluctance of the very men who would most benefit from the reforms to actively support the improvements. A powerful culture of virility and machismo surrounded the men doing these dangerous jobs. They were proud of the skills and confidence they had acquired to do their duties, and, in some sense, there were widely held opinions that when a man got hurt, he had failed to live up to the esprit de corps.[36]

There was, in fact, a real "Casey Jones," who was killed in a heroic effort to slow his speeding train and protect his passengers in the famous collision outside the town of Canton, Mississippi, in April 1900. The sense of duty Casey represented ran deep. Railroad jobs were as respectable and well-paid as any available to men in the working class. When things went wrong and a man got hurt, it was the man who was to blame; to shift responsibility elsewhere was cowardly.[37]

The judiciary was also decidedly stacked against the worker who sought to place liability on the railroads. The common law guide was that any man who took a job with the railroad understood and accepted the risks. Courts generally ruled against a plaintiff trying to place liability on the company for mistakes for which another employee was responsible. The rail companies were generally united in holding a hard line against accepting any responsibility. However, as the carnage piled up higher and higher, that line was getting harder to hold. Coffin's persistence was gaining some traction in the press by the late

1880s, and lawmakers in both Des Moines and Washington DC were also starting to take notice.

Coffin, in alliance with professional associations representing both train car manufacturers and train engineers, spent the better part of two years lobbying the Iowa Legislature on bills he wrote that would require the automatic coupler and the air brake. In 1890 his efforts paid off, with Iowa becoming one of the first states in the nation to require all railroads to equip their trains with "proper, efficient, and safe automatic couplers and brakes."[38]

Although he was celebrated in some corners, Coffin's single-minded attention to improving railroad safety left him politically vulnerable. His seat on the Railroad Commission was intended to represent agricultural interests, and many in the farming community felt Coffin had done little to advance their primary issue: shipping rates. When Coffin's term ended in 1888, Governor Larrabee chose to replace him with a former lieutenant governor and prominent merchant who was more acceptable to the farmers.[39]

Coffin didn't skip a beat and took his campaign to Washington, pushing Congress to adopt a nearly identical bill in February 1893. "In the year after President Harrison's approval of the measure there were 2,837 railroad men killed and between 20,000 and 30,000 injured," Coffin wrote a decade later, noting that by 1897 the number of trainmen killed had been reduced to just 1,700, with 5,000 fewer injured.[40]

7

The Mulct Law

Liquor dominated the campaign in which Governor Larrabee came into office, and it would again dominate as he left. The restrictive Clark Laws were clearly not working as intended, and whoever followed Larrabee as governor would need to know the degree of their failure. In December 1887, Larrabee issued a request to the state's district judges to report to him on the status and conditions in their jurisdictions. The response was overwhelmingly negative.

"I have to say that outside the enormous expense entailed upon this county by fruitless efforts to convict its violators, I see no appreciable difference," wrote Charles H. Phelps, First District judge in Burlington, in December 1887. Phelps went on to declare the "penalties are so severe, its practical destruction of valuable property" are so extreme that "many temperate and right-minded people" find the Clark Laws "unjust."

Judge J. J. Ney of the Tenth District Court, located in Independence, said that violators continued to operate with impunity. "I ordered six writs of injunctions last summer against as many saloonkeepers, but they filed bond, and I have been told they continue to keep their places open."[1]

Larrabee could not have been too surprised. The public dissent over prohibition had been growing for months. In August 1887 a heady group of young Republican businessmen in Des Moines held a convention for the sole purpose of adopting an anti-prohibition platform. They hoped to present it to their party later that year, when its statewide meetings were held. One of the leaders of this group was Larrabee's progressive protégé, Albert B. Cummins.[2] Next, in the election of 1888, Peter Dey, a former mayor of Iowa City, became the first Democrat in more than thirty years to win a statewide race by being elected to a seat on the Railroad Commission, which only recently had become an elected office.[3]

The Democrats were careful, however, not to overplay their hand, believing that most people were tired of the Clark Laws and had certainly had enough of men like Frank Pierce. They advocated a return to local rule, where the voters of each township or county would decide whether to allow the return of the saloon. The Democrats also proposed levying a very expensive license fee of at least $500. And, rather than rushing full throttle by selecting an aggressive pro-liquor candidate for governor, they selected a moderate, a teetotaler, and a well-known former Republican named Horace Boies.

"We know of scores of excellent Republican businessmen who say they voted for prohibition and would like to see it enforced throughout the nation, but declare that it is a failure," the editor of the *Cedar Rapids Gazette* observed in October 1889.[4]

Boies characterized the Clark Laws as "merciless in their severity."[5] He also believed that a total ban on alcohol was unenforceable. But neither was he supportive of the unregulated saloon. The combination proved a powerful message, and he won the election with just under 50 percent of the vote, becoming the first Democrat elected governor since the 1850s. As monumental as Boies's victory was, voters did not give him a mandate. Republicans lost eighteen legislative seats but retained the majority in both houses, thus ensuring that the status quo would be maintained, at least for a time.[6]

As much as anything, a report by the *Des Moines Register* in July 1890 crystalized public opinion in favor of repealing the Clark Laws because of their corrupting influence. The paper found that during one six-month period, Polk County taxpayers were charged $30,000 (nearly $1 million today) for administrating liquor cases, of which $11,000 ($340,000 today) went to five judges and the rest was scattered among prosecutors, high-ranking police, and the searchers.

Like almost everyone, the editors of the *Cedar Rapids Gazette* were outraged. "It is a deliberate conspiracy to use the law of the state for personal enrichment," the paper charged. "It is apparent that the so-called enforcement of prohibition by the justices and constables of the city is nothing else than a combination scheme for plundering the treasury of this county. It can be deliberately charged without fear of disproof that they don't want the illegal sale of liquor stopped. They don't propose to kill the goose that lays the golden eggs."[7]

When the Iowa secretary of state released its annual report on the cost of liquor prosecutions in 1890, the reality of the pilfering in Polk County was made clear: court costs ran just over $100,000 to win just thirty-three convictions and collect just $2,910 in fines. Overall, the Clark Laws were costing taxpayers $713,000 per liquor conviction.[8]

Thus, in the election of 1891, the Democrats did even better. Boies was returned to office by a wider margin, while Democrats took control of the state senate. Perhaps more telling was that Democrats won six of eleven congressional seats. Dissatisfaction with prohibition was, once again, the catalyst.[9] "The election is over and Iowa has gone—not Democratic, but anti-prohibition," wrote a reader to the editors of the *Des Moines Register* in the wake of the election. "Now the duty of every good citizen in my opinion is to submit to the will of the people. Let us have a license by county option and have it soon."[10]

The only response that the Republicans could muster was to join the anti–Clark Law crowd. In advance of the 1893 governor's race, Republicans adopted a party platform that called for the end of prohibition but left open what would replace it. Voters rewarded them, replacing the Democrats' two-time incumbent, Boies, with Frank D. Jackson, while also giving the GOP big majorities in the general assembly.[11]

While the 1893 election stood as a major setback for Iowa prohibitionists, they were by no means ready to acquiesce. Perhaps of greatest consequence was the split between J. Ellen Foster, juggernaut of the Iowa prohibitionist movement, and Frances Willard, the national president of the Woman's Christian Temperance Union. Willard had relied on Foster for decades as an adviser and field lieutenant. There was, however, a fundamental difference of opinion as to how closely the WCTU should align itself with political parties. Willard wanted to fully embrace the Prohibition Party in those states where it was active or another third party that advocated temperance. Despite Foster's history of success in working with the lawmakers of Iowa, Foster advocated for the WCTU to be nonpartisan. Deep down, she believed that the prohibitionist cause was a moral one and the machinations of party politics could only corrupt the message.[12]

A confrontation took place at the national meeting in November 1889, when Foster made a bid to replace Willard as president and lost badly. On the final night of the convention, Foster led the entire Iowa delegation out of the meeting in protest. She later told reporters she regretted that such an action was necessary but hoped it would "force many women to think critically and come to logical conclusions."[13]

The outcome was that Foster established a rival organization called the Woman's National Republican Association, which, ironically, as the name implied, was allied with the GOP. By 1890 she had moved to Washington DC, where her husband took a job with the Treasury Department, and she soon found work as an emissary on social issues for the McKinley administration and later for presidents Theodore Roosevelt and William Taft. She died in August 1910.[14]

With the WCTU of Iowa in tatters and the State Temperance Alliance nonfunctional, the job of redesigning public policy over liquor regulation fell to the backroom dealmakers. At the outset of the legislative session in January 1894, an agreement was worked out to repeal the Clark Laws, but few spoke publicly about what might replace them. The mere mention of the "local option" was a non-starter because of its abysmal performance history for stopping anyone, anywhere from making, selling, or drinking booze. There were not, however, too many other options. Negotiators would have to get creative and find something new.

An epiphany came not from a novel form of regulation but from how that regulation was expressed. They called it the Mulct Law, and its key feature was to require saloonkeepers, brewers, and distillery owners to prepay a fine for operating an illegal enterprise. A decade later Trumbell White, an Iowa native turned New York media luminary, called the Mulct Law "an act by which prohibition still remains on the statute books, while the state sells indulgences to violate the law."[15] Historian Dorothy Schwieder calls it "one of the strangest laws in Iowa history."[16]

The bill was carefully worded so that nothing in the act should be understood "in any way" to "mean that the business of the sale of intoxicating liquors is in any way legalized." Nor should it be "in any way" understood that the state was providing "any manner or form of a license." The imposition of the $600 "Mulct Tax" on saloon owners, to be paid before the doors opened, required written consent from the majority of voters in a city or county.[17] The enabling legislation survived in the state senate by a mere two votes; it was signed into law in March 1894 and ordered to take effect immediately, with promulgation in the newspapers. About half of Iowa's ninety-nine counties—which represented all of Iowa's largest population centers—agreed to participate. As quirky and legally mind-bending as it was, the Mulct Law was probably the most successful of Iowa's temperance dictums, lasting twenty-one years, until 1915, as the national push toward prohibition was gaining momentum.[18]

One location remained steadfast in its official opposition to both the saloon and the Mulct Law—the town of Vinton, where, decades later, Myrtle Cook, president of the Benton County Woman's Christian Temperance Union, would be murdered.

"All who believe that the saloon is the supreme curse of this country should use every effort to prevent Vinton being cursed with an open saloon," Reverend Charles W. Skemp wrote to the editor of the *Vinton Eagle* shortly after the Mulct Law was adopted in August 1894.[19]

While Iowans debated whiskey and beer questions, fallout from the Panic of 1893 spread across the nation. The collapse of the Philadelphia and Reading Railroad helped set off the financial crisis, which led to the failure of hundreds of banks and thousands of businesses. Unemployment and homelessness soared.[20] In protest of the federal government's failure to help, masses of unemployed men organized a march on Washington in the early spring of 1894. Known as Coxey's Army, for the Ohio businessman who inspired the idea, the men reached Washington, but their presence had little impact on public policy.[21]

Meanwhile, another "industrial army" was forming near the wharf in Oakland, California. This was a bigger group: as many as fifteen hundred men led by Charles T. Kelly, a printer by trade who had also worked as a recruiter and organizer for the Salvation Army. Kelly demanded that his followers maintain a military-like code of conduct but with democratic principles. Crews elected captains whose primary job was to oversee a common treasury that paid for meals and other necessities. Their goal was to roam the country looking for work. If some did find jobs, that would be great; others would keep going all the way to Washington DC if needed. One crew captain told a news reporter that they were headed first to New Orleans. "We intend to go where we can get work," he said. "In our party are 31 loggers, 15 miners, a railway ticket agent, two cooks, a waiter, and seven brakemen. Most of us came here from the [Puget] Sound. We are honest men and want to work."[22]

One of the enlisted men in "Kelly's Army" was nineteen-year-old Jack London. With his time as an oyster pirate on the San Francisco Bay behind him and the glory of the Klondike still ahead, he joined up just as the army was leaving Sacramento. Penniless but fearless as only someone young and strong can be, London stayed on through most of April 1894 as the men made their way from Omaha to Des Moines.[23]

Either by force or invitation, Kelly's Army made their way aboard an eastbound Southern Pacific train at Sacramento. The governor of Utah tried to stop them before they crossed the state line, but sympathizers intervened and cleared their passage by rail onward to Wyoming and then Nebraska. When they reached the eastern terminus of the S and P line at Council Bluffs, Iowa, the army's advance stalled.[24]

Chicago & Northwestern Railroad Co., which controlled the rails running east across Iowa, viewed Kelly and his men as a threat. Nathaniel M. Hubbard, general counsel for the line and a longtime adversary of former governor William Larrabee, first issued orders barring any of Kelly's men from riding on Chicago & Northwestern cars. Next, Hubbard pressured Iowa's Republican governor, Frank Jackson, into calling out the militia in case there was trouble. "If these tramps and bums try to capture one of our trains, there will be trouble," Hubbard said. "Our road was not built for charitable purposes. The movement must be stopped right here and now."[25]

Accepting the fact that no train transport would be made available to his men, Kelly marched them out of Council Bluffs and followed the rails to the tiny hamlet of Chautauqua, about four miles away. The line of men stretched nearly a half mile long and proceeded out of town without incident.[26] Although Governor Jackson did order five companies of the Iowa National Guard to take up positions around Kelly's camp, he got on a train in Des Moines to get a closer look, bothered by the political optics of having soldiers surround a group of peaceful, unarmed men. Jackson blamed Hubbard for overstating the threat and ordered the militia to stand down. Kelly then announced his plan to lead his men on foot to Des Moines, 130 miles away.[27]

London, who kept a diary of his time as a political vagabond in Iowa, was delighted with the adventure—at least at first. "In 10 minutes after the army arrived, the camps were formed, fires built, and dinner under-way," he wrote. "Each company's lieutenant goes to the commissary and gets rations. Though the rain, sleet, and hail was coming down in torrents, we made quite a meal on stew, bread, and coffee. As night came on, the wind increased and grew bitter cold, blowing from the north. The men soon scattered in search of lodgings. The owner of an elevator gave permission to occupy it and in less time than it takes to write it, was occupied by 300 men."[28]

As the army moved east, the sole of one of London's shoes gave out, and soon he was practically walking barefoot. He went as far as he could, checking in each night at the commissary to see if there was another pair of shoes available, but there wasn't. He arrived at the outskirts of Des Moines on April 30. The townspeople were generous, feeding and providing shelter, until Kelly was offered wood and tools to build enough flatboats to float the entire regiment down the Des Moines River, eventually to Keokuk and the Mississippi.

London took leave of the army when he reached Hannibal. "I can't stand starvation," he scribbled. From there, he and his friends found room on a cattle train bound for Chicago, where, at the post office, London found letters and badly needed cash from his mother. London's later life would be filled with risk and adventure, but never again would he expose himself to quite the same conditions as he experienced out on the windswept prairie of Iowa that early spring.[29]

Kelly and some of his men eventually made it to Washington DC, but the impact of the industrial armies on Congress was minimal. It wouldn't be until FDR and the New Deal legislation of the early 1930s that the federal government assumed its role as a safety net of last resort and took responsibility for helping address unemployment.

Attorney Albert S. Cummins almost certainly made no money working for the farmers on the barbed wire case. What that lawsuit did do, however, was make Cummins a household name throughout rural Iowa and solidify his reputation as a champion of the common man. He was happy to accept both honors as he began maneuvering to achieve a long-held ambition to become a U.S. senator. Once he dropped the barbed wire case, Cummins set to work finding better-paying clients. One of them, Frederick Hubbell, was one of the wealthiest men in

Iowa. An early investor in Des Moines real estate, Hubbell cofounded the Equitable Life Insurance Company of Iowa and was a partner in the Des Moines Water Works Company. He owned steamboats and railroad lines. Hubbell lived in the city's most lavish and well-known mansion, known as Terrace Hill, which, since the mid-1970s, has been the official home of Iowa's governor.[30]

Through his association with Hubbell and other important businessmen, Cummins had, by his midforties, acquired all the trappings of a member of the social elite of Des Moines. He and his wife built their own mansion across Grand Avenue from Terrace Hill. He rode to the office each day in a covered carriage with a coachman and a pair of fine horses.

Like his mentor, former governor Larrabee, Cummins had one foot among the farmers and the middle class; the other foot was set firmly among the affluent Republicans. He had spent just one term in the Iowa Legislature, where he was recognized as one of the leaders of the new progressive wing of the party. They favored greater state control over corporations and the elimination of monopolies and believed that markets free of tariffs and trade restrictions would benefit Iowa farmers. They had also concluded that the prohibition of liquor was a proven failure and wanted to return to some form of local control. These were radical positions, but when Cummins expressed their merits, they somehow became more mainstream.

In 1892 one of Iowa's two U.S. senators, James Wilson, announced his retirement. This rare opportunity set Cummins into motion to capture his most prized ambition. The election of U.S. senators in Iowa, as in many other states at the time, was restricted to members of the legislature. Thus, the election process was tightly controlled by the party leaders, who were tightly controlled by the railroad lobby. Because of his work as a whip for Governor Larrabee's package of railroad reforms years before, Cummins found his candidacy blocked. Joseph W. Blythe, general counsel for the Chicago, Burlington, and Quincy Railroad, used his influence to convince lawmakers to name his father-in-law, John Gear, a former governor and congressman, as the replacement for Wilson.

Cummins tried again in 1900, when Gear's first term expired, but he lost once more. At this point, Cummins revised his strategy and decided to bide his time, given that Gear was seventy-five years old. In 1901 Cummins announced that he would run for governor. He won and, from that office, he laid the groundwork that would eventually take him to Washington.[31]

One of the few cultural events of international importance to take place in Iowa during the late nineteenth century began when a tall, dark, and distinguished-looking man stepped off a train platform near a small hamlet tucked into the northeast corner of the state. It was June 1893, and the visitor was Antonin Dvorak, who had traveled from New York with his wife and son in hopes that the town of Spillville and its largely Czech-speaking populace would cure his longing for home.[32]

There was no more famous or transformative musical talent in the world. His works had been played to wide acclaim in some of the most prestigious concert halls in Europe. That he had been lured away from Prague to take on the role of musical director of a newly organized American music academy made international headlines.[33] It was money, however, that brought the composer to New York. Jeannette Thurber, a wealthy music patron, offered Dvorak a salary of $15,000 ($500,000 today)—more than twenty-five times what he had been earning in his position with the Czech national conservatory. Thurber had lofty goals, and she would not be denied. She felt strongly that the works of Melville, Whitman, Twain, and Crane, among others, had established the American literary voice, whereas American musicians remained poor mimics of their European teachers. Well aware of how Dvorak spun Slavic folk music into important symphonic compositions, she believed he could help find an original American sound. She wanted him and no one else, and at the time she had the money to make it all happen.

His contract called for him to work a minimum of three hours a day, six days a week at her new school. His time was divided between giving instrument lessons and teaching composition.[34] Among his students were Black musicians from Harlem, who exposed Dvorak to spirituals and gospel songs. During that first year in America, Dvorak completed what many consider his masterpiece, the symphony *From the New World,* which made novel use of the melodies and rhythms born in the slave plantations of the American South.[35]

Dvorak had the summers off, and after his first year in America, evidence suggests he was considering a trip home. He told his secretary, Joseph Kovarik, who was also a cello student, that he was homesick for his beloved Bohemia. Kovarik told him of his hometown in Iowa, with its Czech citizenry and verdant and undulating countryside. It sounded ideal.[36] Despite his fame, Dvorak slipped into Iowa virtually unnoticed by the press. The only attention his visit received came in the *Saint Paul Globe* in September 1893.[37] Still, his summer in Spillville was apparently a happy one. He spent many afternoons walking along the Turkey River. On Sundays, or when he got the urge, he would play the organ in the town church. As often as possible, he shared beer and conversation at the tavern. Having such a rich and famous visitor made some in town uncomfortable, and there were whispers about how much he drank.[38] He had returned to New York by September, again without drawing any attention from Iowa's newspaper editors. He was in the audience when *From the New World* premiered at Carnegie Hall in December.[39]

Dvorak died in May 1904, and his obituary, published in the *Des Moines Register*, like those published in newspapers all across the United States, included no mention of his summer spent in Spillville.[40] News of the great composer's time in the Hawkeye State would not be reported in Iowa's biggest papers until decades later.[41] In 1920 Cosmopolitan Productions released a silent film called *Humoresque*, which featured Dvorak's famous piano sonata of the same name. It was a big hit and revived interest in the renowned Czech composer and his music.[42] In February 1922 a feature story that ran in the *Des Moines Register* highlighted Dvorak's music as a central part of the movie and went on to claim that Dvorak's *Humoresque*, once again a world-famous tune, had been written during his summer in Iowa. The report claimed that not only had *Humoresque* been written while Dvorak summered in Spillville, but the symphony *From the New World* as well. The source of this wishful thinking was Freeman R. Conaway, a former newspaperman and one-time public affairs deputy to Governor William Larrabee. Unfortunately, Conaway was wrong on both counts.[43]

Kovarik, Dvorak's secretary and friend, tried for years to correct the record. The symphony *From the New World* was finished before Dvorak left for Iowa, and *Humoresque* was published in 1894, long after Dvorak was back in New York. The one notable piece that Dvorak did write in Spillville was his String Quartet No. 12, the "American" quartet, published in 1893.[44]

8

God Hates the Four-Flusher

Among Iowa's many football stars, the best known is Marion Morrison, who went to Hollywood and became John Wayne. His hometown was Winterset. Morrison played on the line at the University of Southern California before a body surfing accident tore up his shoulder, angered his coaches, and cost him a scholarship.[1] Iowa has had plenty of famous entertainers too: Glenn Miller was from Carlinda and played the trombone. Johnny Carson, born in Corning, did magic. Meredith Willson wrote Broadway musicals and came from Mason City.[2]

The best ballplayer to come out of Iowa was probably Bob Feller, a Hall of Fame pitcher for Cleveland from the late 1930s through the early 1950s. No less an authority than Ted Williams called Feller "the fastest and best pitcher I ever saw during my career." Feller hailed from Van Meter.[3]

Decades earlier, another native son held the honor as the best Hawkeye to play baseball—Adrian "Cap" Anson, who was born and raised in Marshalltown. He starred in twenty-seven seasons of top professional ball, most of it as the player manager of the Chicago White Stockings, the predecessor organization to the Chicago Cubs. Anson and the White Stockings were then the biggest draw in the game, winning five National League pennants between 1880 and 1886. (The American League didn't organize until 1901.) Anson was the first man to collect more than 3,000 hits. He led the league in runs batted in eight times and retired with a .334 career batting average.[4]

Anson was also an innovator. He was an early adopter of the third base coach, as well as the "hit-and-run" play and the rotation of pitchers. He is additionally credited with being among the first managers to bring his team to the warmer climate of the South for spring training.[5] Anson, however, also holds an infamous place in history as probably the first hardline enforcer of baseball's "color barrier." The first game marred by Anson's racism is thought to have taken place in September 1883, when he brought the White Stockings to Toledo for an exhibition game against the town's minor league club. The opposition had a promising rookie catcher named Moses Fleetwood Walker, who was Black. Anson announced to the press before the game that he would pull his team from the field if Walker was in the lineup. Walker, nursing a badly bruised hand, was initially going to sit out the game. Perhaps not wanting to give in to the major leaguers, the Toledo manager—whose team played in the American Association—revised the lineup at the last minute and put Walker in right field. The stands were already full, and if Anson followed through with his threat, he would lose his share of the gate. "We'll play this here game," Anson said. "But won't play never more with the n——."[6]

Another rookie likely on the field that day was a promising center fielder for the White Stockings named William Askley Sunday Jr.

An Iowa native, Billy Sunday, as he was known to millions in later years, became one of America's leading evangelists and an ardent prohibitionist. Between 1910 and 1925 his revivals drew tens of thousands of attendees.[7] He was among the first preachers in America to reach into millions of homes via radio. At the peak of his career, he was earning more than $1 million a year at a time when the average American worker made less than $14,000 annually. He was welcomed to the White House by presidents and considered John D. Rockefeller Jr. a friend.[8]

If Sunday was on the field that day in Toledo, there's no record of the soon-to-be Christian disciple speaking up for the Black catcher. Such moxie from Sunday that day would have been hard to summon. He was just nineteen years old, having arrived in Chicago with goose grease in his hair and just a dollar in a pocket of his secondhand suit. And Anson, at six feet and some 240 pounds, was an intimidating presence, as well as one of the game's biggest stars. Racism among the white players was probably rampant, and if Sunday wanted to play, he couldn't rock the boat. It wouldn't be just the bigotry that he would have to put up with, but also the coarse language, promiscuous behavior, and drinking—especially the drinking.

A career .250 batter, Sunday had deer-like speed and gifted hand-eye coordination that made him an ideal center fielder in the days when most ballfields weren't confined by fences. He played in 499 major league games between 1883 and 1890. His best year was probably his last one, split between the Pittsburg Alleghanies and the Philadelphia Phillies, when he stole eighty-four bases and scored eighty-four runs. He was only twenty-eight years old when he decided to hang up his cleats and pick up the Bible.[9]

Sunday's remarkable life began as humbly as any on a failing farm near Ames, Iowa. His father, a private in the Twenty-Third Iowa Volunteers during the Civil War, died while in uniform after contracting measles at the age of thirty-four. Before he was ten, Sunday and his brother were sent by his mother to live in an orphanage, one of the soldiers' homes that had been established after the war mostly to care for the children of men killed in action.[10]

"My father went to war four months before I was born," he wrote in a 1914 autobiography. "I have butted and fought and struggled since I was six years old. I know all about the dark and seamy side of life, and if ever a man fought hard, I have fought hard for everything I have ever gained."[11]

It was at the orphanage in Davenport that Sunday came to appreciate hard work and discipline. At the age of fourteen, he returned to Ames, where he worked first as a bellhop at a local hotel and then as an errand boy for Colonel John Scott, a former lieutenant governor of Iowa. His life changed forever when he won a Fourth of July footrace. The field included a couple of track stars from nearby Iowa Agricultural College, now Iowa State University. Undaunted, Sunday rolled up his overalls and ran barefoot. News of his speed reached the fire brigade at Marshalltown, which was badly in need of a ringer to anchor the department's tournament relay team and, perhaps, someone to play outfield for the town baseball team. They convinced Billy to relocate after finding him a job with the local undertaker. He had never played baseball before but quickly found that his athletic skills fit nicely into the game. He reportedly dominated the 1882 championship against Des Moines, scoring five runs and making spectacular plays in the field. News of Sunday's exploits soon reached Cap Anson, who was then on a visit home to Marshalltown. He heard nothing but praise of the town's center fielder. The following spring, Anson invited Sunday to Chicago for a tryout.[12]

Billy's inexperience and raw skills kept him on the bench during his first seasons with a White Stockings club who were then the best team in the country, having won the National League title three years in a row. As he was being schooled on the finer points of the game, Billy served as the team secretary, juggling hotel reservations, train tickets, and players' baggage. When he did get into a game, he struggled—once striking out thirteen consecutive times his first year. Anson, tiring of Billy's performance, got him to choke up on the bat and cut down on his swing to take advantage of his speed. He never became a great hitter, but he improved enough to get a lot more playing time, and Billy became one of the league leaders in stolen bases.[13]

His religious epiphany came on a warm June afternoon in 1886. Chicago was at home playing a series against the New York Giants, and on an off day, players from both clubs got together to roam the barrooms and brothels of the city's Tenderloin District. Billy might have nursed a beer while tagging along. As the group moved from one saloon to another, Billy found himself on the corner of State and Van Buren Streets, where a "gospel wagon" was parked and a three-piece band was playing religious hymns. The sounds and words of the hymns were familiar and spoke to him. A wave of emotion left him weak-kneed and short of breath. His teammates didn't notice, but one of the men playing in the band did. He put an arm around Billy's shoulders and led him down the block to the Pacific Garden Mission, where Sunday would transform from a gritty ballplayer to a minister of the Gospel.

"I rose and said to the boys, 'I'm through. I am going to Jesus Christ,'" Sunday recalled later. "We've come to a parting of the ways.' I turned my back on them. Some of them laughed and some of them mocked me; one of them gave me encouragement; others never said a word."[14]

Sunday didn't give up baseball right away but spent the off-season in Chicago working and studying at the Young Men's Christian Association center. The White Stockings sold his contract to Pittsburg in 1888, and then the Alleghenys sent him to the Phillies the next year. He asked for and received permission from the Philadelphia team to be relieved from his contract after the 1890 season, which prompted the Cincinnati Reds to offer him the staggering sum of $5,000 ($154,000 today) to play for them. Sunday was newly married and thought hard about the offer—that salary was enough to buy outright a new house in a good neighborhood of Chicago.[15] "There's nothing to consider," his wife, Nell, told him. "You promised God to quit." Thus, Sunday accepted the position of assistant secretary at the Chicago YMCA, which paid $83.33 a month.[16]

His job was to walk the city's Tenderloin District, looking for converts. He waited outside the police stations and hospitals. He ventured down back alleys and into seedy hotels. Sunday honed his speaking skills when asked by the deacon at the YMCA to fill in and give a sermon. "We never had a man on our staff who was more consecrated, more deeply spiritual, more self-sacrificing," said L. W. Messer, an official with the Chicago YMCA. "He was especially strong in his personal effort among men who were strongly tempted and among those who had fallen by the way."

The Panic of 1893 rattled Chicago's railroad economy and, among other things, resulted in donations to the city's YMCA largely drying up. Sunday was notified that his contract would not be renewed, and with his first child on the way, he desperately needed to find work.

Chicago that year was also hosting its famed World's Fair, which would draw millions of visitors. One of those coming to town was an emerging evangelical star named John Wilbur Chapman. Chapman, who would go on to become one of America's most important revivalists, was still making his name and needed a passionate advance man. Chapman was well aware of Sunday's fame as a ballplayer and was confident the young missionary could help bring baseball fans into the pews. Chapman hired Sunday on the spot, doubling his salary to $40 per week.[17]

Sunday spent two years with Chapman, traveling all over the country. In addition to setting up the revival camp and coaxing the local press into early coverage, Sunday was given opportunities to sermonize. Chapman, dignified and unemotional, tended to be upbeat and positive before his audience. He often spoke of God's love of his flock and stressed the salvation that came with redemption. Initially, Sunday carefully followed Chapman's manuscripts, but with time Chapman allowed Sunday's own voice to emerge. Sunday's message was far darker, peppered with warnings of eternal damnation. "Do you think your scoffs can extinguish the flames of hell?" he once said. "Do you think you can annihilate hell because you don't believe in it?"

His use of common language was also distinctive. "I don't believe all this tommyrot of false doctrines," he fumed. "You might as well sit around beneath the shade and fan yourself and say 'Ain't it hot?' as to expect God to give you a crop if you don't plow the ground and plant the seed." He was also known to throw in a joke or two. "God likes a little humor, as evidenced by the fact that he made the monkey, the parrot, and some of you people," he said with a grin.[18]

Chapman abruptly ended his traveling ministry during the holidays of 1895, leaving Sunday out of work again. This time, Sunday and his wife had a second child. Although his five-foot-eleven frame remained lean and fit, a return to baseball was no longer possible. While he contemplated his options, a telegram arrived from a small town in northern Iowa inviting him to come and hold a week-long revival meeting.

"I had no money. What should I do? I laid it before the Lord," Sunday recalled. "There came a telegram from a little town named Garner, out in Iowa, asking me to come out and conduct some meetings. I didn't know anybody out there, and I don't know yet why they ever asked me to hold meetings. But I went."[19]

From there came more offers: Jefferson and Waterloo, Sioux City and Marshalltown. Soon, Billy Sunday's "kerosene circuit" was born as he, his family, and a dozen or so assistants, musicians, and stagehands moved from town to town between Iowa, Illinois, and Wisconsin. His name was well known throughout the Midwest because of his years as a White Stocking, but it was his power as an orator and his gift for showmanship that brought him thousands of followers. He added song and dance bands as part of the routines and, on occasion, performed acrobatic tricks himself.

A law adopted in 1902 gave judges the authority to impose a sentence on alcoholics who had run afoul of the law to terms at either of Iowa's two mental institutions. The idea for the bill came from H. H. Abrams, a former head of the Anti-Saloon League, who cloaked the proposal as an attempt to provide better care for the habitual alcohol abuser, but in fact it was meant to be punitive. A year's term was the minimum, but five years could be ordered in severe cases. The courts retained authority to send a patient back to the hospital if he or she relapsed after being released.[20]

Complaints from alcoholics about mistreatment by the staff at the mental hospitals began almost immediately. "If I was almost crazy before I left Des Moines, I will soon be as insane as the rest of the jabbering maniacs with whom I am forced to daily come in contact," began a letter smuggled out of the Mount Pleasant Insane Asylum in November 1902. The writer, W. S. Richmond, was sentenced to a three-year term at the hospital after being found to be a dipsomaniac.

"For thirty-six hours after I came here, I was forced to sleep in a perfectly nude state," Richmond said. "That part would not be so bad, but I don't get enough to eat. This institution boasts of maintaining this ward on 5 cents a day. You would not wonder at it when you see the bill of fare."[21]

With no special training or direction, the hospital staff could do little to treat alcoholics, but their pleas for more resources went unanswered. "We have no experts in the treatment of inebriety at the state hospitals," said John Cownie, chairman of a newly created state oversight agency called the Board of Control. "No provision has been made by the legislature for that," he said. "Many persons who are sent to the hospitals for inebriates think they will get some special treatment. There is nothing of that kind. All the physicians in charge of inebriates do is give them tonics calculated to build up their systems."[22]

A breaking point was quickly reached as more alcoholics were sentenced to terms in the state mental hospital. "The present state of affairs under which insane persons and dipsomaniacs are confined in the same institution is rapidly becoming intolerable," the *Ottumwa Daily Courier* noted in January 1903.[23]

It took two years, but in December 1905 Iowa became only the second state in the union to open a dedicated treatment hospital for alcoholics, locating the facility near the center of the state at Knoxville.[24] "I look on drunkenness wholly and solely as a disease," W. S. Osborn, the hospital's first superintendent, told the *Des Moines Register* in 1907. "Crime and degeneracy are the results, rather than the causes of inebriety. I am within bounds of exact facts when I assert that 50 percent of all inmates in all the penal institutions in Iowa today are either inebriates themselves or the offspring of inebriates."[25]

Another shining example of the Iowa progressives of the early 1900s pushing public policy was the debate over criminal pardons and clemency. Lawmakers in Iowa gave the governor the power to grant conditional pardons beginning in 1878, but even twenty-five years later, there was growing unease that governors were too reluctant to exercise their pardon powers and that judges were often too harsh in their sentencing. By 1900 prison wardens and academics studying the issue were calling for a separate board dedicated to the parole process, inmate job training, and sentencing guidelines for judges.[26]

Into this debate came the case of boy murderer John Wesley Elkins.

In 1901 Elkins was twenty-four years old, having spent half of his life behind bars at Anamosa. He worked as the prison's chief librarian and had spent much of his free time reading and taking advantage of the limited educational opportunities. Elkins was never a behavior problem for the guards and was respected among the inmates for his intelligence and thoughtfulness. Still, the doctors were worried as he suffered from fainting spells and a depressed and weakened condition. Every year, parole was a possibility, but the record was stacked against him: only eleven convicted murderers had been released from Iowa prisons in more than a quarter century. In 1901 Clayton County attorney L. M. Fisher became interested in Elkins's plight. He visited the prison and spoke with the inmate. Elkins did not deny his actions but tried to explain how, as only a twelve-year-old, he had acted out against the severe mistreatment of his parents and had yet to develop the moral capacity to distinguish right from wrong. Fisher came away convinced that Elkins should be pardoned. He quickly contacted the county's two state legislators and got promises that they would look into Elkins's case.[27]

There remained many in Clayton County who remembered the double murder. A prevailing opinion was that criminals were born and could not be rehabilitated and that Elkins, if allowed back into the community, would kill again. Or, perhaps worse, he would pass on the penchant for viciousness to generations of his heirs.[28]

"I can remember Wesley Elkins, an unusually bright and attractive lad," said State Senator Hiram C. Bishop, who represented Clayton County and was a former school superintendent. "But if you looked closely, you could see a peculiar expression in his steel-like eyes. I believe murder was born in the boy's heart. His mother plotted murder before him. To let such a person loose upon a community, even after years of imprisonment, would not be a safe proposition."[29]

James Harlan, a professor at Iowa's Cornell College, was of the opposite opinion and worked tirelessly for Elkins's parole. He traveled to Anamosa to meet with the inmate many times. He then traveled to newspaper offices all over the state, bringing with him the latest thinking from the emerging scientific discipline of criminology. These new criminologists were beginning to make the case that there was no link between heredity and violent behavior.[30]

State law gave the governor wide discretion to commute a prison sentence, except for someone convicted of first-degree murder. The governor could reject a pardon plea from a murderer, but before such a request could be granted, the general assembly had to hold a public hearing on the question.[31] Elkins brought his appeal to the governor's office several times before lawmakers finally took up his case in 1902. Cummins had just taken office, and advocates for progressive reforms crowded the capital. Debates on women's suffrage, compulsory education for minors, and the establishment of a juvenile court system were all part of the new agenda.

The state senate had blessed the parole request by the end of March, but the house turned it down before reversing itself in early April. A few weeks later, Governor Cummins signed the parole order that allowed Elkins to walk out of prison.[32]

He would never return. He was given permission to move to St. Paul in 1904, where he worked as an accountant for a railroad company. He married and eventually retired to Southern California, where he died peacefully at the age of eighty-three.[33]

While progressives cheered the Elkins parole and his subsequent peaceful life, there was a competing public policy that drew on a very different perspective on human behavior: eugenics. The theory that the human race could be improved through state-sanctioned selection of desired, heritable characteristics had been developing since Francis Galton, a British scientist, invented the concept in 1883.[34]

Connecticut became the first state to ban marriage for anyone who was epileptic or "feeble-minded" in 1896; it put in place a harsh three-year prison term for any violation. Kansas, New Jersey, Ohio, Indiana, and Michigan soon followed with similar restrictive laws. In Iowa, eugenics-inspired legislation was introduced in 1902, but it wasn't until 1911 that a law passed authorizing the sterilization of "criminals, idiots, feeble-minded, imbeciles, lunatics, drunkards, drug fiends, epileptics, and syphilitics as well as moral and sexual perverts, and diseased and degenerate persons."[35]

An Iowan named Harry Laughlin would become one of the world's leading advocates for the use of sterilization, immigration restrictions, and mass incarceration to "purify the breeding stock" of the white race. Born in Oskaloosa, Iowa, in 1880, Laughlin would work side by side with a biologist who became director of the infamous Eugenics Record Office: Charles Davenport. Their work, which was funded by the Carnegie Institute, would become central to the doctrine of the Nazi Party, which awarded Laughlin an honorary doctorate from the University of Heidelberg in Germany in 1936.[36]

9

A Kill Fee

When attorney John Looney established the *Rock Island News* in March 1905, the editors of its much larger rival, the *Rock Island Argus*, were initially impressed. "Editorially, the paper announced a strictly independent political attitude, with a single purpose to reflect correctly the news without bias or prejudice," the editor of the *Argus* respectfully noted. "The further declaration is made that it will not undertake to regulate the universe—certainly a very wise and laudable policy on the part of any journal."

The *Argus* was also careful to point out that Looney's name was conspicuously absent from the paper's masthead as well as from its incorporation papers and other official business filings. Looney's reputation as a thug and a political insider was already well established, and the *Argus* wasn't sure what to make of this new venture. "Newspapers, like all things, are what they make of themselves."[1]

A tall, slender man whose temper and rash decision-making often put him at a disadvantage against bigger, more clear-thinking adversaries, Looney was nonetheless one of the most successful mob bosses in the Midwest. His reign began in the mid-1890s and lasted until 1925. He was years ahead of the gangs in Chicago and controlled a larger criminal operation than the Prendergast organization in Kansas City. Looney was the model for Paul Newman's mob boss character in the 2002 movie *Road to Perdition*. Unlike the benevolent role that Newman played, the real John Looney was viciously corrupt and cold blooded.[2]

An often-repeated story tells of a young Al Capone being sent by his boss, Johnny Torrio, to meet with Looney down in Rock Island. Although the authority of the tale is somewhat murky, Torrio apparently wanted in on Looney's lucrative prostitution ring, which reportedly employed as many as three hundred young women working in brothels up and down the Mississippi. Capone probably wasn't fully aware of who he was dealing with and was apparently less than respectful. Looney tossed Capone out on his ear. When Capone returned to Chicago, he told Torrio he never wanted to deal with the Irishman again.[3]

Rock Island was part of what would become the Quad Cities—which consisted of Davenport and, later, Bettendorf on the Iowa side of the Mississippi River and Moline and Rock Island on the Illinois side. Rock Island wasn't the biggest of the group, but it had five railroad lines, which made it the regional transportation hub. The commercial district was busy. There were electric lights on the streets downtown, well-organized Police and Fire Departments, and a library. Davenport was almost twice as large at the turn of the century, with a bigger economy and more cultural venues. But Davenport also had "Bucktown," which encompassed six blocks along the eastern riverfront and was home to forty brothels and more than two hundred saloons operating twenty-four hours a day. Someone had to take control of all that vice and loose change.[4] As Looney's criminal operation grew, so did the amount of attention he received from the city's major daily, the *Argus*. In March 1904 the paper told of how Looney was the instigator of a melee that broke out at a political event where the police were called—but because Looney had most of the cops on his payroll, the officers jumped in on Looney's side and beat back his opponents.[5]

"There is but one side to a proceeding where anarchy and ruffianism are arrayed against lawful procedure," railed the *Rock Island Argus* after the incident. "Riot was his [Looney's] motive, and the police, instead of interfering to prevent such a condition, aided and abetted it."[6]

The bad press was becoming too much for Looney's outsize ego to bear. In response, he bought a downtown building that was home to one of the best restaurants in town, as well as a well-appointed gentlemen's club and a brothel upstairs. A second-floor suite became the offices for the *Rock Island News*, Looney's newspaper. Initially, the paper printed a variety of legitimate stories, along with potent pushback on anything that the *Argus* reported that Looney found objectionable. It was not long, however, before Looney realized that the paper could also be used as a highly effective extortion tool. Looney's men were known to threaten well-heeled members of the Rock Island establishment with a smear story and demand a "kill fee" to stop its publication.[7]

One story that did get published, in September 1911, accused Rock Island mayor Harry Schriver and Jake Ramser, a prominent businessman, of running a nudist resort on the edge of town. A few days after the completely fictitious story ran, Ramser confronted Looney in a downtown barbershop. Looney drew a gun and shot Ramser in the hand. The bull-like Ramser charged ahead anyway. Looney was tall but rail thin, and Ramser disarmed him before delivering a severe beating.[8]

A year later, Looney again smeared Mayor Schriver, linking him in a front-page story with a well-known prostitute. The mayor flew into a rage. He filed criminal libel charges and got a judge to shut down Looney's paper. Police officers loyal to Schriver arrested Looney and brought him to jail. But before locking him up, they led Looney into a room where Schriver was waiting. Looney took another beating, suffering a broken nose, a likely concussion, and several deep head wounds caused by strikes from a heavy object. Looney was hospitalized, and for a day or two it appeared he might not recover.[9]

He did.

About a week later, Looney and a couple dozen of his henchmen infiltrated a peaceful political rally on the steps of city hall. On Looney's signal, his men turned the protest into a riotous mob aimed at the mayor. The crowd shelled the city offices with rocks, bricks, and bottles. Police fired shots into the melee, killing two and wounding nine, but were still unable to gain control and had to retreat inside city hall behind barricades. Order wasn't restored until the National Guard arrived hours later.

"The whole trouble from its incipiency may be traced to the fact that I enforced the law against disorderly saloons and chop suey joints," Mayor Schriver explained the next day. "That is what brought forth the attack upon me by the Looney paper and it is at the bottom of the entire disturbance. It is deplorable, but we are not going to quit now until we rid the city of the elements of disorder and defiance."[10]

More bloodshed took place in October 1922, when Looney and his son Connor were ambushed by a rival gang as they approached the doors of a downtown hotel. A gunfight ensued and lasted for nearly an hour. Connor was killed. No charges were filed against Looney, but the gun battle was too much for the state authorities to ignore, and the Illinois attorney general put serious effort into ending Looney's reign as crime boss. Six months later, the Rock Island mayor, the police chief, and the city attorney were each found to be in the employ of Looney and were convicted of political corruption charges. From there, state investigators began building a case against Looney, pressuring his former partners to testify against their boss. In July 1925 he was found guilty of conspiracy, and six months later he was convicted of ordering the killing of a Rock Island saloonkeeper who refused to pay Looney a tribute.[11]

At the time of the murder of Myrtle Cook in September 1925, Looney was locked away in a Peoria jail, waiting for a bail hearing. He wasn't set free again until he was paroled in 1934. His turf was quickly divvied up among a half dozen or more gangs, including one mobster who may have been responsible for the killing of Mrs. Cook.[12]

Robert Hyde and Charles Martin were out on the town in Des Moines. It was a Monday night in July 1906, and the two young Black men met up with a couple of girls and spent much of the early evening jumping from club to club on the east side of the Des Moines River, dancing and drinking. The weather had been nice all day, free of the heavy coat of humidity and summer's ever-present threat of a thunderstorm. People were out enjoying the cool night air, getting ice cream and sodas or just walking along the river. Harry Lynch and his wife were among them. Both were actors playing that week in a vaudeville show at downtown's Iowana Park Theater. The Lynches were white, and they had likely been drinking too. About 8:30 p.m., at the corner of Sixth Avenue and Mulberry Street—where the new Polk County Courthouse was being built—the Lynches and the Black couples approached from opposite directions on a part of the sidewalk that narrowed to accommodate a trolley stand.[13]

Des Moines was then a bustling city of sixty-two thousand that included by far the largest Black community in Iowa. Their neighborhoods boasted a significant number of professionals—including doctors, teachers, and lawyers. Many Black families owned their own homes and ran thriving businesses. Despite their success, they still comprised less than 3 percent of the city's population and endured more racial hostilities than many churchgoing whites would have liked to think.

That summer, tensions between the races were heated all over Iowa.

In early June, a Black circus performer in Des Moines allegedly assaulted and raped a white girl. In the northwest Iowa town of Le Mars, a mob formed around a Black man after someone accused him of assaulting a white woman. And just a couple days later, a Black man was arrested in Des Moines and charged with shooting a trolley car conductor to death in a dispute over a fare.[14]

The altercation between the Lynches and the Black couples escalated when both refused to give way on the narrow section of the sidewalk. According to a report in the *Des Moines Register* the next day, the Black men were the aggressors. One of them, the paper said, grabbed Harry Lynch by the shoulders and tossed him into the street. The second Black man took Mrs. Lynch by the arms and pushed her off the sidewalk toward her husband. She screamed, attracting the attention of several white men nearby. One of them was Private John Hearns of Troop E, Eleventh Cavalry, stationed at nearby Fort Des Moines. "His southern blood was aroused," the *Register* reported. "Thinking that the men might attack the woman again, he jumped to her assistance. Grabbing a negro by the throat with each hand, he carried them to the sidewalk."

A crowd quickly gathered around the two Black men, according to the news report. Stones were thrown. Someone called out, "Mob him!" Another yelled, "Kill him! He struck a white woman!" There was an appeal from within the crowd for a lynching, and "several men rushed to a streetcar and tore a trolley rope off," the report claimed. The police station was just a block away, and before events could escalate further, a phalanx of officers rushed in and encircled the Black men. The *Register* estimated that close to a thousand people were assembled, calling for blood. A patrol wagon parted the surge, and the cops put the Black men inside and made their way back to the safety of the station.

"We had said nothing to them," Mr. Lynch claimed in the *Register* report.[15]

The *Register*'s version of events found skeptics among the Black readers of the paper. One of them, S. Joe Brown, was one of Iowa's leading civil rights attorneys and president of the newly organized Des Moines African American Council. It is likely that Brown knew Hyde or Martin, as both young men were born and raised in Des Moines. And Brown would certainly have been familiar with the tone and substance of the one-sided approach that the mainstream white press took in reporting almost any unsavory interaction between the races. The bottom line was that Brown didn't believe the *Register* got the story right. He probably met with Hyde and Martin as well as other witnesses. When Brown went to the paper to seek a correction, he was probably well armed.

Another story ran the next day, and while it could not be considered a retraction, to the paper's credit, they offered a far more balanced report on what occurred. They quoted Brown as saying that it was the white couple who triggered the dustup by refusing to give the Black people half of the narrow sidewalk. "The soldier, Hearne, seeing the difficulty and that it afforded an excellent opportunity to display his Southern chivalry, rushed up and assaulted the negros," Brown explained. The two young Black men, the *Register* quoted Brown, "resisted the assaults, and a rough-and-tumble fight ensued, in which the negros took care of themselves very well."

Brown conceded that the conduct of Hyde and Martin could not be condoned, especially if alcohol were involved. But overall, looking at the facts objectively, he said he was appalled at how quickly such an incidental disagreement could flare into a near-lynching. "It was one of the most disgraceful as well as unjustifiable outbursts of the hatred of Northern whites against negros, as well as the inflammability of the mob, that has ever disgraced the history of the grand old state of Iowa," Brown said. He pointed out that performances of Thomas Dixon's *The Clansman* had recently played to packed houses in Des Moines (the play on which the infamous film *Birth of a Nation* was based). Dixon's play had one sole purpose, Brown asserted, which was to "poison the minds of Northern white men against my people."[16]

Lost to the vagaries of time was the judicial outcome of the assault case against Hyde and Martin, but Attorney S. Brown would run for judge later that same year and for a seat on the city council in 1910. Although he lost both races, Brown—along with his longtime law partner, George Woodson—took on and won some important civil rights cases.[17]

Brown was born in 1875, the youngest of six children and the grandson of former slaves. The family most likely came north after the Civil War, settling in the tiny town of Keosaugua, Iowa, less than ten miles from the Missouri border. Van Buren County was not known as being especially hospitable to newly freed Black people, but both Keosaugua and nearby Bentonsport were Quaker communities that had been active in the Underground Railroad before and during the war. By 1867 there were 42 Black residents of Keosaugua out of a total population of 688.[18] When Brown was ten, the family moved to Ottumwa, which had boomed in recent years to a population of more than 5,000, attracted by the many factory jobs for unskilled laborers. Coal mining flourished all over Wapello County. Ottumwa was also one of central Iowa's major railroad hubs, and by the early 1890s, with the success of the Morrell meatpacking company, the city was also a critical part of the nation's food supply chain.[19]

Both of Brown's parents died shortly after moving to Ottumwa, and Brown was forced to fend for himself while still an adolescent. He was attending the lone public school in Ottumwa and was apparently bright enough to gain attention from one of his white teachers, who helped find him a job as a bellhop at a local hotel. After he graduated from high school, these benefactors sought out a scholarship for Brown to the University of Iowa as well as another hotel job in Iowa City. Brown received a liberal arts degree in 1898 and then a bachelor of law degree as well. Instead of going directly into practice, however, he spent a year as the school principal in Buxton, Iowa. Buxton was a town organized by the Consolidation Coal Company, which openly recruited Black workers from the South, paid them the same wages as white workers, and provided integrated housing, along with many other accommodations. This was the only place in Iowa at the time where a Black man could teach or oversee the education of white children.[20]

Brown's time in Buxton would shape the rest of his life in several ways. It was there that he met his wife Sue, who would partner with him in the organization of the Iowa branch of the National Association for the Advancement of Colored People and serve as its first president from 1915 to 1917.[21] Brown would also meet his law partner, George Woodson, there. Woodson, who was a few years older, graduated from Howard University Law School in 1895. They shared a Des Moines–based practice for more than twenty years.[22]

Buxton also influenced Brown's strongly held belief that the races could live successfully side by side. The Consolidation Coal Company was a subsidiary of the Chicago and Northwestern Railroad, which relied on a steady supply of coal from the Buxton mines. Because of prior experience with labor strife, the company executives purposely opened the town to Black workers. The company was adamant that white workers who objected to these conditions need not apply. While Brown worked at the Buxton school, the town population was close to five thousand, of which about half were Black.[23]

After leaving Buxton and the education system, Brown and Woodson set up shop in Des Moines, taking on the normal assortment of civil cases. However, they were also open to civil rights complaints and criminal defense. In November 1905 Brown picked up a murder case involving one of his former neighbors in Buxton. The victim was a miner, and the accused was his wife. The press painted an ugly portrait of Lulu Austin, "a large, athletic looking negress" who was much larger than her husband, ill-tempered, frequently intoxicated, and had threatened to kill her spouse many times in the past. It was noted that Lulu used a pocketknife. "His body is literally hacked to pieces," the *Ottumwa Tri-Weekly Courier* reported. "Numerous wounds are to be found on his left arm, as if he had tried to ward off many vicious knife thrusts."

Brown had Lulu plead self-defense, and once the jury heard all the evidence of the husband's history of domestic violence, they acquitted her.[24]

Brown often took up capital cases involving Black defendants on appeal. Quick verdicts from all-white juries were common nationwide and were, in some cases, used as a legal alternative to mob lynchings. Brown reversed scores of such cases, including some that went before the Iowa Supreme Court, where he became the first Black attorney to argue before the high court in the state's history. The record shows that he also defended white immigrant clients. He won the release of a German accused of manslaughter in 1915.[25]

His most consequential case before the high court came very early in his career, in 1905, when a Black member of a Polk County jury was barred from eating dinner with the rest of the panel in a nearby boardinghouse. Brown won the case at the lower level, arguing that because the boardinghouse had many times provided meals to county juries, it legally constituted "a public place" and could not discriminate based on race. He won a verdict of $50, and when the man who ran the boardinghouse refused to pay, Brown obtained a court order to seize the man's treasured trotting horse.[26]

Brown would help found and serve as the first president of the Iowa Colored Bar Association in 1925, having been denied membership in the American Bar Association because of his race. He died in 1941.[27]

January 1906 began an important year in the career of Governor Albert Cummins. His record in defense of the common man and in defiance of the monied interests was already secured. He had pushed through a model child labor law that barred all children under fourteen years of age from working indoors, the result of which was to send nearly all of them back to school. He also signed legislation outlawing poisonous additives like formaldehyde from being used as preservatives, which was a common practice in the meatpacking industry.[28] Now he was preparing to take his progressive legislative agenda up a notch and put himself once again fully in the crosshairs of the state's most powerful political player, the railroads.[29]

By tradition, no governor of Iowa had ever run for a third term, but in 1906 Cummins would do just that. The establishment wing of the party, which was closely aligned with the railroads, brought forward three candidates to challenge Cummins for the GOP nomination. Each of them shared the same basic message in opposing Cummins and his progressive agenda: there was no need for all these revolutionary reforms; Iowa was just fine as things were, and the status quo was appropriate, so voters should stand pat. Thence came the fight between the Progressives and the Standpatters that would come to define politics not just in Iowa but nationally for the next decade.[30]

Adding to the political drama playing out against the backdrop of the gubernatorial campaign were historic reforms contained in Cummins's legislative agenda that year: he wanted to ban the railroads from giving away free train tickets to elected officials and key government employees and to end the practice of party leaders choosing candidates for state and federal offices. The railroad's free-pass program had been used as perhaps its most effective lobbying tool. Not only legislators were corrupted by free travel but also judges and editors of big newspapers. "The system has taken on such proportions and is so greatly used to influence public opinion and bribe public officials that it should be abolished, root and branch," Cummins said in an address to the legislature in January 1906.[31]

The primary election bill was of even greater political importance. It was through the leadership of Iowa's Republican Party that the railroads maintained their stranglehold over the state. By breaking that chain and giving voters the right to choose their candidates in the primary elections, Cummins believed a better form of democracy would be forged. "Corporations have, and ought to have, many privileges; but among them is not the privilege to sit in political conventions or occupy seats in legislative chambers," he said in 1902. "Corporations, as such, should be rigorously excluded in every form from participation in political affairs."[32]

The rail barons and their supporters in the legislature might go along with the ban on free passes, but they knew that losing the power to select candidates would bring an end to their dominance. "I believe as a general thing the men selected by the state gatherings of the party are its highest grade men, its men of ability and integrity," said State Senator Shirley Gilliland, an unabashed foot soldier of the establishment. "On the other hand, the primary election law will give to the riff-raff of the cities a power in the selection of candidates which it seems to me is at least to be dreaded."[33]

To which Cummins responded: "I must not be misunderstood as even hoping that a primary election law will bring about the millennium in politics," he said. "There will still be fraud, selfishness, deceit; but I am sure that when this law is passed, we will have taken one step towards purer and better government."[34]

To get the primary law through the legislature, Cummins needed more time. His election to a third term was critical. In his battle to win the GOP nomination, which in Iowa at the time was the defining challenge, Cummins enlisted the help of his mentor, former governor William Larrabee, who helped swing the party delegates to Cummins. Larrabee called the 1906 election "a contest to see whether the corporations shall control this state or whether the people led by Governor Cummins shall."

A compromise was worked out in which Cummins was selected as the party's candidate for governor in exchange for Cummins's acceptance of some Standpat positions in the party platform. Cummins went on to win his third term in November, but by less of a margin than he had won twice before.[35] There could be no question that Cummins saw the direct primary as a major victory for the voters, but he clearly had personal motivations as well. Cummins's long-held ambition to become a U.S. senator was repeatedly frustrated by the backroom deal-makers led by the railroad attorneys Joseph W. Blythe and Nathaniel M. Hubbard. The primary election law was adopted in April 1907, and only a few weeks later, Cummins announced he would run in the 1908 primary election for the U.S. Senate.[36] His opponent would be the incumbent William Boyd Allison, one of the favorites of the railroad cabal. Before Cummins could get out of the gate, however, fate would intercede. Iowa's vexing and seemingly never-ending fight over liquor returned to the political forefront and dealt Cummins another frustration.

For more than a decade, the liquor issue in Iowa had seemed to have been solved, or at least held in check. The Mulct Law, adopted in 1894, gave tolerant populations the option of allowing the saloons to stay open while also granting to those communities where temperance was the prevailing opinion the corresponding right to ban the sale of liquor. In January 1907 the state auditor released a report on the revenues generated by payments of the Mulct Tax. This was the first time that the state had tabulated the taxable income related to liquor sales since 1889. What stunned readers of the auditor's report was that all of the state's largest counties allowed liquor sales.[37] That revelation stirred up the temperance lobby, which had been politically sidelined since the Mulct Law's adoption. Prohibitionists were outraged that liquor was available almost everywhere. Complaints quickly followed that not only were the saloons flourishing but the owners were openly ignoring the few restrictions that the Mulct Law imposed on their operations. The ban on selling beer on Sundays, for instance, was widely ignored. Also ignored was the mandated closing time of 10:00 p.m. The Mulct Law banned tables and chairs inside the barroom and required owners to keep windows unobstructed and doorways wide open so that anyone passing by could see who was partaking. No such restrictions were being enforced, especially not in the river towns along the Mississippi.[38]

Only two weeks after the auditor's report was released, an arsonist attacked the home of a Burlington doctor who had filed lawsuits against saloon owners, accusing them of violating the Mulct Law. In February 1907 lawmakers in Des Moines debated legislation that would authorize the state to hire a division of marshals whose only job would be enforcement of the Mulct Law. In May, injunctions were filed against seventy-nine saloon owners in Dubuque.[39] The biggest and most dramatic confrontation that summer took place in Davenport, widely recognized as Iowa's most liquor-friendly town both because of its large German American community and its sprawling red-light district. The bars in Davenport were all furnished with tables and chairs. Screens and tinted windows provided customers with privacy. Many had private backrooms and second floors where prostitutes conducted business. Virtually all of them were open at all hours, and none closed on Sundays.[40]

On the morning of August 3, 1907, a prohibitionist named T. H. Kemmerer filed injunctions against twenty-seven Davenport saloon owners for violating the terms of operation ordered in the Mulct Law. A week later, Kemmerer and his attorney returned to court to file complaints against sixty-eight more saloons.[41] With every bar in town threatened, the drinking men of Davenport held a massive protest just days later. Led by the Germans, a crowd estimated at five thousand marched peacefully through the streets of the business district and then gathered at Washington Square, the heart of the German neighborhood. A 150-member band played John Phillip Sousa's "Stars and Stripes Forever." Flags and banners hung from the street posts. Some of the protesters had signs. One read: "Sane laws we uphold, but insane restrictions we will fight." Former Mayor C. A. Ficke was among the first to stand and address the crowd. "The purpose of this meeting is not to defend the Davenport saloons," Ficke said. "A few of these are such disreputable dens that they ought to be suppressed, and the administration ought to see that they are suppressed. This meeting is rather a protest against the unfairness of punishing men who maintain respectable places. It is also a protest against placing the entire population of the city under guardianship because of the misdeeds of a few men."[42]

A reporter covering the protest for the *Quad-City Times* noted the next day that the assembly remained completely peaceful, there was no drinking among the participants, and no arrests were needed. But in the weeks that followed, as more of the saloonkeepers were brought forward in court, the atmosphere in Davenport changed markedly. Following a court appearance in October, T. H. Kemmerer—the temperance activist who had prompted the crisis by bringing the first suits against the bar owners—was attacked and beaten by a cane-wielding sixty-three-year-old German newspaper editor. Kemmerer wasn't badly hurt, but after he filed an assault charge against the editor, a mob surrounded the courthouse, threatening Kemmerer's attorney, who had to brandish a revolver before finding safety in a nearby office.

Out-of-town newspapers sensationalized the events in Davenport, claiming that lawlessness ruled the streets. Demands were made on the governor to call out the National Guard. A Des Moines minister suggested churches throughout the state coordinate a day of prayer for the sinners of Davenport.[43]

Governor Cummins wanted nothing to do with the smoldering chaos. He knew he was vulnerable on the liquor question, having long before gone on record as opposing the state prohibitory law. Cummins was himself probably not much of a drinker; his objection to prohibition was that it didn't work. He believed that the Mulct Law was a poor remedy, but he also believed that enforcement of the law was a local, not a state, matter. His critics recognized their opportunity and seized upon the crisis in Davenport, getting friendly editors to condemn the governor for being soft on the liquor violators or, worse, to imply that Cummins had been paid off. "Possibly the Davenport saloon interests have some reason for feeling pretty sure there will be no gubernatorial interference in the interest of law enforcement," jeered an item in the *Sioux City Journal*.[44]

There was no good option for the governor. The river towns had been among his most loyal voters. Using the militia or some other heavy-handed enforcement tool would cost him dearly in the coming senate primary. Yet, ignoring the lawlessness would hurt him even worse. The pressure mounted as the judges and prosecutors in Scott County refused to act against the saloons. Finally, in mid-December, Cummins announced that he had directed the Iowa attorney general to take all actions needed to enforce the state liquor laws in Davenport and elsewhere.

The move did cost him. After all his work to give voters the power to select primary candidates, Iowa's "whiskey counties" abandoned him and strongly backed his rival, the Standpatter William Boyd Allison.[45] But the whimsy of history, of course, wasn't done with Cummins yet.

Allison won the primary and would have been reelected in the fall. However, he was also seventy-nine years old and had been in ailing health throughout the summer campaign. On the afternoon of August 1, at his home in Dubuque, Allison fell unconscious and died three days later. A complex series of legislative maneuvers followed, and after another special election in November 1908 Cummins was finally Iowa's junior U.S. senator. He would remain in the office for sixteen years.[46]

Fig. 1. Charles Mason, Iowa's first Supreme Court justice, 1903. New York Public Library.

Fig. 2. J. Ellen Foster, leader of Iowa's Women's Christan Temperance Union during the 1880s. From F. E. Willard and M. A. Livermore, eds., *A Woman of the Century* (Buffalo NY: Charles Wells Moulton,1893), 296.

Fig. 3. LEFT: Joseph Eiboeck ran an influential German-language newspaper in Des Moines that was strongly anti-temperance. New York Public Library.

Fig. 4. BELOW: Anamosa State Prison, 1911. Fortepan Iowa.

Fig. 5. ABOVE: Boy-murderer Wesley Elkins. Illustration from *National Police Gazette,* November 9, 1889. National Police Gazette.

Fig. 6. RIGHT: U.S. Senator Albert B. Cummins, ca. 1911. Courtesy Library of Congress, Harris and Ewing Collection, LC-DIG-hec-00432.

Fig. 7. Governor William Larrabee, ca. 1886.
New York Public Library.

Fig. 8. Train wreckage near Washington, Iowa, 1881. Iowa State Historical Society.

Fig. 9. Train wreckage near Marshalltown, Iowa, 1890. Photograph by Theodore A. Brown. Internet Archives.

Fig. 10. Saloon in Paullina, Iowa, 1900. Iowa State Historical Society.

Fig. 11. Evangelist Billy Sunday, born near Ames, Iowa, in 1862, played seven seasons of Major League Baseball. Courtesy Library of Congress, Bane Collection, LC-DIG-ggbain-06295.

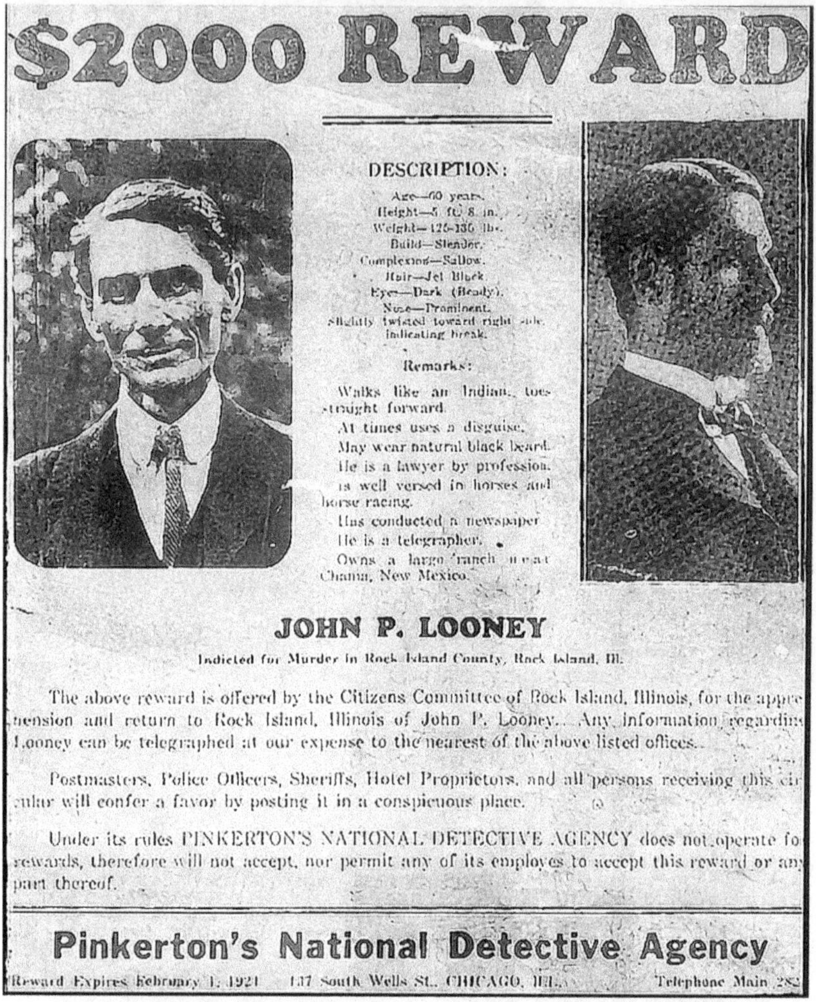

$2000 REWARD

DESCRIPTION:

Age—60 years.
Height—5 ft. 8 in.
Weight—125-135 lbs.
Build—Slender.
Complexion—Sallow.
Hair—Jet Black.
Eyes—Dark (Beady).
Nose—Prominent.
Slightly twisted toward right side, indicating break.

Remarks:

Walks like an Indian, toes straight forward.

At times uses a disguise.

May wear natural black beard.

He is a lawyer by profession.

Is well versed in horses and horse racing.

Has conducted a newspaper.

He is a telegrapher.

Owns a large ranch near Chama, New Mexico.

JOHN P. LOONEY

Indicted for Murder in Rock Island County, Rock Island, Ill.

The above reward is offered by the Citizens Committee of Rock Island, Illinois, for the appre-hension and return to Rock Island, Illinois of John P. Looney. Any information regarding Looney can be telegraphed at our expense to the nearest of the above listed offices.

Postmasters, Police Officers, Sheriffs, Hotel Proprietors, and all persons receiving this cir-cular will confer a favor by posting it in a conspicuous place.

Under its rules PINKERTON'S NATIONAL DETECTIVE AGENCY does not operate fo[r] rewards, therefore will not accept, nor permit any of its employes to accept this reward or any part thereof.

Pinkerton's National Detective Agency

Reward Expires February 1, 1921 137 South Wells St., CHICAGO, Ill. Telephone Main 282

Fig. 12. Wanted poster for John Looney, 1922. At the height of his power Looney ran the largest organized crime organization in the Midwest. Pinkerton Detective Agency.

Fig. 13. S. Joe Brown, attorney and civil rights leader, 1925. National Bar Association.

Fig. 14. Suffrage parade in Boone, Iowa, October 29, 1908. Iowa State Historical Society.

Fig. 15. Farm family near Dubuque, Iowa, 1910. Noble Photograph Collection, Iowa Women's Archives, University of Iowa Libraries.

Fig. 16. Iowa farmer harvesting grain on McCormick reaper, 1920s. Malcolm Price Laboratory School, University of Northern Iowa.

Fig. 17. U.S. Army recruiter signing candidates for Black officer training, Fort Des Moines, 1917. Photograph by Paul Thompson. National Archives.

Fig. 18. Seventeenth Provisional Training Regiment officer graduation with commissions, Fort Des Moines, October 15, 1917. Photograph by Hebard-Showers Company. Iowa State Historical Archives.

Fig. 19. Children with racing pedal car, Vinton, Iowa, 1924. Fortepan Iowa.

10

The Suffragists

Reverend Gertrude von Petzold, an Oxford-trained minister and one of the first women ever to lead a congregation anywhere in Europe, arrived in Iowa around 1908. A German native, she came to England as a young adult believing the academic community there would be more welcoming to a female scholar. Her graduation from St. Andrew's and Edinburgh universities was widely acclaimed, and members of a progressive Unitarian church in the northern city of Leicester quickly offered her a job. She attended the Fourth International Congress of Religious Liberals in Boston in 1907 and became aware of some like-minded Unitarians active in Illinois and Iowa. She took over a ministry in Des Moines on a temporary basis when the regular pastor went on a months-long speaking tour. She made an immediate impression.[1]

The women's rights movement in England was far more advanced than it was in America. London's suffragists had long since grown impatient. Their militancy escalated from heckling members of Parliament and staging large demonstrations to outright rebellion. This rebellion included destruction of government offices by setting fires and smashing windows.[2] Von Petzold was not necessarily an advocate of such tactics, but she spoke of them with admiration. "While [von Petzold] would not go [on] record as sanctioning the radical steps taken in England," the *Des Moines Register* reported in January 1909, "she said that measures should be taken of sufficient vigor to impress the world with the sincerity of the cause."[3]

Suffrage leaders in Iowa, like those in many other states, were also growing impatient. A quarter of a century had passed since the general assembly first passed a resolution that would have put the question of female suffrage before voters. Time and time again, the same resolution was introduced, but never again would a majority of the male lawmakers support giving their wives, mothers, and daughters the right to vote. The suffragists had the same problem that the prohibitionists did when it came to amending Iowa's state constitution: the measure had to be adopted in two successive sessions before it could go on the ballot, and the men were just not interested.

"We attempted one session to furnish each member of the legislature just the arguments and inducements that he asked for," Mrs. Evelyn Dame, chief lobbyist for the suffrage groups, lamented in 1907. "One legislator said there wasn't anything that would induce him. One said if his supporters would come to him and ask him to vote for it, he would, and we got his supporters to go to him. They seem to think that if they vote for that resolution, they will be voting for equal suffrage. The fact is we must get that resolution thru two successive legislatures and then voted on favorably by the people at the next election. In 1884, the legislature passed our resolution, but the next legislature refused to pass it, which forced us to begin all over again. We have been trying to get started ever since."[4]

The first public suffrage demonstration in Iowa took place in October 1908 on the dusty streets of Boone, a small town about fifty miles north of the capital. The three-day convention, which drew several hundred delegates, ended with a parade. The press made much of the fact that two young English girls were in attendance, alluding to the roiling civil protests that were disrupting public life in London.[5]

Following the event in Boone, the Iowa Woman Suffrage Association set up offices in Des Moines and prepared their game plan for the 1909 legislative term. House Representative Fred H. Hunter of Ankeny, who would later serve as mayor of Des Moines, introduced the suffrage resolution again on January 11, 1909, the first day of the session.

"I do not care what people think or whether I am ever elected to the legislature again," Hunter said. "I am going to do what I think is right, and I do believe the women should be given the right to vote."[6]

Yet, there was still no consensus. Some lawmakers believed a better first step would be to give women the right to vote in only some elections, for city or school matters, for instance.[7] There were others who did not believe women even wanted the right to vote. "For several years, the ladies have been permitted to exercise the right of suffrage in state and national elections in four western states," the editor of the *Cedar Rapids Gazette* observed. "When women were given suffrage in these states, it was freely predicted that the idea would spread to other states. But it does not seem to be spreading. One of the greatest sources of opposition to woman suffrage is the women themselves. Hundreds of thousands of them are not only not asking for the ballot, but are opposed to being given the ballot."[8]

He was not wrong. American women of the early twentieth century were far more split on the question than might be expected. The role of men as leaders of the household and as their representatives in public life was well established. To many women, enfranchisement jeopardized the woman's place as the center of the home and family. The vote would change everything in ways that no one could predict. In the Midwest and in Iowa, the divide over suffrage among women was surprisingly strong. Life on the farm required women to take on the duties of men in their absence. This fact didn't necessarily translate into a demand from farm women for a say in how the government was run. There was instead an acceptance of a secondary role—to a point, that is. "On the surface, they accepted gendered language that deemed them wives, mothers, sisters, and daughters in relation to the men who seemed to rule midwestern politics and culture," historian Sara Egge said. "In practice, however, midwestern women rejected male dominance. While they did not express a desire to thwart patriarchy, they also refused to acknowledge it as a limitation on their burgeoning political identities. They embraced the accepted channels of female authority and then transcended them."[9]

Also standing in the way of suffrage were the anti-prohibitionists. No one doubted that if women ever won the right to vote, they would outlaw beer and whiskey the very first chance they got.[10] The politics of suffrage even fostered its own form of xenophobia. Carrie Chapman Catt, an Iowa native and national suffrage leader, argued that the best way to mute the growing political influence of the immigrant male populations in American cities was to give native-born women full citizenship. Catt, who served two stints as president of the National Woman Suffrage Association between 1900 and 1920, pointed to the German American community and their affinity for liquor as both anti-democratic and anti-American.[11]

On March 11, 1909, the suffrage resolution once again came to the floor of the Iowa Senate, apparently without notice to the public, because the gallery was empty. There was no debate. The clerk read the bill into the record, and then they voted: 38 against, 11 in favor. In all, the senators spent less than fifteen minutes on the bill.[12]

One of the few witnesses was Reverend von Petzold, who had emerged that spring as one of the leaders of the suffrage movement in Des Moines. She was apparently close enough to the senate floor to appreciate the vigor and delight some of the senators took in rejecting the bill. One of them, who had been especially disrespectful, was Senator Shirley Gilliland, the prominent Standpatter and foe of Governor Cummins on all things progressive. Von Petzold told reporters that Gilliland had his feet up on his desk as the roll call began. "For quite a while, I saw nothing of him but his legs and feet until suddenly with a magnificent jerk, down to the feet, up comes the head," von Petzold recalled. "And then, he roars out his answer to the roll call. There is suggestion of brutality in his voice, of savage satisfaction; the kind which a big boy bully experiences after having beaten down a small play fellow."[13]

She found the senate's Republican majority "ignorant, undemocratic, insulting, rude, and unfair," the *Des Moines Register* reported. "I am surprised that the senators of Iowa are so far behind the times. It is possible that they do not know that the advice of women is needed on every subject under the sun, and do they not know that most of the great problems before us cannot be settled satisfactorily with[out] the advice of those whom they call frail?"[14]

Republican senator W. P. Whipple attempted to come to Gilliland's aid but probably only poured gasoline on the fire. "I fear that the good woman [von Petzold] must have been unduly excited at the time," Whipple told the *Register*.[15]

Flare-ups between the two sides erupted for months. In June, perhaps in hopes of calming the waters, Senator Gilliland agreed to debate von Petzold as part of the annual Chautauqua meeting that was to be held in July at the state fairgrounds in Des Moines.[16] Six thousand attendees crowded into the main stock pavilion at the fairgrounds to hear the bitter rivals face off. No real victor could be declared, mostly because everyone in the audience already held convictions on the question. Not surprisingly, the senator defended the status quo and questioned what advantage giving the vote to women would achieve. The main argument put forward by von Petzold was that a democracy derived its power to govern through the consent of those governed, which at the time, in Iowa, did not include half of the population.

There were some fireworks. Gilliland, at one point, said that the women of Iowa were very happy fulfilling their primary obligation to society by being the mothers of the next generation. Here, von Petzold pounced, calling Gilliland "wicked" for limiting the ambitions of women to just motherhood. This attitude, von Petzold charged, was what "filled the industrial school at Mitchellville with fallen girls." There was a noticeable gasp from the audience that such a fine lady would say something so crude in a public setting. Gilliland wisely chose not to respond in kind.[17]

The debate and surrounding controversies brought von Petzold celebrity status and some unwanted attention in the months that followed. In what might have been an early version of social media trolling, handbills were published and distributed in downtown Des Moines by a mysterious group calling themselves the Anti-Suffrage Central Committee. The handbills, which used colorful and provocative language, seemed to target Reverend von Petzold personally. The author or authors promised to debate von Petzold and to put an end to the "suffrage sophistry" and the "overly militant fever" displayed by the equal rights proponents. The announcement was signed by Ezra Simpkins, identified as the committee's secretary. When contacted, von Petzold told reporters that she had attempted to find the committee and Ezra Simpkins to no avail. Observers noted that the handbills lacked a printer's mark, which might have provided some clue to who paid for the circulars. Because the handbills continued to be distributed during December 1909, the leaders of the suffrage movement could not ignore or laugh off the campaign. In early January 1910 the women hung Ezra Simpkins in effigy at a rally in Des Moines, and a few days later the sponsors of the Simpkins campaign announced that they had terminated the effort.[18]

As the 1910 election approached, the suffragists launched a novel and risky campaign to overturn the state senate vote. They screened candidates by asking if they would support the suffrage bill, and they went public with the answers. Such a move would have alienated them from some male voters whom they would ultimately need to support them. However, as von Petzold had counseled, the gloves needed to come off. "It is a better political move to defeat every candidate for the legislature who is not in favor of suffrage than to have to storm the citadel at the state capitol a year hence to get complete capitulation," the *Des Moines Register* reported her saying.[19]

In March 1911 a key hearing was held before the Iowa Senate on yet another version of the suffrage bill. This time, the public was given plenty of notice for the hearing, probably to allow the women opposing the suffrage bill to organize. One of the more active opposition groups was led by Mrs. Earl S. Cullums, wife of one of the city's most prominent physicians. Like Cullums, the female opponents of suffrage in Iowa tended to be wealthy, native born, and Protestant. They typically held positions of public authority of some kind and viewed women voters as a threat to that stature and certainly a threat to the stature of the men in their families.[20]

At the March 1911 hearing, Mrs. Cullums, the rich doctor's wife, reportedly gave an eloquent speech that silenced the suffragists. "Is it the voter who makes the home?" Cullums asked. "Or is it the home that makes the voter?"[21]

The great suffrage champion Reverend von Petzold had returned to England by this time, but sitting in the Senate chamber was the movement's most formidable nemesis, Senator Shirley Gilliland. Following Mrs. Cullums's remarks, Gilliland took the floor to blister the equal rights amendment one last time.

"I am here to say that we do not need decorated dishpans and hobble skirts in politics in this state," Gilliland sneered. "I am here to say that the home will not be improved by giving women the ballot. The saloons, the red light districts, graft, corruption—all of this will not be eliminated wherever it exists by giving women the ballot."[22]

While the vote was much closer than two years earlier, the result was the same. The suffrage amendment was defeated in the Iowa Senate 27 to 21.[23]

At the turn of the century, there were fewer than a thousand automobiles in Iowa. By 1914 there were more than three hundred thousand cars: one for every 5.5 residents, the highest per capita rate of auto ownership in the country.[24] As the number of car owners grew, so did their influence on state lawmakers. The new car license law, approved in April 1911, imposed a fee of $8 on all passenger cars with twenty horsepower, and forty cents for every increment of horsepower above that.[25]

Later, in July 1911, William C. Hayward, Iowa's secretary of state, called on the traffic cops of Iowa to stop issuing tickets to drivers whose cars lacked license plates. His staff, who were responsible for issuing the new plates, were overwhelmed with applications, and the factory contracted to provide them had a fire and fell desperately behind on the job. "It is impossible for this department to meet the demand," he said. "In the vault, there are from 5,000 to 6,000 letters all unopened. Every one of the persons who wrote those letters has done his best to comply with the new law. For the time being, he will have to go without a number or even a receipt to show that he had applied."[26]

What the car drivers of Iowa needed were new and better roads. Only a fraction of the nation's 2.2 million miles of highway were concrete, and there were no major connections between large cities. In Iowa, the rich black soil that produced a bounty of farm crops became thick and nearly impassable after it rained.[27] "Some of the Elks who drove to Davenport in their machines during the reunion of the Iowa State Association, will leave their machines at home and go by train when they attend the next state convention," the *Des Moines Register* noted in June 1912. "Thirty or forty miles out of Davenport, the autoists were overtaken by torrential rain. The soil was like gumbo and the mud acted on the wheels like soft glue."[28]

The man put in charge of fixing the roads in Iowa was Thomas MacDonald. He came from Montezuma, Iowa, where his father ran a grain and lumber business, an enterprise that would basically shut down every time it rained because of the muddy roads. He graduated from Iowa State University in 1904, and a year later he became Iowa's first highway engineer.[29]

He traveled the state, largely on horseback, meeting with county officials and inspecting road conditions and bridge projects. When he found incompetence or worse, he had no real authority to force county supervisors to undertake corrections and had to find other methods of influence. In some instances, he found unscrupulous business relationships between county officials and road contractors that led to shoddy or overpriced work.[30] One of his earliest contributions came after discovering that most of the county road money was spent fixing older wood bridges, which seemed to need almost constant attention. It was MacDonald who impressed on state officials to begin using steel bridges reinforced with concrete spans, a policy that was bitterly fought by the army of private contractors making a killing on repairing the wood structures.[31]

Under MacDonald's leadership, Iowa had, by the 1920s, one of the nation's most modern and efficient highway systems. By then, he had gone to Washington DC to take over what would become the U.S. Highway Administration; it was there that he would spend the next thirty-four years.[32]

The original backbone of the national highway system was proposed in 1912. Carl G. Fisher, who made a fortune manufacturing and selling headlights to America's burgeoning automobile industry and opened the Indianapolis Speedway in 1909, envisioned a modern highway connecting Times Square in New York with the Palace of the Legion of Honor in San Francisco. The cities and counties through which the road would pass, he proposed, would be asked to provide the manpower and materials needed to build the road. He wanted the highway completed in time for the opening of the 1915 Panama-Pacific Exposition in San Francisco.[33]

Even with local money, millions of dollars in startup costs would be needed. Believing that his colleagues in the automobile industry would quickly back the proposal, Fisher wrote to the nation's most successful automaker, Henry Ford, in September 1912, asking for his support. Ford refused, telling Fisher that the American taxpayer would never again consider paying for better roads if private financing were used for the transcontinental project. Others disagreed. Frank Seiberling, president of the Goodyear Tire Company, pledged $300,000. Time and money were also committed by Henry Joy, the president of Packard Motors, who took over the management of the entire operation. Joy became so engrossed in the highway project that in June 1913 he drove west from Detroit scouting for the best route through the Midwest. He got as far as Omaha, where he stopped at a Packard dealership and asked for directions to Wyoming. There weren't any, the dealer replied and, indeed, just a mile or two beyond the town limits, Joy found himself stranded on the Nebraska countryside.[34]

If the route west was a cipher, getting from the Eastern Seaboard to Chicago was easy. Starting in New York City, the highway would follow mostly existing roads in New Jersey and Pennsylvania before crossing Ohio at Marion and then Indiana at Fort Wayne. Governors from a number of western states lobbied extensively to be included as the route took shape. Promoters of the road in Colorado proposed spending $1 million on one of the two routes that they believed would bring the roadway through their state. Joy, who had been named president of the Lincoln Highway Association, was careful to keep the final route selection under seal until everything was ready.[35]

There was little question that the road would need to cross Iowa, just as the Central and Union Pacific railroads had done a generation before. The exact route and which towns in Iowa would be included were also closely held secrets. The announcement came on September 14, 1913, and the final route would bring autos over the Mississippi River at Clinton and then on to Cedar Rapids, Marshalltown, Ames, and finally Council Bluffs.[36]

Initially, it was thought that the highway would be used primarily by tourists and that cities along its route would benefit by bringing in the leisure dollar. No one was thinking that the highway would become arteries for the delivery of goods by trucks. The railroads could not conceive of the day when traffic on highways would compete with them for freight and passengers. Within a few short years, however, the Lincoln Highway was linked to a modern, well-engineered network that brought the automobile traveler to virtually every major American city.

Other unintended beneficiaries of the highways were the bootleggers of the Midwest. With Chicago at the center, liquor could be moved efficiently and quickly east to Indiana and Ohio and west to Iowa. Indeed, two towns in eastern Iowa were on the Lincoln Highway path—Belle Plaine and Tama—both neighbors of Vinton, where Myrtle Cook was murdered in 1925.

11

Last Call in Marshalltown

The Billy Sunday Ministry opened 1909 on the road in Spokane. He lectured and prayed for six weeks in December and January, attracting more than six hundred thousand parishioners. Among those attending were about six thousand whom Sunday had convinced to take a vow of abstinence, or, as he liked to call it, "hitting the sawdust trail."[1] Toward the end of his visit, law enforcement officials in Illinois sent word that Sunday's life had been threatened. Bootleggers in Springfield allegedly hired a couple of ex-cons, recently released from the federal prison at Joliet, and they were coming west to kill Sunday before he could convert any Illinois drinkers. While Sunday took the threat in stride, he bought himself a revolver, which he kept in his hip pocket, and went on with the show. After leaving Washington, he played a few nights in Los Angeles in early February and then took his family on a well-earned vacation on the island of Catalina.[2]

When Sunday reached the Illinois capital in March, there were no signs of the contract killers, but the evangelist did have a violent altercation. A former resident of the mental institution in Jackson, Illinois, attacked Sunday with a horsewhip; the assailant even got in a few blows before the one-time major league outfielder wrested the lash away. He claimed that Sunday should be punished for his public use of coarse language. The police said that they would send the man back to the hospital in Jackson after he had spent a few days in the county jail.[3]

The revival in Spokane marked a turning point in Sunday's career. He was no longer preaching in small towns and backwater crossroads. He was now in demand in the big cities of the Midwest and the East. His ministry employed more than a dozen musicians, roadies, and advance men. He could demand and usually receive a big indoor stage, with heat in the winter. Some cities didn't have a hall or auditorium big enough and had to build one. "Billy Sunday Tabernacles" were erected in Los Angeles, Baltimore, Wichita, and Kansas City.[4] The shrines were ubiquitous, if sometimes short-lived, landmarks. Often, after Sunday's team packed up and moved on, the tabernacle was taken down and the wood was recycled for other uses, sometimes to build the Sunday church in the next town.[5]

Following his services in Illinois, Sunday accepted an invitation to preach in Marshalltown during the last week of April 1909, which would be something of a homecoming for him. It was there that he spent his high school years, first played baseball and discovered his skills in public speaking. There was, however, some question whether Marshalltown could muster all that would be needed to host one of America's most famous evangelists. He made the commitment to come to Marshalltown in November 1908, which didn't give the city much time.[6] The fact that winter was quickly closing in didn't help. Volunteers came from all over to help build the tabernacle. "Age is no bar to employment on the tabernacle unless the applicant is crowding the century mark," noted the *Marshalltown Evening Times-Republican* just days from the construction deadline. "Eli Mendenhall, in his 96th year, offered a day's work but was advised to wait until his services were needed. Joseph Tuffree, age 99, has not yet applied, but John Galloway, over 80, was astride the roof yesterday, hammering away like a mechanic at 40."[7]

The five-week revival began on Sunday morning, April 26, 1909. There were three sessions that drew a combined audience of nearly twelve thousand, which was equal to the population of the entire city of Marshalltown.[8] "The temporary tabernacle was built to hold 5,000 people, but at the first service, it was packed and you couldn't get within 200 feet of the doors," N. S. Ketchem told the *Des Moines Register.* "Billy made a hit by talking in a reminiscent vein and telling of his impression as he walked up the street of his old hometown after such a long absence. He referred by name to a dozen old landmarks and local characters who everyone had forgotten. He told of how he started playing baseball as a member of the team that represented a Marshalltown hardware store and how 'Pop' Anson happened to come along and pick him up."[9]

In the last week of his Marshalltown engagement, Sunday devoted a session exclusively to men, in which he gave his famous "Booze

Sermon." An estimated six thousand men turned out, and nearly two hundred took an oath that day never to touch liquor again. Over the course of his career, Sunday would claim to have used the Booze Sermon to persuade more than three hundred thousand men and women to adopt a life of sobriety. At services held in Ohio, Pennsylvania, and Kansas during the campaign of 1911–1912, he counted thirty-six thousand who took the pledge; the next year, close to eighty-one thousand were converted in revivals held in North Dakota, Indiana, and West Virginia. There were reports of some ten thousand in Des Moines alone.[10] Throughout his stay in Marshalltown, Sunday hammered away not just at the evils of whiskey but on the passivity of the men in the city who might not drink, themselves, but remained tolerant of the saloons that legally operated under the state's Mulct Law.

"There's one word that is spelling the doom of the saloon," Sunday told his audience in Marshalltown. "That is votes. If the church people will but vote right, the saloon will be down and out in no time. The people of this country have been damned and cursed by it as by nothing else, and I tell you it is doomed."[11]

His words had the desired impact. Only days after Sunday's operation left for its next booking, petitions circulated in Marshalltown asking the city council to revoke saloon permits. Two weeks later, the county attorney filed suits against six saloons for selling liquor to minors.[12] The litigation was joined by the Anti-Saloon League (ASL), which was just beginning to exert its power nationally.[13] The cases, however, dragged through the courts, and a year later a district court judge found that the Marshalltown saloons were operating within the law.[14]

The ASL did not lose very often. Established in Ohio in 1893, it was a political machine focused on changing the laws in every state to put every saloon in the country out of business.[15] The organization handpicked candidates willing to fight for prohibition and helped fund and manage their campaigns. Once their candidates were elected, the ASL kept close tabs on their investment, holding them to their commitments once the voting began.[16]

The ASL in Iowa achieved most of its early success not in the legislature but in the courtroom. Just as it had attacked the saloonkeepers of Marshalltown, the ASL looked for technical violations of the Mulct Law. Selling liquor at a restaurant, for instance, was forbidden, although wine, whiskey, and beer were served at almost any nice bistro. Restaurateurs would claim that the waiters were providing a personal service to the customers and that the house had nothing to do with the transaction. The ASL disputed that claim in court and won closure of the loophole. Prescription booze sold by pharmacists was another place where ASL attorneys went to work. In the end, pharmacists who couldn't produce paperwork clearly identifying their customers were subject to fine and loss of their license.[17]

The Iowa ASL claimed to have closed 185 saloons in 1911 alone. They also pointed to actions pending against another 200 in such cities as Burlington, Cedar Rapids, Keokuk, and Fort Madison, promising success against at least half of them. The state's estimated three thousand barrooms in 1905 were down to fewer than seven hundred by 1912.[18]

Efforts in Iowa to get the general assembly to repeal the Mulct Law and reimpose prohibition were less effective. Petitions signed by more than one hundred thousand voters were submitted to the state senate in November 1910, and organizers said they would have another one hundred thousand signatures by the time lawmakers convened their first session in January.[19]

"Either the liquor traffic is right or wrong," said Reverend Charles Hall, a Baptist minister from California who had come east to support the temperance campaign. "If it is right, it certainly ought to have free course, run, and be glorified. If it is wrong, it ought to die. We believe it is wrong and believing that, in the name of the home and the commonwealth, we are determined to outlaw it in this great state."[20]

This growing campaign was enough to arouse Colonel Joseph Eiboeck, the feisty German newspaper editor and veteran of the liquor battles waged in the 1880s. He was, by 1911, seventy-three years old but still publishing his widely read German-language daily and still very tuned in to events surrounding the capital. Eiboeck had good reason to be alarmed. The strength of the temperance movement nationally could not be ignored. In the summer of 1911, prohibition was the dominant legislative issue in a half dozen statehouses—including in Maine, Texas, Kansas, and Kentucky. Meanwhile, the pressure to ban alcohol was building in six other states that approved women's suffrage laws by the end of 1911; three more were likely to adopt suffrage in 1912. The fight in Iowa over women's suffrage rights was returning to the forefront of the legislative agenda, which meant that prohibition would too.[21]

"We feel that the prohibitory laws are directed against our habits and customs of life and that they are an unwarranted interference with them," Eiboeck said. "We want true temperance and true morality. We don't want drunkenness. We simply want to be let alone in the enjoyment of harmless habits of life that we brought with us from the Fatherland and which should be no one's concern but our own."[22]

Liquor was one of the few issues on which the two wings of Iowa's Republican Party seemed to agree: the Progressives didn't believe the whiskey bottle could be legislated out of society; meanwhile, the Standpatters were, as always, content to leave things alone. Bills proposing to put a liquor ban back before voters were turned down in 1909 and 1911.[23]

Members of the Iowa Equal Suffrage Association took early trains on the morning of February 20, 1913, to ensure their arrival at Des Moines ahead of the 10:00 a.m. state senate committee. Some, from as far away as Council Bluffs and Clarion, probably came to town the day before. Scheduled for a hearing that day, once again, was the suffrage bill. The association members planned to pack the gallery even though they had been assured by lawmakers that the bill had been marked for failure.

The women-led opposition, confident that the senators would once again turn down the voting rights measure, decided that it wasn't worth their time to show up for the hearing. Mrs. Earl S. Cullums, the physician's wife and suffrage critic who had played an instrumental role in killing the bill two years before, told reporters there was no need to be present.[24] Mrs. Cullums misjudged the mood of the lawmakers. Impressed by the large showing from the Iowa Equal Suffrage Association, the senate committee moved the suffrage bill right along to the floor, where it passed overwhelmingly. On the day it came before the lower house, the Speaker took a moment before the vote and sternly reminded the visitors that no public outbursts or demonstrations were allowed inside his chamber. The suffragists ignored the admonishment and broke into a wild celebration that didn't end for fifteen minutes.[25]

Even after the governor signed the bill, the ordeal wasn't even close to finished. Iowa law required that the measure come back before lawmakers a second time and win passage again before the question could be placed on the ballot. The male voters of Iowa would have nearly three years to think about it.[26]

12

The Hyphenated Americans

A dry spell, humorist Josh Wilson wrote with a grin in the summer of 1913, was a climatic event dreaded by the farmers of Iowa, while their counterparts in Texas would consider the same weather conditions as the blessed onset of the rainy season. "A threatened drought in Iowa every summer may be depended on with as much certainty as the arrival of the 4th of July," Wilson mused from his perch at the *Cedar Rapids Gazette*. "From the time the corn crop is knee high till it is out of the way of frost, the Hawkeye agriculturist holds himself in a combatant state of resignation and gloomily allows that we are liable to have a dry spell at any moment. He clings steadfastly to his horror of a drought till it's time to begin to worry over the prospect of a hard winter."[1]

If the farmers of Iowa shared an unease over the weather, they also shared an unrivaled success. Iowa growers produced a record corn crop in 1912, delivering 421 million bushels to market. Collectively, agriculture products from Iowa were valued at over $1 billion in 1914.

"Iowa alone produces more corn than Nebraska, Kansas, and Oklahoma combined," the State Department of Agriculture proudly reported in 1914. "She produces more oats than the total of three states of North Dakota, South Dakota, and Missouri. In her poultry products, she is again in the lead and gaining steadily on New York and Wisconsin in their dairy output."[2]

Such output sent land values skyrocketing. Speculators jumped into the market. "The Harvey Powers farm just west of town changed hands twice within a few hours," the *Des Moines Register* reported in August 1912. "Mr. Powers sold the place to James A. Harp for $116 per acre, and a few hours later, Mr. Harp sold the farm to C. A. Schrader for $120. The farm contains about 160 acres."[3]

In November 1913 the heirs to a 180-acre dairy farm near Marshalltown put a notice in the paper of a public auction. They promised a free lunch to anyone who showed up. They also said that they would take bids on the pastures and $50,000 worth of improvements as well as every animal and farm implement on the property. On the day of the auction, the roadsides were jammed with parked autos; an estimated three thousand people turned out. There was not much of a drama; the sale was completed within twenty minutes. The winning bid came from Eli Messer, a young farmer from Dysart, who offered a record price, just over $500 an acre. "Shall I write you out a check for this right now or wait and come to the bank?" he asked the auctioneer.[4]

The influential farm journalist Henry A. Wallace, who later served as the secretary of agriculture under Franklin Roosevelt, pointed out in January 1914 that a speculative bubble might be forming. "Land that now sells at $100 an acre does not produce more bushels of grain that it did when it sold at $50, $40, or $30," he warned. "It rents for more money because crops bring more money. Therefore, if present prices of land are to be maintained, we must, in the first place, do better farming and thus increase the acre yield. We must also do better marketing and we must strive to get a larger share of the consumer's dollar."[5]

Farm income rose from $7.8 billion in 1913 to $9.5 billion nationally in 1916. Heeding Wallace's advice, farmers were finding better methods and using more automation. Had war not broken out in Europe in 1914, which sent farm prices skyrocketing even higher, demand for American farm products would have fallen well short of the mounting supply. However, once the United States entered the fighting, farm production became a matter of national security under the slogan "Food will win the war."[6]

Shortly after President Woodrow Wilson took office in March 1913, someone in the administration issued an unattributed statement that was picked up by papers all over the nation: the Wilson White House would be dry. This was an interesting development since the new president was known to enjoy the occasional scotch and had expressed his opinion that the liquor question was a private one and held no upside for him politically.[7]

In the November 1914 election, voters in four states—Colorado, Oregon, Washington, and Arizona—adopted constitutional amendments barring the manufacture and sale of alcoholic beverages. A month later, a majority in the U.S. House of Representatives supported the passage of national prohibition, but their numbers fell just short of the two-thirds needed to pass the bill on to the Senate.[8] The drive for national prohibition of liquor was building for another reason: women's suffrage, and in 1914 Iowa found itself at the center of both issues.

A full-time temperance lobby, the Iowa Constitutional Amendment Association, opened offices in Des Moines and began candidate screening in January 1914.[9] Just as the suffrage leaders had targeted specific races to improve their chances four years earlier, temperance activists fanned out across the state, identifying favored candidates and promising assistance come November.[10] Not only were they vetting potential candidates for the legislature, but they were also very interested in who might be running for lieutenant governor. The lieutenant governor served as president of the state senate and was empowered to make committee assignments, including to the panel on intemperance, where prohibitory bills had recently been killed.

"The fight will center on lieutenant governor," said A. U. Coats, president of the Amendment Association. "For the last four sessions of the legislature, we have had 'wet' lieutenant governors, and in appointing committees on temperance, he has selected a majority of 'wets.' The temperance people feel that the election of a 'dry' lieutenant governor is of more than ordinary importance."[11]

As a result, the temperance coalition surprisingly chose to back O. P. Myers, a Democrat, for the lieutenant governor position. The Republican incumbent, William Harding, was considered a pawn of the liquor interests. "[Harding] as lieutenant governor has persistently labored for the liquor interests of our state," began a resolution adopted by the Gideons Association in October 1914. "He has persistently made [an] effort to smother all moral and temperance legislation."[12]

Harding won and, in January, when he announced committee assignments, the temperance people were not happy. "We are fully aware that Mr. Harding is 'wet,' but we thought that there was some chance this time that he would play fair with us," said Coats of the Amendment Association. "We were sadly mistaken."[13]

The prohibitionists did prevail in Iowa's house of representatives, which had voted several times to repeal the Mulct Law. A breakthrough in the state senate didn't come until "wet" members of the Committee for the Suppression of Intemperance attempted to exclude the press from its meetings. Their thinking, apparently, was that members on the fence would more likely vote with the liquor interests if their ballots were secret. While the wets succeeded in getting the press excluded, the dry coalition forced all the temperance bills to the senate floor, in full view of the press and public. As a result, the full senate voted to repeal the Mulct Law, 27 to 22, on February 12, 1915. The action meant that Iowa's existing prohibitory law, placed in the state constitution more than fifty years before, became the operative authority with regard to liquor. Lawmakers gave the saloon owners, brewers, and distillers until January 1, 1916, to close down their businesses.[14]

The Iowa attorney general immediately announced that he would be submitting a bill to fund a new division of the state police, whose job would be to enforce the liquor ban. Legislation was also quickly introduced that would give the police the authority to search automobiles without a warrant if the transporting of liquor was suspected. While they still could, liquor distributors and saloon owners in Des Moines organized fleets of trucks and cars, all loaded with booze and all bound for delivery to bars and storage garages in Omaha and Rock Island.[15]

Seeing their job done with liquor, the energized senate leadership next took up the suffrage amendment. In the prior session, both houses of the legislature had supported placing the question before the voters. Now, the same resolution needed to pass a second time. Leading the Iowa suffragists this time was a no-nonsense political veteran named Flora Dunlap. Dunlap had been mentored by Jane Addams in Chicago and had come to Des Moines a decade earlier to run one of Iowa's first shelters aimed at supporting low-income families. Like Addams, Dunlap found her mission in the streets, which helped win her the backing of city leaders. She was a champion of education and became the first female member of the Des Moines School Board in 1912.[16]

There was a sense of assurance that the suffrage amendment would pass and that male voters would support it. That perception was so prevalent that much of the work Dunlap and her team undertook in 1914 was to prepare women to utilize their new voting rights. They organized a "suffrage school," where an all-female faculty taught women students how to vote, conduct political campaigns, give public speeches, and, indeed, run for office.[17] They were that confident.

"The time was when a woman who favored equal suffrage was thought 'queer,'" the editor of the *Keokuk Daily Gate City* wrote in May 1914. "But now-a-days to oppose suffrage marks a woman as being queer, and very few men can be found anywhere who speak against it."[18]

At the Republican state convention held in Des Moines in July 1914, the delegates adopted a party platform that favored equal rights for women. In November, male voters in Montana and Nevada approved women's suffrage rights. And on February 24, 1915, the Iowa State Senate approved, for a second time, the voting rights resolution. Suffrage would finally go before Iowa's male voters in June 1916.[19]

During the first week of December 1915, exports out of the Port of New York more than doubled that of any week in either 1913 or 1914.[20] Just during the month of April 1915, boxes filled with guns and ammo valued at more than $30 million moved out of the New York Custom House on their way to British and French troops.[21] The trade was so lucrative that idle manufacturing plants all over the United States retooled their shops and were soon reaping big munitions profits.[22]

Iowa farmers were making money too. Corn was selling for between $2 and $3 per bushel; wheat was fetching as much as $3.60 per bushel.[23] While the war was no doubt more than an abstraction to the farmers of the Midwest, it was far enough away that any guilt felt over the blood money was not stressful or lasting. But for the ninety thousand German immigrants of Iowa, the war was as real as the bullets and the bombs the American manufacturers were sending across the Atlantic.[24]

In early August, only a few weeks after the war began, President Woodrow Wilson pledged that the United States "must be neutral in fact as well as in action." Then came the discovery that Colt's Armory Company was selling machine guns to the Canadian government, which in turn was shipping the guns to England. On September 3, 1914, Congressman Richard Bartholdt, who represented the heavily German neighborhoods of south St. Louis, raised a question before members of the House Foreign Relations Committee about the Colt's contract, strongly suggesting that the arms sales violated the president's neutrality pledge.[25] Standing behind Bartholdt and fully supporting his allegations was another German American member of the committee, Representative Henry Vollmer of Davenport, Iowa.

After much debate, the committee agreed to call on the president to explain how the Canadian gun sales didn't violate the neutrality pledge.[26] Weeks later, the State Department issued a statement insisting that the government had no authority to prevent private enterprise from selling goods to a willing buyer and that this had no impact on the neutrality pledge.[27]

Bartholdt, born in Schleiz, (near Bavaria), was one of the longest-serving members of Congress, having first been elected in 1893. He was known as a pacifist who also had strong ties to the German crown, enough that President Taft appointed Bartholdt a special envoy for a peace mission to Berlin in 1911.[28] Vollmer, on the other hand, was a newcomer to Washington, having won a special election in February 1914 to replace a Democratic attorney from Muscatine who had died just a few months earlier.[29] Vollmer's father was born in Hanover and immigrated to Iowa around 1864. The younger Vollmer received an undergraduate degree from the University of Iowa and studied law at Georgetown University. He came home, passed the bar, and set to work. Bright, ambitious, and politically astute, Vollmer was elected mayor of Davenport at the tender age of twenty-six and won reelection three times before throwing his hat into the ring for Congress.[30]

Iowa's second house district represented a diverse population, from the professionals in Iowa City to the restless river towns of Muscatine and Davenport. One of Iowa's largest communities of German immigrants lived there, and while the majority of voters were decidedly "wet," they honored party allegiance little, flipping back and forth between Democrats and Republicans whenever it suited them. Just two months after winning the seat, Vollmer surprised everyone by announcing that he would not seek reelection. While his explanation was vague, there is evidence that he had been targeted by Republican supporters of suffrage and prohibition.[31]

Had he decided to run, however, the German American community most certainly would have lost an important voice of caution in the prewar debate over arms shipments to the Allies. Freed from the yoke of reelection, Vollmer could be blunt about the war. "It would be the most disastrous conflict ever recorded in history," he told reporters in July 1914. "Nothing that has transpired heretofore would compare with it. I believe that such a war would be a great detriment to the

US, to the whole world in fact, for we could not progress when a large portion of humanity was impoverished."[32]

He was also free to lead public pro-German war efforts. He helped raise money for the Red Cross on the German side of the battlefields. He was a keynote speaker at a pro-German event in Davenport in August that raised $25,000 for German relief. Days later, he spoke to a large picnic event sponsored by Germans from Black Hawk County. Vollmer told the crowd that it was the "intense jealousy" of the English toward the economic power of the German Empire that had led the British to start the war.[33]

Thus, when Bartholdt rose before the Foreign Relations Committee in September, Vollmer was also able to give full-throated endorsement. As the congressmen waited for Wilson's response on the Colt machine-gun sales, they charged ahead and organized a protest on December 1 in Chicago, where they jointly announced plans to introduce legislation banning U.S.-made arms shipments to the Allies. Within days, the arms embargo bill received support from a half dozen other congressmen, along with progressive crusader Senator Robert LaFollette of Wisconsin. Iowa lawmakers introduced a letter of support in Des Moines. The German American press took up the story nationally.[34]

Bartholdt and Vollmer posed a real threat not only to the American munitions industry but, more importantly, to the Allied generals. Pushback came on December 15, in the form of a story published in *The Sun*, one of New York's smaller but still influential dailies. The reporter quoted a Wall Street attorney named Maurice Leon, who boldly accused Vollmer, Bartholdt, and a third congressman who favored the arms embargo of acting as "agents of Germany."[35] Leon was well known to the New York press as both an expert in international law and a financial adviser to the French government.[36] "This is a characteristic German maneuver," Leon told the *Sun*. "I have no doubt but that these three Congressmen are carrying out the expressed wishes of Count von Bernstorff, the German Ambassador to this country and Dr. Bernard Dernburg, the German publicist."[37]

The charge of treason fell flat. Following the *Sun* story, Bartholdt took to the Senate floor and denied acting in any way that could be interpreted as "high treason against the government of the United States." The accusation, he said, couldn't be taken seriously considering the fact that the charge emanated from a New York spokesman for a foreign belligerent, which, according to reports, "would be at its rope's end but for the contraband supplies which it receives from the United States."[38]

The chairman of the Foreign Relations Committee was William J. Stone, who, like Bartholdt, was from Missouri and whose district also included German American wards of St. Louis. Although Stone was a Democrat, he was not especially close to President Wilson and, therefore, seemingly indifferent to the political pain the embargo bill might cause the administration. Stone allowed the Bartholdt-Vollmer bill to move forward. In addition, Stone sent a letter to William Jennings Bryan, then Wilson's secretary of state, pointedly asking if the administration's policy was to discriminate against the people of Germany and Austria in the context of arms sales.

Bryan, who would resign his cabinet post in protest only a few months later because he believed Wilson had taken sides, was anxious over the arms sales but not yet ready to break with the president. In a six-thousand-word reply to Stone, Bryan vigorously defended Wilson, arguing that it had "never been the policy of this government to prevent the shipment of arms or ammunition into belligerent territory." He dismissed the notion that the federal government had any responsibility to prevent trade that might violate the neutrality pledge. "No such obligations exists; it would be an unneutral act."[39]

Bryan closed: "It is the business of a belligerent operating on the high seas, not the duty of a neutral, to prevent contraband from reaching the enemy."[40]

Once Wilson's position became fully articulated, House leaders killed the Bartholdt-Vollmer embargo bill, but they could do nothing to stamp out the question over America's role in the war. The neutrality debate escalated dramatically in early May 1915, when a German U-boat captain homed in on an unarmed passenger ship off the coast of Ireland, the *Lusitania.*

Of the 1,960 people on board, 1,193 were killed, including 128 Americans.

Former president Theodore Roosevelt spoke for many when he said that America could no longer sit on the sidelines. "It seems inconceivable that we should refrain from taking action," he said when learning of the attack. "This represents not merely piracy, but piracy on a vaster scale of murder than any oldtime pirate ever practiced."[41]

The muted response from the president played well on the prairie. "President Wilson makes it easy for Americans to follow him when he talks such pure Americanism as he did in his address at Philadelphia last night," wrote the editors of the *Quad-City Times.* "The president believes that peace is a much finer thing than war."[42]

Harvey Ingham, editor of the *Des Moines Register,* agreed: "The sinking of the *Lusitania* was deliberate murder. But what of dropping bombs on defenseless cities? What about the assault on Dunkirk from 20 miles away? What of the use of gas? When will we recognize that all war is savagery, always accompanied with rape and torture, loot[ing] and arson. The sinking of the *Lusitania* is murder. But so is everything else that is going on in Europe."[43]

Some Iowans even took up the argument that the Germans were free to attack the ship because it was thought to be carrying ammo. "The Germans had a perfect right to sink the big ship," wrote Samuel H. M. Byers, who had served on the staff of Gen. William Tecumseh Sherman during his famous run through Georgia during the Civil War and would later serve as a U.S. envoy in several European capitals. "[Germany] will sink more, and the only safety Americans have for property or lives is to stay home and stop pretending to be neutral, but be neutral in fact."[44]

As much as Roosevelt was still admired, most Iowans would stand with President Wilson at a time of national crisis. "It is regretted that one of the few jarring notes should have been sounded by one who himself has been an occupant of the White House," the *Sioux City Journal* remarked. "But there are times when even Theodore Roosevelt should be silent, and this is one of them."[45]

Roosevelt was having none of it and continued to criticize Wilson throughout the summer. The former president also called out Congress for the dismal state of the American armed forces. After an assassination attempt on banker J. P. Morgan in July 1915, Roosevelt added a third and even darker refrain to his stump speeches: the threat to U.S. security posed by "hyphenated Americans."[46] Addressing a crowd estimated at thirty thousand, in San Diego on July 27, Roosevelt noted that Morgan's assailant was German-born and that the efforts of the banker's butler probably saved his life. "If, when J. P. Morgan was attacked in his home by a hyphenated American, the butler stood quietly by and remarked that he did not believe in violence and that he was neutral?" Roosevelt said, hitting two targets in the same sentence. "Mr. Morgan might not have been alive today. But the butler did not attempt to be neutral."[47]

He later called the hyphenated American "an active force for wrongdoing," in an August speech at an officer training camp in Upstate New York. "The effort to hoist two flags on the same flagpole always means that one flag is hoisted underneath, and the hyphenated American invariably hoists the flag of the United States underneath. We must all be Americans and nothing else."[48]

In September Roosevelt, in a piece for the *Metropolitan Magazine*, condemned anyone who didn't fully support American arms exports to the Allies. "The foolish professional pacifists who advocate refusing to sell munitions of war to the Allies are proposing a course of action as wicked as it is base," he argued.[49] There was little doubt that Roosevelt, in making reference to the "professional hyphenated American," was speaking directly of the members of the National German-American Alliance and other German lobby groups. He was also speaking of congressmen Richard Bartholdt and Henry Vollmer.

"The Americans who are now striving to prevent the sale of munitions of war to the counties endeavoring to secure the redress of Belgium's wrong, that is, the allied powers, are playing the game of a ruthlessly militaristic and anti-American Germany against their own country as well as against the interests of humanity at large," Roosevelt said.[50]

Roosevelt's assaults initially failed to connect with most Iowans. "No foreigner ever came to the American shores to live and rear his family whose first ambition was not to associate himself with the American community," the editor of the *Des Moines Register* commented in November 1915. "The hyphen is not of German, nor of Polish, nor of Italian origin. It is purely American."[51]

In an odd twist, however, it was President Wilson who came to share Roosevelt's thinking—both on the deplorable state of the U.S. military and the disloyalty of immigrant Americans. In November 1915 Wilson gave perhaps his most important prewar speech, at the Manhattan Club in New York. There, he made the case that war was looming and that the United States was not ready. He outlined a military preparedness plan that called for the training of four hundred thousand soldiers and an uptick in modernizing the navy. These were merely prudent steps to take. "No thoughtful man feels any panic haste in this matter," Wilson said. "The country is not threatened from any quarter. She stands in friendly relations with all the world."

Wilson then lashed out at the immigrant community, echoing Roosevelt's words of alarm. "There are citizens of the U.S. born under other flags but welcomed under our generous naturalization laws to the full freedom and opportunity of America, who have poured the poison of disloyalty into the very arteries of our national life," he said. "It is necessary that we should promptly make use of processes of law by which we may be purged of their corrupt distempers."[52]

The sudden shift in policy left Iowans uncomfortable with exactly what the president was planning to do with the expanded military. "Statesmen throughout the world might rest assured that the United States intended no aggression, but they would not," the *Des Moines Register* editorialized after the speech. "They would no more rest assured than France did when the German army was increased in 1904 or thereabouts."[53]

Even more troubling was Wilson's harsh questioning of the loyalty of American immigrants.

"If we are to have an issue made of the loyalty of the foreign born, as President Wilson would seem to force upon us, the challenge might as well be taken up at once," the *Des Moines Tribune* opined. "The fact is that the foreign-born population of America have shown more restraint under the strain of war than thousands of the home born, who have been hot on the trigger from the very start. There is no higher patriotism in America than among the foreign born, and this whole cry against them is part of the hysteria of the hour."[54]

13

Wet to Dry Again

The first mention in Iowa of D. W. Griffith's infamous film, *Birth of a Nation,* came in mid-February 1915. A prior Griffith effort, *Avenging Conscience,* based on "The Tell-Tale Heart" by Edgar Allen Poe, was playing at the Palace Theater in Muscatine. A reviewer from the local paper was delighted with *Avenging* and couldn't get over the realism, the storytelling, and the director's groundbreaking cinematic techniques. In the last paragraph, the reviewer mentioned that Griffith's newest film, *Birth of a Nation,* was already booked to open in New York in March. Admission, he pointed out, would be $2—a stunning amount given that a matinee showing of *Avenging* cost just ten cents.[1]

Throughout 1915 no one could escape hearing or reading something more about Griffith's latest movie—not even in Iowa. There had never been anything like it before. The cost of producing the film was said to be more than $500,000. The director employed a cast of more than eighteen thousand, as well as three thousand horses and hundreds of other animals. The film was based on the novel *The Clansman* by Thomas Dixon, which was published in 1905. Both the film and a theatrical version of the novel played in theaters and opera houses all over America and were immensely popular among white audiences—even in the North. Audiences seemed unconcerned with the racism and Dixon's baseless attempt to recast the Southern slave owners as tragic victims of the Civil War.[2] Griffith was born in Kentucky and raised by a father who served as a colonel in the Confederate Army. He made little effort to deviate from Dixon's original storyline.[3] People lined up in New York and Los Angeles, eager to see the movie, even with the $2 entry fee. A special screening was held in the White House for the president and his family. The movie was the nation's first blockbuster.[4]

Iowa's white population, which represented about 99.4 percent of the state's 2.2 million residents, seemed as though they couldn't wait for the film to arrive, many of them having attended a performance of the play based on Dixon's novel ten years earlier.[5] Most of the adults in Iowa would have also been very aware of challenges made by Black ministers and progressive whites to block the movie from opening in some towns. After a court fight, the mayor of Chicago allowed the film to open in his city in early June. "The only objection raised," the *Quad-City Times* noted, "is that a Negro is the villain and therefore it has been asserted that it would promote race hatred." The controversy, the paper decided, was overblown, pointing to a court ruling that favored the film's producers. "Every race is entitled to the same standing before the law," the *Times* quoted the judge. "If we bar a play from production because the villain is black, we could bar him because he was white, or yellow, or brown, or red."[6] The leaders of the National Association for the Advancement of Colored People raised objections to the film in early March, only weeks after it opened in New York.[7] In April, a man was arrested after throwing rotten eggs at the screen during the film's showing at the Liberty Theatre in New York.[8] Only days later, the Methodist Episcopal Conference of New England condemned the film as being "untrue," "cruel," and "demoralizing."[9]

In June 1915, while the theater owners in Des Moines were still unsure of exactly when the film might become available to them, the congregation of the First Baptist Church in Des Moines passed a resolution opposing the film showing in their city.[10] The Sioux City Opera House was the first venue in Iowa to begin showing *Birth*, just before Thanksgiving, 1915. By then, the producers were allowing theater owners to charge just twenty-five cents for the afternoon shows.[11] The editor of the *Sioux City Journal*, who might well have been first in line, assigned himself the job of sorting out what all the fuss was about. He concluded that while the film was historically accurate in capturing the North's "mania for revenge" against the Confederates following the war, it was also decidedly "one-sided" in its depiction of the Reconstruction South. But that exaggeration, he said, was no more extreme than those employed in *Uncle Tom's Cabin*, a novel that helped fan the passions of abolitionists in the 1850s.

"It recalls—somewhat spectacularly, to be sure, but none the less effectively—that the conquering [U]nion, in its hour of triumph, was not nearly as magnanimous as it might have been toward its stricken foe—that the mania for revenge was rampant in the land and found outlet in numerous ways which reflected little credit upon the government in Washington," the *Journal* said.[12]

Reverend J. H. Garrison, a prominent member of Sioux City's Black community, also saw the movie and came away deeply disturbed. Garrison and a collection of Black and white citizens equally offended by the film called on the mayor to eliminate some scenes from the second half of the movie, which, they argued, were so inflammatory that they might provoke violence. "The mayor told the delegation that he thought they were viewing the picture from the wrong angle," the *Sioux City Journal* reported:

> He said that the whole play developed the theme that the colored men of the south had been tools in the hands of the white carpet baggers, that every crime of the reconstruction period was traced to the activities of the white man.
>
> The mayor said he carried from the theater a hatred of the white carpet bagger rather than an impression that the negro was to blame for the period of lawlessness created after the war.
>
> In the end, the mayor said he would not interfere with the owners of the Opera House showing *Birth*.[13]

The film was scheduled to open at the Berchel Theater in Des Moines on April 30, 1916. The Black community in Des Moines, which, while still segregated, was the largest in Iowa, could demand more than empty promises from city hall. Well ahead of the film's opening, Mayor James R. Hanna promised to invite a delegation of Black ministers to a private screening of the movie, along with the city police chief. "The result of which exhibition will determine what, if any, action is to be taken by city authorities," the Black-owned *Iowa Bystander* reported on January 28.[14]

The editor of the *Bystander* was John L. Thompson, who was also an attorney and most certainly a close colleague of Iowa's two most prominent Black civil rights attorneys, S. Joe Brown and George Woodson. All three were also part of the leadership of the Des Moines chapter of the NAACP.[15] Not long after the mayor made his promise to preview the film before its general release, Thompson wrote an editorial responding to the many times he had been asked his opinion about the controversy by his white acquaintances and business associates. Although he probably had not seen the film yet, all he needed to know to form an opinion was that it was based on Dixon's novel. Mr. Thompson wrote:

We are surprised that so many pretended intelligent white people are so eager to have this inferior picture played which causes so much prejudice, quarrels, and friction between the races, inflaming each with hatred toward the other. If Mr. Dixon and his crowd want to be fair about portraying the *Birth of a Nation*, they should start with Abraham Lincoln emancipating a race, thereby making a new nation on this continent, cementing the North and the South and eradicating slavery and thus display the rise of the colored man as well as the rebel soldier who held the slaves in bondage for years. Instead of portraying the colored lieutenant governor trying to force a white woman to marry him, he could have pictured the thousands of slaveholders who were living in open adultery and raising families by colored women.[16]

Attorney George Woodson announced in March that lawmakers friendly to the cause would be introducing legislation giving the state the authority to censor moving pictures considered to pose a threat to the public. The governor said he was not opposed to such a bill but noted that most cities and counties already had authority to prevent public screenings of immoral or inflammatory films. Woodson said that local officials were not making use of that power and needed oversight from the state.[17] In response, the Des Moines City Council invoked a public safety ordinance just two weeks before the film was to open and notified the owners of the Berchel Theater that they could not show the film. "It would take a guard of a dozen men at that theater all the time that play was there," said Councilman Ben Woolgar. "I haven't the money nor the men to handle a situation I feel would arise."[18]

Having already spent heavily on promoting the film's arrival, the owners of the Berchel Theater vowed to screen the film as planned while filing court papers seeking an injunction against the city council's action. "You can rest assured that the play will be shown," said Jack Gethcell, a part owner of the theater. "We know what we are doing. Politics may govern the city councils, but we have the advice of the best legal talent in the city and we know our rights."[19]

Before a district court judge could rule, Gethcell and his partners went ahead and opened their doors in defiance of the city council's order. When the judge did decide on the injunction, he upheld the right of the city council to prevent public events that might risk citizen safety—at least until a full hearing on the matter could be conducted. Gethcell and his partners held their afternoon matinee anyway, which brought the chief of police and a gaggle of officers to the theater. They arrested the manager and two projectionists and put a chain lock on the theater doors.[20]

The trial took a full week. The city's case rested on whether the movie could evoke by itself such passions as to induce physical confrontation. Called to give his opinion on the first day was Reverend B. F. Fellman, pastor of the Calvary Baptist Church, who said Black men were characterized again and again as villains, while whites were victims. "Such a story might create prejudice," Fellman said. W. T. Lincoln, a Union Army veteran, testified that the crowd cheered more loudly for the southern anthem "Dixie" than it did for the "Star Spangled Banner." Reverend J. F. Nugent, pastor at the Catholic Church of Visitation in Des Moines, said he found nothing immoral about it, nor "anything that could in the least harm any race or people."[21]

District Judge Joe Meyer ruled against the city, finding that it had failed to show that the film did or might cause violent outbreaks. "My conclusion, based on the evidence before me, is that the average, intelligent, fair-minded citizens of this community will not be prejudiced against colored people or have created in them any race hatred or antipathy by reason of the exhibition of the photoplay in question," Meyer wrote.[22]

Martin Stickles, a failed farmer and chronic alcoholic, was the last man arrested for public intoxication in Cedar Rapids prior to the repeal of the Mulct Law. A few hours later, as the clock turned December 31, 1915, into January 1, 1916—Frank Quinn became the first drunk taken into custody in Cedar Rapids under the state's newly authorized prohibitory regime.

As a young man, Stickles seemingly worked productively on his father's farm outside Cedar Rapids before the liquor disease caught him. His drinking problem brought him public attention from time to time in the pages of the *Cedar Rapids Gazette*. Once, the paper documented how Stickles and his hired hand came to town one afternoon, got drunk, lost one another, found one another, got drunk again, and lost each other a second time.[23] After promising a judge in 1911 that he would take the "cure" in exchange for having his fine reduced to $5, he was back before the same court within weeks on the same charge.[24] Two years later, he was brought before the police court and complained bitterly over the fines being assessed—which he probably never paid. His protest was enough, however, for the judge to double them.[25]

Stickles also complained after being arrested on New Year's Eve, 1915. He pled not guilty and demanded a trial. The judge granted Stickles's wish but allowed just one witness, the police sergeant in charge of the night detail. The sergeant testified that Stickles was drunk and unconscious on the sidewalk when they found him. He had to be carried to the patrol wagon and then from the wagon into the jail. Stickles was fined $100 plus court costs, which he probably also never paid.[26]

Frank Quinn was an entirely different sort of carouser. He was probably in his early twenties and also handsome and confident enough to win a reputation around town as something of a lady killer. He made the front section of the *Gazette* in December 1910 when he was arrested on a charge of seduction. In Cedar Rapids, at that time, criminal seduction was loosely defined as attempts by a man to corrupt an unmarried woman, which, if proven, could bring a maximum sentence of twenty years in prison.[27]

The case against Quinn started when a police officer became curious about him keeping company with a young woman in the early hours at the Cedar Rapids train station. The officer questioned them and wasn't satisfied with their answers, so he took them both down to the station. In court, Quinn said he was going to Des Moines and that the girl was just tagging along, although both admitted they had spent the prior night together after meeting at a dance. The judge decided that Quinn probably wasn't anything more than an average masher but sent him to jail for fifteen days for disorderly conduct.[28]

When Quinn became the first arrest in Cedar Rapids under prohibition in the early morning hours of New Year's Day, 1916, it was unclear where he had been drinking. Hamm's bar on Third Avenue, thought to be the last saloon in town, had closed the night before, and last call had come early at 7:30 p.m. Few drinking establishments anywhere in the state remained open much later. Before the night was over, sewers all over Iowa had swallowed up thousands of gallons of beer because brewers had no place else to put it.[29] In Waterloo, anyone convicted of public intoxication throughout December was kept locked up until after the New Year. "When they get out, they will find the saloons closed, and maybe some of them will be able to stay away from liquor for good," said Police Judge J. H. Meyers.[30] One of the last official acts of the Keokuk City Council in 1915 was to grant a liquor permit to a saloonkeeper for the purpose of selling a single glass of whiskey on New Year's Day in violation of state law. Barkeeper Philip Nickel was to document the sale and then turn himself in to the state attorney general in an effort to test the validity of the legislature's repeal of the Mulct Law. "I was not looking for a fight on the mulct law repeal at Keokuk, but we will be able to take care of all the scraps the saloon men want to stage," Attorney General George Cosson said in a statement. "The repeal law is going to stick, and we are going to win no matter where or how the wets want to engage us in battle."[31] It took six months, but the Iowa Supreme Court ruled on June 30 that lawmakers had the authority to repeal the Mulct Law and had executed that power appropriately.

For the seventh time since statehood, Iowa had reversed itself on the liquor question, going from wet to dry.[32]

President Wilson, who remarried in mid-December, probably spent an uneventful New Year's Eve with his new bride, which might have included highballs.[33] Worry over the war would have occupied the president. His preparedness plan to upgrade and expand the U.S. military was languishing. Voters in the Midwest and the South, who were isolated from the realities of the war, remained unconvinced that there was a need for a bigger, stronger military. And they were strongly opposed to the higher taxes that would be needed to pay for the buildup. As a result, Congress also remained on the fence.

In early January 1916 Joseph Tumulty, Wilson's private secretary and one of his most trusted advisers, told the president that he needed to sell the program himself. "I cannot impress upon you too forcibly the importance of an appeal to the country on the question of military preparedness," Tumulty wrote to Wilson.[34] The decision was made that the president would embark on a campaign swing through the Midwest at the end of the month, with a tentative itinerary that included stops in Cincinnati, Cleveland, Toledo, Chicago, and Des Moines.[35]

When news reached Iowa of Wilson's potential visit, the White House was inundated with welcoming telegrams—many coming from ardent Republicans who had never supported a Democrat in their lives. "We are sure the people of Iowa City, without regard to party distinction, would welcome him heartily," the editor of the *Iowa City Press Citizen* promised. "If the local leaders of the [Democratic] party will take the initiative, they may count on all possible assistance from the [R]epublicans to second the motion."[36]

Even before the president's staff had much of a chance to map out Wilson's visit to Des Moines, the Greater Des Moines Committee stepped in to offer the White House a plan for how Wilson's time in their city should be spent. The Wilsons would arrive just before 7:00 p.m. on February 1 at the downtown train station. Two separate receptions and dinners would be held—one for the president at the Des Moines Club, which had the city's most exclusive dining rooms. Meanwhile, Mrs. Wilson would have dinner at either the Chamberlain Hotel or the Golf and Country Club. After dinner, the president and Mrs. Wilson would have a chance to collect themselves in a suite at the Chamberlain before being escorted to the Des Moines Coliseum, where the president would give his speech at 8:15 p.m. The president's train would leave for Kansas City at midnight.[37] As soon as these plans were made public, the Greater Des Moines Committee was itself inundated with demands from the city's elite and near-elite for invitations to one or both of the presidential events. The guest list for the presidential dinner was limited to 150 men; even fewer women would be invited to sit with Mrs. Wilson. The scramble for tickets became downright shameless. "One officeholder laid down the law to the Greater Des Moines committee secretary," reported the *Des Moines Tribune,* "insisting that his wife 'should not be left out of the invitations to the dinner for Mrs. Wilson.'"[38]

Helen Keller, author and political activist, happened to be in Des Moines on a lecture tour as the hysteria over Wilson's visit was playing out. A reporter caught her on the way out of her hotel and asked her about the president's preparedness plan. She was not a fan. "That money might be employed to improve our cities," Keller said. "We have been traveling for weeks through cities of the east, west, and south. In them we found great sections that were unfit for human habitation."[39]

Four days before the big day, a telegram arrived in Des Moines from the White House politely but firmly declining participation in any dinners or receptions during Wilson's "five-hour" stay in town. Joseph Tumulty, one of Wilson's top aides, sent the message, noting that the president would not be accepting similar invitations and instead wanted to conserve his strength and concentrate on his speech. "The president has found by experience that it is wise for him to have the program of his visit as simple as possible."[40]

Disappointed but probably not surprised, the elite of Des Moines moved on and prepared to do what they could to make the president's visit as memorable as possible.

The national press quickly labeled Wilson's planned Midwest tour a bold gambit. He was attempting to bypass Congress, taking his preparedness plan directly to the voters. The strategy had few precedents, and it was rife with pitfalls. Key to Wilson's success, some suggested, was winning over Iowa, which some commentators believed was ground zero for opposition to military expansion. A Washington correspondent for the *Des Moines Register* explained:

Probably there is no other state in the whole list the president will visit where the nature of the reception and the nature of the impression made in the presidential visit will be watched more carefully than in Iowa. The leading politicians of all parties and factions are planning to get careful reports from the grass roots advising them how Wilson is received and what effect his visit had had. It is understood some of the leading newspapers will send men about a few days behind the president to ascertain in what frame of mind he has left the public.[41]

Wilson had in his corner, however, one of Iowa's most favored sons, Billy Sunday. "Am I for preparedness? Ha! You bet your sweet life!" he said during a sermon on January 4 in New Jersey. "I believe in the biggest battleship and the biggest torpedo that can spit 250 pound[s] of gun-cotton and turn a battleship in[to] a bunch of junk. Yes, I believe in preparedness with a big P."[42]

On the day of the presidential visit, the city of Des Moines was emerging from an ice storm with temperatures not expected to rise much above zero all day.[43] The presidential train pulled out of Chicago on the morning of February 1, with an expected arrival in Des Moines in the late afternoon. Wilson planned to make platform speeches at Joliet around 11:00 a.m. and Moline around 2:00 p.m., and then came brief stops in Davenport, Iowa City, Newton, and Grinnell.[44]

At Moline, a large and enthusiastic crowd greeted him, undaunted by the subzero temperatures even as a bone-chilling prairie wind swirled. After finishing his remarks, Wilson brought his wife forward to great cheers. The small but insistent voice of a young boy near the platform caught Wilson's attention, as well as that of a good portion of the crowd. "Hey, Mr. President, please step back," the boy called out, pointing a camera toward the train platform. "I want to get a picture of your wife."

Initially taken aback by the request, Wilson complied and then, smiling, he nodded to the boy. "Well," Wilson remarked. "I admire your taste."

"And we admire your taste," someone in the crowd shouted back.[45]

They arrived without incident in Des Moines, on time, and were taken to a suite at the Chamberlain Hotel. They dined privately and were attended by a single waitress, Peggy Connors. "Only Miss Connors can tell today whether it was suffrage, home management, politics, or what was the engrossing subject of their dinner talk," the *Register* reported the next day. "Miss Connor may know, but it is doubtful if ethics will permit the telling."[46]

Wilson, renowned for his skill as a public speaker, was at the top of his game in his appearance before at least eight thousand in the Des Moines Coliseum. Right away, he won them over by addressing the elephant in the room. "Someone who does not know our fellow citizens quite as well as he ought to know them told me there was a certain degree of indifference and lethargy in the Middle West with regard to the defense of our nation," Wilson said. "I said, 'I don't believe it but I am going to see.' And I have seen. I have seen what I expected to see—great bodies of serious men, great bodies of earnest women, coming together to show their profound interest in the objects of this visit of mine."

The crowd, reportedly the largest he had addressed since leaving Washington on the tour, gave him frequent applause—especially when the president referenced his desire to keep America out of the war. "No voice has ever come to any public man more audibly, more unmistakably, than the voice of this great people has come to me, bearing this impressive lesson: 'We are counting on you to keep this country out of war,'" the president said. "And I call you to witness, my fellow countrymen, that I have spent every thought and energy that has been vouchsafed to me in order to keep this country out of war."[47]

The president left for Kansas City at midnight, as planned, and probably didn't see the main headline in the *Des Moines Register* the next morning. The message that it carried was clear: "President Wilson Spends a Day Amid Peace Loving Iowans." An editorial in the *Muscatine Journal* may have expressed the feeling even better: "President Wilson was informed that the middle west was opposed to the preparedness plan," the *Journal* editor wrote. "His reception in the many states which he has visited reveals the west to be strongly in support of the sane measure of national defense which the president proposes."[48]

In November 1915 male voters in four key states—New Jersey, Massachusetts, New York, and Pennsylvania—turned down ballot measures to give women equal suffrage. Most political analysts attributed the outcome to fears that a liquor prohibition would quickly follow women getting the vote. In Iowa, where the saloons had been closed the year before by the legislature, suffrage leaders didn't have the same concerns as they campaigned ahead of the June 1916 election.[49] Ever resolute, Flora Dunlap, president of the Iowa Equal Suffrage Association, announced in January that they had organized campaign groups in eighty of Iowa's ninety-nine counties, as well as men's advocacy groups in the state's largest counties. "We believe that Iowa will be the twelfth of the progressive states to give the ballot to women," Dunlap said.[50]

In February Dunlap unveiled a plan to raise $25,000 ($3.5 million today) to be spent in an all-out surge during the last two months of the campaign.[51] In May the women-led suffrage opposition committee held a big meeting in Ottumwa, with John P. Irish as the keynote speaker. Irish, a longtime temperance foe and former editor of the Iowa City paper, came back from California just to join the fight.[52] "The laws which gave man the ballot are founded on the laws of God, which gave man physical strength and courage to defend his nation," he said.[53]

As returns were still being counted, Dunlap declared victory after suffrage support surged ahead on election night. By the next afternoon, her fortunes had reversed. News came from Des Moines that the suffrage measure had been defeated, 52 percent to 48 percent. The heaviest opposition came from the river towns.[54] Dunlap called it a "deferred victory" and assembled her troops in Des Moines the very next day to plot out where the movement would go from there. Despite record fundraising, the Equal Suffrage Associated had debts of $7,000 and needed to not only pay those bills but raise thousands more for yet another run. "Let us begin immediately to get enough votes to carry the next election," Dunlap said. "Get more women interested."[55]

14

The Hangings at Camp Dodge

Only weeks after the United States broke diplomatic ties with the German Empire in February 1917, the War Department announced that an officer training school would be established at Fort Des Moines. Two sessions were contemplated: one during July and the other through August.[1] The military authorities at Fort Des Moines, already on high alert, quickly followed with an order that all "unnaturalized Austrians, Germans, Bulgarians, or Turks" living within a half mile of the garrison would have to find new homes.[2] In May, military police raided a homeless encampment near the fort, killing an Italian immigrant and arresting two others. They reported finding "a large quantity of rifles and cartridges." "Secret service men are of the opinion that a German 'junta' exists in south Des Moines," the *Quad-City Times* reported.[3]

The War Department was intentionally quiet about exactly who would be trained at the new officer school in Des Moines. In May 1917 it became clear why: it would be Black officers.[4]

At the start of the war, the army had about ten thousand Black enlisted men; the navy had perhaps five thousand. Between them, only a handful were officers. The War Department needed men, and Wilson was under pressure not only to include Black men as part of the draft but also to give the best among them a chance to command.[5] Once the decision was made, the location of a training camp for Black officers became key. No southern state could be considered, due to the more overtly racist nature of the South. There were already racial tensions in manufacturing centers of the North, driven by the migration of Black people from the South to war-related jobs. Iowa, and particularly Des Moines, became an inviting choice. The city had a Black population of nearly six housand, which represented just 6.6 percent of the city's nearly ninety thousand residents—but the Black neighborhoods were also vigorous and well-integrated. The city also successfully hosted an all-Black regiment in 1903 at Fort Des Moines without incident.[6] And the editors of the *Des Moines Tribune* promised that there would be "no more orderly or better conducted military camp in the country."[7]

A total of 639 Black officers graduated on October 15, 1917. A significant number of them were sent immediately across town to the army's large regional induction and training center, Camp Dodge, about twenty-five miles from Fort Des Moines. Along with the 15,000 or so white soldiers stationed at the camp were several thousand new Black draftees newly arrived from Alabama.[8]

There remained some skeptics that the freshly minted Black officers were capable of actually leading companies of new Black enlisted men. The editors of the *Des Moines Register* found it necessary to point out both the "opportunity" and "responsibility" that the new Black officers faced. Just days before the new recruits from the Deep South arrived in Iowa, the paper warned of "false notions about the north," and "new freedom suddenly to be realized" by the Black soldiers from Alabama.[9]

There was no second class of Black officers waiting to move into the Fort Des Moines barracks. While officials in Washington proclaimed that future Black officer training would take place with candidates at existing white camps, only a few Black people were ever commissioned following the closure of the Iowa program.[10] Within six months of the formation of the Black companies in Des Moines, an incident took place that would seal the fate of the training school and turn back the clock on the integration of the military: on the night of May 24, 1918, a white girl was allegedly raped by three Black soldiers based at Camp Dodge, almost certainly commanded by Black officers.[11]

The victim said that she had come to the camp to see her fiancé and that they had gone to a remote part of the base. She claimed the Black soldiers approached, and one identified himself as a military police officer. She and her boyfriend attempted to leave, she said, but were attacked instead. The boyfriend was allegedly knocked unconscious, and the victim was carried into the brush. The attack ended when the boyfriend revived and started calling for help.[12]

News of the assault was suppressed for three days by the mainstream press, and even then few facts except the allegation of the crime were shared. The military trial for those accused began within a week, and judgment followed less than four hours later. Three of the accused would be hanged.[13]

"This government has an awful problem on its hands in the making of soldiers out of half savage blacks from southern plantations," began an incendiary editorial from the *Marshalltown Evening Times-Republican*, which advocated for the death penalty in the case.[14]

"With the exception of those accused and the victim, there were no other witnesses. Military officials testified that two of the three attackers confessed to the rape. The third man denied ever participating but was executed anyway. Almost every soldier at Camp Dodge, perhaps fifteen thousand men—both Black and white—were required to attend the execution."[15]

Wilson's obsession that aggressive reporting on the war might undermine military operations led to the adoption of the Espionage Act in June 1917. The measure restricted any speech, written or oral, that "willfully" caused harm to the military. The postmaster was also given the authority to halt the delivery of any publication that contained language promoting "treason, insurrection, or forcible resistance."[16] One of the first prosecutions undertaken by federal authorities under the Espionage Act took place in the summer of 1917 at Davenport, a hotbed of discontent over the war. The case began when a pacifist and former British soldier named Daniel H. Wallace was invited to speak at the Davenport Opera House on the evening of July 25, 1917.[17] The event had been organized by men active in the German American community of Davenport. One was Fred Vollmer, an attorney and brother of former congressman Henry Vollmer; another was Dr. Henry Matthey, one of the town's most successful physicians and surgeons.[18] Wallace, director and organizer of a Chicago-based pacifist organization called the League of Humanity Bureau for Conscientious Objectors, was of interest to the Germans of Davenport, who wanted their young men to know there were legal alternatives to the draft. The Germans of Davenport were probably unaware that Wallace's offices in Chicago had been raided by federal agents only a month before. Officers had broken up the meeting, seized printed material believed to be seditious, and detained eight, including Wallace.[19]

Notice of the talk was not advertised in the mainstream press of the city, but it drew an audience of about fifteen hundred. There were reports that undercover officials from the War Department were also inside on the night of Wallace's talk. He began by telling the audience about serving on the front lines of the European war, of the misery and bloodshed. He explained to them the rights of men under the U.S. Constitution to avoid military service by declaring themselves "conscientious objectors." He drifted into illegal speech by declaring that any man who enlisted was signing "your own death warrant," that "American lives are England's meal ticket," and that he would rather "stand up against the law and be shot than fight on foreign soil."[20]

The *Quad-City Times* (then known as the *Davenport Democrat and Leader*) quickly condemned the meeting as a "disgrace" and denounced Wallace and an associate as "two ranting freaks" who maligned their government, slandered Belgium, praised Germany, damned the Red Cross and the Salvation Army, and indulged "in language that would have closed a burlesque show the first night."[21]

Within days, federal indictments were issued against Wallace, Fred Vollmer, and five others. By mid-October, Wallace was convicted and sentenced to twenty years at Leavenworth. Judge Martin J. Wade called Wallace one of the "most dangerous men" ever to come before his court. "The very audacity of this man going about the country collecting money sowing the seeds of discord and discontent," Wade said.[22]

Vollmer negotiated an agreement with the prosecutors and pled guilty to aiding and abetting Wallace; he was fined $3,000. "I committed a technical violation by applauding some of the anti-British statements of the speaker," Vollmer said at sentencing. "But I earnestly deny that he was brought to Davenport for the purpose of opposing the draft law or that I had any idea that he would make the kind of address that he did."[23]

Dr. Matthey was not so fortunate. During his trial, a witness testified to hearing Matthey talking subversion to another man on the night of the Wallace speech. Among the things overheard was that "Americans had no business to be onboard the *Lusitania,* that they had been warned to keep off," that England had started the war, and that the United States should keep out of it.[24] The jury found him guilty of violating the Espionage Act, and he was sentenced to a year's term in federal prison. His appeal took four years to reach the U.S. Supreme Court, which refused to intervene. In April 1922, just days before he was ordered to report to Leavenworth, President Warren G. Harding granted him clemency.[25]

Another test of loyalty during the war took place in the tiny hamlet of Sutherland in western Iowa. Businesses and homeowners in early 1918 began posting signs that read: "German language strictly forbidden." According to the *Sioux City Journal*, some local residents of German descent notified the authorities that the signs were a violation of the freedom of speech. Not so, a U.S. Marshal ruled. "Good for Sutherland!" the *Journal's* headline declared.[26]

In February 1918 the Davenport School Board voted to drop German-language classes from the curriculum.[27] Next, in early May, came an order from the Audubon County Council on Defense barring the use of German on local telephone lines. And just a few weeks later, Governor William L. Harding issued the "Babel Proclamation," which banned the use of any foreign language in schools, churches, trains, and most other public places as well as on the telephone. "Freedom of speech is guaranteed by federal and state constitutions," the governor said. "But this is not a guaranty of the right to use a language other than the language of this country."[28]

A few weeks later, Mrs. Herman Lippold, Mrs. Henry Lippold, Mrs. James Holst, and Mrs. William Matzen, all of Scott County, were fined collectively $225 for speaking German on the telephone. Apparently, Mrs. Herman Lippold was the most chatty among them and got hit with a $100 penalty.[29]

Senator Albert Cummins had no use for and a general dislike of most Democrats, but he had a special loathing for Woodrow Wilson, whom he considered a power-hungry egomaniac. Cummins was among a group of senators who frustrated Wilson's attempt to arm U.S. merchant ships against attacks by German submarines. Wilson denounced them as a "little group of willful men representing no opinion but their own."[30]

Cummins wanted the United States to remain neutral. He opposed the preparedness plan and only reluctantly voted in favor of the war, hoping right up until the end that another option could be followed. On April 6, 1917, he said:

I have believed and still believe that there is another, better and more effective course than the declaration of war. If I believed that there was a bare opportunity that a fight for that better way would be successful, I would not hesitate to consume the time of the Senate in submitting my reasons for its adoption, but I know that war is to be declared and I intend to give my first energy to the promotion of unity among the people of the United States.[31]

Just as Iowans had rallied to the Union Army generations before, they stood ready to send their young men to battle in Europe. "All together, eyes to the front, forward march!" declared the *Iowa City Citizen.*[32]

A parade and patriotic meeting were organized among the Germans of Davenport just days after Congress acted. Former congressman Henry Vollmer was a keynote speaker.[33]

James Norman Hall was born in Colfax, Iowa, and went to England in the spring of 1914 in search of a writing career. Instead, he enlisted in the British infantry and would later be trained as a pilot. He was shot down behind enemy lines in May 1918, well before many American soldiers were even out of basic training back in the states. Years after the war, Hall did become a celebrated writer, as coauthor of *Mutiny on the Bounty.*[34]

George C. Herring Jr. came from Creston, Iowa, and was among the nearly 280,000 American doughboys to cross the Atlantic in June 1918. For months, the Allies had waited for the vast American army to have an impact on the war, but General John Pershing refused to break up his troops to fight under the British or French flag. "It is maddening to think that though the men are there, the issue may be endangered because of the shortsightedness of one General and the failure of his government to order him to carry out their undertakings," wrote Lloyd George, the English secretary of war to the British ambassador in Washington.[35] Herring's unit participated in what was considered the first all-American offensive when U.S. troops took heavily fortified German positions at St. Mihiel in northeastern France. Herring survived the war and would return home, earn advanced degrees, and teach history at the University of Kentucky. He thought of himself as a "thoroughly Americanized German American," who had "no qualms about fighting against the homeland of his ancestors."[36]

Levi Whitfield Ruhl was born in Poweshiek County, Iowa, and served as a corporal in the Iowa National Guard during Pershing's campaign to root out Pancho Villa in 1916. He enlisted in July 1917 and was assigned to the 126th Field Artillery as a second lieutenant. The 126th saw little action, and Ruhl returned home to be elected Benton County sheriff in 1922 and again in 1924. Ruhl served as one of the primary investigators in the murder of Myrtle Cook in September 1925.[37] He would later run unsuccessfully for state senate as a Klan candidate in 1926.[38]

At least 4,000 thousand men and women from Iowa were killed in action or died of influenza during World War I, and close to 140,000 served.[39]

15

Shootout at the Carbarn Café

Efforts to establish a state-run police force first gained momentum in 1912 following the gruesome murder of an entire family in the rural town of Villisca. There were eight victims, including four children. Their heads and faces were crushed by blows from an axe. All of them were murdered while they slept. There were no signs of a struggle. No suspects were identified, and no motive theorized.[1]

James M. Carl, chief of police in Cedar Rapids, was among the first to argue that the inability of detectives to solve the Villisca crime was emblematic of a wider system failure. He pointed out that the state government played no unifying role in law enforcement and that the legislature's only real response to horrific crimes like the Villisca murders was to offer a reward. "In the Villisca murder case, there was practically no clue to work on," he said. "Practically nothing was done to bring the guilty person to justice. Only a reward of $300 was offered. Police officers do not work in the hope of reward. Instead of offering rewards, the state should employ competent men to track the criminals in such cases."[2]

In 1915 Attorney General George Cosson proposed legislation giving his office the authority to hire special agents that would be put into the field to help county sheriffs and local police with major cases. Lawmakers agreed to fund the new investigative bureau, but they limited the number of agents to four and gave the authority over their use to the governor.[3]

It wasn't until after the war that the state force was given enough resources to take up the job in earnest. There had been a noticeable uptick in crime after the war. Prohibition and the beer gangs that it fostered added to a general sense of insecurity. Whether real or imagined to many, the sense that evil lurked just ahead was strong and pervasive enough, even in Iowa, that public officials tried to respond.

Reverend C. L. Gould, a prominent minister from Anamosa, blamed Hollywood.[4] Iowa governor William Harding called it a "crime wave" and blamed the proliferation of the modern automobile, which gave "cunning, highly trained criminals" easy transport. J. Edgar Hoover, writing in a column for an Iowa law enforcement magazine, put the blame on "shyster lawyers, sob-sister judges, [and] criminal coddlers."[5]

By 1921 the legislature had elevated the state's team of agents into the Bureau of Criminal Investigation, with seed money of $37,000 (nearly $600,000 today) coming from the Iowa Bankers' Association, whose members had been plagued by a spate of recent robberies.[6] One of the first agents hired was James Risden, a former deputy sheriff from Cedar Rapids. He would spend forty-two years at the agency, serving as bureau chief from 1925 until 1933, when the Democrats took power. He then returned in 1939 as a field agent when Republicans were back in charge and stayed there until he retired in 1957.[7] One of his first cases as bureau chief was the investigation into the murder of Myrtle Cook in 1925.[8] Among his very first assignments working for the state bureau was to help chase members of the notorious Red Burzette gang after a bloody shootout in Sioux City in July 1919.[9]

Donald "Red" Burzette was born in 1895 and raised in the northern Iowa town of Clear Lake, which was made famous a half century later as the site of a tragic plane crash that killed three of America's greatest early rock 'n' roll stars: Buddy Holly, Ritchie Valens, and J. P. "the Big Bopper" Richardson.[10] Clear Lake in the 1900s was a summer tourist destination where families could camp or rent a bungalow along the shore of Iowa's third largest lake. Red Burzette's father scratched out a living as a laborer. In the 1910 census, Red was recorded as working in the town's sewer system. It is unclear if he served during World War I, but most news accounts later suggest that Red and his older brother Everett organized an auto-theft ring around 1915 or 1916.[11]

Red, Everett, and their younger cousin Melvin formed the core of the gang, along with two well-trusted and violent associates, Tex Maynard and Jim Davis. The first murder tied to the gang took place in March 1919 near the town of Hull, Iowa. The victim, identified as Claude C. Letner of Sioux City, was found face down in a plowed field just a few steps from where his car sat overturned in a ditch. He had been shot once in the back of the head. The *Sioux City Journal* initially reported that Letner was on his way back from attending a funeral and was thought to be carrying a large amount of cash. Later, it was determined that Letner was probably a bootlegger and was carrying not cash but booze when ambushed by the Burzette gang. They were again suspected of hijacking the shipment of another bootlegger in southern Minnesota three months later, getting away with more than a hundred cases of whiskey with a total value of about $130,000 in today's money.[12]

Before the gang had a chance to spend any of the loot, there came the bloody shootout at the Carbarn café on July 22, 1919.

Red Burzette, Maynard, and Davis were returning home to Sioux City early that morning, probably just after closing the deal on the stolen whiskey, their pockets still jammed with cash. Their progress was slowed by a flat tire. When they reached town, the gunmen pulled into a service station that had just opened for the day. One of them, probably Maynard, drew his gun on the attendant and demanded that he get to work on the flat right away. The café was right next door and, believing they had frightened the young attendant into compliance, the three men went to get breakfast. The kid, named Malcolm McLeod, was the son of a Sioux City cop, and as the Burzette crew were taking their first sips of coffee, McLeod phoned the police station. Before the gangsters could finish their eggs, Sioux City detectives James Britton and Maurice Farley, along with Captain John Shannon, were making their way across town. Britton and Farley had worked on the Letner murder case and suspected Burzette and his boys were responsible.

The cops ran through the door of the café and got the jump on the three gunmen, ordering them to give up. Instead, Burzette brought his revolver out and began firing away. Britton and Farley fired back. Maynard and Davis joined the melee. Barely five feet separated the cops and the gunsels. Both Burzette and Britton took fatal shots. The *Journal* reported that seventeen bullets were exchanged in less than ten seconds. Davis and Maynard were badly wounded but would survive and later be charged with murder in the death of Britton.[13]

Still at large were five other members of the gang, who went into hiding until the end of October, when they probably ran out of cash. Led by thirty-five-year-old James O'Keefe and twenty-seven-year-old William Convey, the remaining members of the Burzette crew pulled the daring daylight robbery of a bank in Westfield, Iowa, near the border with South Dakota. The haul was about $4,000 (about $66,000 today), but in their haste to get away, one of them forgot to cut the telephone line. As the robbers neared Sioux City, they were intercepted by police and taken into custody without a fight.[14] The robbers were quickly brought before a district judge in Plymouth County. All five criminals pleaded guilty and were held in the county jail at Le Mars, awaiting transport to the penitentiary at Fort Madison. On November 14, around 6:30 p.m., Plymouth County sheriff Hugh Maxwell and members of his family began serving the prisoners their dinner. O'Keefe and Cullon surprised the lawman with drawn pistols that had been smuggled into the jail. The sheriff reached for his firearm, but Cullon shot first, hitting Maxwell in the side. The sheriff's son, Deputy William Maxwell, came to his father's aid and was shot in the right eye. One of the gang members bludgeoned the sheriff's wife with a table leg, knocking her unconscious. Before exiting the jail, the gang rounded up the sheriff's two younger daughters and locked them in one of the jail cells. Deputy Maxwell died that same night.[15]

Although O'Keefe and company were able to get someone to smuggle a gun into the jail, they didn't think to secure reliable transportation once free. After four full days on the lam, the crew were only able to get about thirteen miles away from the Plymouth County jail. Police found them in an abandoned barn near the town of Maurice, and, although heavily armed, they offered no resistance. They had no food and were battered by a brutal autumn cold snap. Two of the gang members had frostbite on their feet; another had developed pneumonia.[16] By the end of the week, all five had been swiftly convicted of first-degree murder and sentenced to life terms. On Friday afternoon, November 21, the five convicted killers—guarded by four sheriff's deputies and two special state agents—were put aboard a special jail car for the train ride to Fort Madison.[17]

But the Burzette mayhem didn't end there.

During services on Christmas morning, 1920, O'Keefe and three other inmates scaled the walls of Fort Madison and escaped into the snowy fields surrounding the prison. Their absence wasn't discovered right away, and a posse of guards and local volunteers found no trace of them as a storm front closed in and covered their tracks with fresh snow. State officials told reporters four days later that they believed the fugitives had met men with cars and had probably been taken to Chicago. It was a clean getaway.[18]

Escaping with O'Keefe were two other Burzette men, Harry Smith and John Cullon, both of whom had been convicted of murder in the Le Mars jailbreak. A fourth convict, James Lane, who was serving ten years for robbery, broke out with them. None of the four were able to enjoy freedom for long. Cullon was arrested in April 1921, by local police in Sedalia, Kansas, on unrelated charges. In May, O'Keefe was shot to death in Oklahoma City by another gangster, who was apparently unhappy with the split on a recent robbery. Smith made it until October before he was recognized in Minot, North Dakota, and rearrested.[19] Everett Burzette and his cousin Melvin would be convicted in March 1926 of the shotgun murder of a school superintendent who had surprised them during a robbery. Everett got a life sentence and broke out of Fort Madison in 1947, after serving twenty-one years. He was recaptured a few weeks later in Ottumwa. He died in prison at age sixty-six. Melvin Burzette was sentenced to twelve years for his role in the school killing. He was paroled in October 1931 but was sent back to Fort Madison in 1955 for passing bad checks and died that same year.[20]

Prior to the rise of Al Capone, one of Chicago's most notorious criminals was Tommy O'Connor, who was long suspected of hiding out in different parts of Iowa. In February 1918 O'Connor was part of a gang that hit one of the cashier offices of the Illinois Railroad. During the robbery, one of the clerks was shot to death. Prosecutors attempted to pin the killing on O'Connor, but he was acquitted. In January 1919 an associate of O'Connor was found shot to death, and once again O'Connor was charged. The case was dropped, however, after the primary witness against O'Connor mysteriously disappeared.[21] In January 1921 police located the witness and reactivated the murder charge, but months went by before they could find O'Connor and bring him into custody.

On the night of March 24, 1921, six Chicago police detectives arrived at the home of one of O'Connor's relatives, where he was staying. As the cops stood in the doorway, O'Connor was said to have quickly opened the front door, shooting Detective Sergeant Patrick O'Neill five times in the face, killing him. Although the other five cops were within arm's distance of the killer, O'Connor escaped, triggering one of the largest manhunts in city history.[22]

Four months later, police in St. Paul, Minnesota, caught up to O'Connor and sent him back to Chicago to stand trial for the murder of Officer O'Neill. By the end of September, he had been convicted and sentenced to hang. However, just days before his execution, O'Connor and several cellmates broke out of the Cook County Jail. It was believed that someone had smuggled a gun past the guards, and O'Connor had used it to force his way out. Once again, O'Connor became the subject of a massive multistate manhunt.[23]

For the next few years, O'Connor sightings took place all over the Midwest, but perhaps nowhere as frequently as in Iowa. Police in Des Moines were convinced that O'Connor was seen eating at a local restaurant in February 1922. In March authorities in Oskaloosa believed they had taken O'Connor into custody after a fellow train passenger identified him. In April investigators were sure he was in on a major burglary of a Des Moines department store. In November 1922 O'Connor was alleged to have shot a man in the arm in Ottumwa.[24]

Records suggest that O'Connor was probably not in all the places that Iowans feared. He was never recaptured, however, so the claims remain unresolved.

In June 1921 Burr Whitter, thirty-six, a farmer from Charles City, ended his life by putting a bullet into his head behind one ear. He left a wife and two children. David Barrett, forty, shot himself in the heart with a shotgun while out in his grain field near Jefferson. Debt and sickness were believed to be responsible. He left twelve children. J. S. Reeder, thirty-eight, checked himself into a hotel in Creston, threw a clothesline over the steam pipe that ran along the ceiling, tied a noose around his neck, stepped up on a stool, and kicked himself off. He had a wife, no children.[25]

All three were soil-hard Iowans. All three had debts they couldn't pay and seemingly nowhere to turn for help. The postwar economy was good for almost everyone but the farmer. Gone was the easy money that bankers in the East were ready to lend. Gone, too, were the price guarantees backed by the government. With the war's end, the railroads were permitted to hike freight rates, which jumped 30 percent in 1920 alone. Concerned over inflation, the Federal Reserve Bank raised interest rates and all but cut off the farmers from this last lifeline of credit.[26]

Meanwhile, the Iowa farmer brought in a record 3.2-billion-bushel corn crop in the fall of 1920, beating the 1912 high mark by more than 9 million bushels.[27] But the demand wasn't there. As prices fell, some farmers held on to their grain, hoping for better terms. A crisis was brewing.

"The banks in Iowa are loaded up with loans to their limit," C. R. MacKay, deputy governor of the Chicago Federal Reserve Bank, told reporters in November 1920. "Banks in the larger cities have loaned to their smaller banks and the smaller banks have been unable to collect their loans at maturity."[28]

All the misery of the Great Depression played out a decade earlier in farm communities all over America. More than six thousand banks failed in the mid-1920s, most of them in the Midwest and the South.[29] Suicides in Iowa jumped from 122 in 1922 to 325 in 1923.[30] Perhaps even more demoralizing was the fact that the pain wasn't felt anywhere else in the economy. The American Federation of Farm Bureaus reported in March 1921 that the price of farm products had risen just 25 percent since 1914. Meanwhile the cost of almost everything else had doubled: clothing was 102 percent higher, fuel and lighting were 127 percent more, and house furnishings were up 180 percent. And Washington had no answers. Henry C. Wallace, the Harding administration's newly appointed secretary of agriculture—and scion to a widely respected Iowa farm family—sincerely advised Iowans, in November 1921, to consider putting ears of corn into their stoves during the coming winter instead of high-priced coal, with the oil from the grain providing the heat.[31]

16

America Is for Americans

It was into this land of despair and divide that the new Ku Klux Klan arrived. Officially reestablished in 1915, the new Klan didn't become a national phenomenon until 1921, when it found millions of receptive ears, not just in the Jim Crow South but also the Far West and, indeed, on the prairie too. Either by design or coincidence, the new Klan's message of nativism, anti-immigration, and white supremacy resonated in the Midwest, where the postwar farm economy had slipped into recession and, in some places, worse. Organizers were careful to distinguish the new Klan from its riotous Reconstruction predecessor. They positioned the new Klan as mainstream and civic oriented. They pledged allegiance to white, native-born Protestantism, promising neutrality to all others. At its height in 1924, there were an estimated five million Klan members nationwide. As many as one hundred thosuand of them were in Iowa.[1]

A pair of public relations executives from Atlanta, Elizabeth Tyler and Edward Young Clark, are credited with creating the new Klan's business model. Men's clubs were the first targets, along with thousands of Protestant ministers, who were exempted from the pricey $10 initiation fee. They put on elaborate membership rallies with free hot dogs and confections, with screenings of D. W. Griffith's *Birth of a Nation,* which remained a novelty and was still generating publicity.[2]

"The Klan is the most amazingly clever capitalization of all recent psychological researchers, offering dull and negligible people an escape from the inferiority complex into the realm of the secretly powerful," wrote William A. White, influential editor of the *Emporia Gazette,* in January 1925. "Their capacity for meeting real injustices is turned into the safe bypaths of hating their neighbor, nosing into their neighbor's religion or despising their neighbor's race and color."[3]

The first Klan recruiter in the Hawkeye State probably showed up in Delaware County in 1920. Delaware would have been a good choice, located between the cities of Dubuque, to the east, and Waterloo, to the west, both of which had large immigrant communities—and, therefore, two of the state's largest Catholic populations. Historian Dorothy Schwieder found the prejudicial voice of the white, native-born Iowa farmer in letters exchanged between a young farmer and his girlfriend during the early 1920s. Schwieder gave him the pseudonym of John Smith. He lived in the tiny northwest Iowa town of Marathon, where he was a proud member of the Klan. "John left no doubt that he viewed Catholics as the Klan's main target and saw them as people he could not trust," Schwieder wrote in a 2002 paper. "Part of John's antipathy toward Catholics was related to bootlegging activities that apparently went on in the Marathon [Iowa] area."[4]

Despite public promises of civility, the new Klan held a special loathing for Jews and Catholics. "The Negro is not a menace to Americanism in the same sense of that of the Jews or Roman Catholic," explained the Klan's imperial grand wizard, Hiram Evans, in 1924.[5] The Catholics, many Klan members believed, were intent on overthrowing the government of the United States and replacing it with a theocracy answerable to Rome. They pointed to the many thousands of Catholic immigrants from Ireland and Germany as proof, claiming the Pope had sent them. Worse were the tales that nuns served as sex slaves for priests.[6] The Klan had even found a woman, named Helen Jackson, who claimed to have "escaped" from a nunnery. They helped put her on the road from 1923 to 1926. She dressed in a mock habit, charged fifty cents admission, and told "true stories" of the brutality and deviancy of Catholic priests. She was most popular in the Klan strongholds of Ohio and Indiana.

"Helen Jackson Never Was a Nun," barked a headline in an ad in the *Logansport Pharos Tribune* (Indiana) in November 1924. "The woman 'lecturer' now in this city neither 'escaped' from a convent nor was she 'converted.'" The ad said that her real name was Helen Barnowski and that she had been brought to town by the Republican Central Committee in cooperation with the Klan. "Like other lecturers on the anti-Catholic platform, she saw, during the rising wave of bigotry, a chance to make easy money." The ad was signed, "Truth Information Bureau."[7]

It was a shared dislike for Catholics that brought prohibitionists and the Klan together. In the Midwest, and Iowa in particular, many had assumed that Catholics were behind most bootlegging operations well ahead of Prohibition. This belief was reinforced by the beer wars in Chicago, which included shoot-outs in the streets. Much of the violence was fueled by the conflict between Al Capone's Italian mob and the North Side Irish gang.

The relationship between the temperance movement and the Klan was problematic and yet also, for a time, a politically potent alliance. It came to national attention in the summer of 1922 when Earle B. Mayfield, a prosperous attorney and businessman from Bosque County in central Texas, threw his hat into the race for U.S. senator. Like Iowa, the Texas plains suffered as much or more than the rest of the country during the economic downturn of the early 1920s. Wheat production fell with the fall in price. Farmers went bankrupt, banks failed, and people were looking for someone to blame. The Klan, recognizing an opportunity, took advantage of it. Mayfield never admitted to being a member of the "invisible empire," but backed by Klan money and Klan organizers, he went from a virtual unknown to the frontrunner in just a few months.[8]

"One of the most peculiar affiliations in the history of American politics has come about in Texas," the *New York Times* observed. "The Anti-Saloon League has combined with the KKK to support Earle B. Mayfield, candidate against former Governor James E. Ferguson for the Democratic Senatorial nomination."

Mayfield's victory was by far the biggest by a Klan-backed candidate, but certainly not the only one. Scores of Klan members or Klan affiliates were elected all over the country in the early 1920s to both state and local offices—often also with the backing of the Anti-Saloon League.[9]

A common theme from Klan candidates, aimed directly at antiliquor voters, was the inability of law enforcement to deal with a wave of crime that jumped nearly 25 percent following the World War I. More specifically, the Klan criticized state and local authorities who either couldn't or wouldn't deal with the illegal liquor traffic. It was on this perch that the Klan took the moral high ground in many communities. In some places—Illinois, for instance—Klan members chased down bootleggers, raided stills, and broke up private drinking halls.[10]

In the Deep South, the Klan's authority over morality frequently took the form of violent intervention. A twenty-eight-year-old Black man was tarred and feathered in Fort Worth, Texas, in 1921 by Klan members who believed him to be "a gambler" who had "immoral relations with women." A Black Houston dentist who had been convicted in court of having sexual relations with a white woman in 1921 was abducted and castrated by Klansmen, who then arranged for him to be delivered to a hospital. In January 1922 a mob of masked Klansmen from Texarkana kidnapped and beat a young Black man for "fooling around with a white woman."[11]

Incidents of violence by the Klan in the Midwest were rare. Far more common were the use of intimidation and the threat of violence. In Peoria, for example, just ahead of an election in November 1922, several carloads of Klan members in full regalia assembled in the town square and, without a word, posted signs threatening "the vengeance of the invisible empire to all sellers and buyers of votes."[12] That same month, Klan members in Des Moines, tired of traffic coming off the highway and tearing through the center of town, put up a billboard. In big black letters, the sign read: "STOP! When you speed you violate THE LAW." The image of a hooded rider on a horse accompanied the message. "That big KKK billboard placed along one of the incoming roads may cause a few chills up and down the spinal columns of some auto drivers," the *Des Moines Register* opined.[13]

In early September 1921 Joseph Pulitzer's *New York World* began publishing the nation's first comprehensive investigative account of the new Klan's dangerous rise to power. "Since the KKK recently began its membership campaign, there have been 64 violations of the rights of individuals by masked mobs wearing the order's regalia," the paper reported. "There have been 21 'tar and feather' parties; 25 individuals have been seized and beaten; two women have been stripped and whipped; 12 general warnings to enforce moral regulations in the name of the KKK."[14]

The Klan reached a high point in national political influence in 1923. A report in the *New York Times* estimated that as many as seventy-five new members of Congress owed "their election in large part to the support of the masked organization." Following the November elections that year, the *Times* declared that the Klan was "in control" of state government in Texas, Arkansas, Oklahoma, Indiana, and Oregon, while also holding some degree of authority in Ohio, California, Michigan, Illinois, and Missouri.[15]

The biggest show of strength by the Ku Klux Klan anywhere in the United States during the mid-1920s took place just a few weeks before the murder of Myrtle Cook in August 1925. An estimated thirty-five thousand Klan members paraded down Pennsylvania Avenue from the Capitol in Washington DC. The march was led by Hiram W. Evans, a Dallas dentist who had seized control of the Klan in a 1921 coup. He wore a purple robe with gold trimmings, and like everyone else in the procession, he was unmasked, as required by the event permit. It was three hours before the entire line would cover the parade route.[16]

An even bigger Klan event took place in Dubuque, Iowa, where more than fifty thousand people paid a twenty-five-cent admission fee to enjoy a carnival on Saturday afternoon, August 30, 1925. The large crowd was thought to be mostly comprised of nonmembers who were less interested in anything the Klan was selling than they were in the performances of stunt airplanes, drill teams, and multiple bands and orchestras. Still, for the Klan in Iowa, the Dubuque event was a landmark. "Early Saturday morning, three airplanes carrying Klansmen from Dallas, Texas, arrived, and another from Des Moines," the *Dubuque Telegraph* reported. Reverend Ira Hawley gave the featured speech, which was intended to assure those gathered that the Klan's goals were honorable. "The principles of the Klan are not anti-Catholic or anti-negro, or anti-Jew," he claimed. "It is pro-Protestant, pro-gentile and pro-white."[17]

Des Moines, among all the cities in Iowa, proved to be the most fertile ground for Klan recruiting. One membership chair, J. G. Ellstrot, claimed to have signed up a thousand new men in just five months. By 1923 the Klan had twenty field men working in every part of the state.[18]

In February 1923 Reverend N. C. Carpenter of the Capitol Hill Church of Christ in Des Moines sent out flyers in advance of a Sunday sermon titled "Why I Am a Member of the Ku Klux Klan." It drew an overflow crowd.

The church pews and aisles were jammed, and many people were turned away, the *Des Moines Register* reported, estimating the attendance at twenty-five hundred and noting that a stenographer took down the pastor's every word for later circulation across the state.[19]

In the municipal elections of 1924, the Klan made its strongest bid for power in Des Moines. In February that year, as leaders in both parties began early campaign planning, the Klan held a massive induction ceremony, just a block away from city hall, where two hundred new members were sworn in. At the conclusion of the event, they lit the "fiery cross," which drew hundreds of onlookers before police and firemen broke things up.[20] The Klan put forward a full slate for Des Moines city offices, including candidates for mayor, street commissioner, and district judge. Their candidate for mayor barely lost, but John W. Jenny, who owned a local grocery store, was elected commissioner of public safety by a landslide.[21]

Statewide that year, the Iowa Klan put everything they had behind William J. Burbank for governor. Burbank, a Republican, was one of the first certified public accountants in Iowa and had been elected treasurer of Black Hawk County three times before becoming the Iowa state treasurer. Burbank narrowly lost in the 1924 primary to John Hammill, the popular Republican lieutenant governor. An analysis of the vote, however, showed that Burbank and the Klan won in six of Iowa's largest counties: Polk (Des Moines), Linn (Cedar Rapids), Black Hawk (Waterloo), and Dubuque (Dubuque).

There were other successes for the Klan in that 1924 election. Reverend E. A. Elliott was sent to Iowa's lower legislative house, representing Polk County. Only a year later, key patrons of his Johnston Station Federated Church called into question some of his votes on Klan-backed bills. Rather than renounce his loyalty to the Klan, the reverend chose to resign from his day job.[22]

One of the boldest public expressions by the Klan in Des Moines took place on the night of April 22, 1925, when suspected Klan members placed scores of burning crosses all over town. Crosses were put up outside the police station, on the courthouse steps, on the Capitol grounds, and all over the Black neighborhoods. Fire units were overwhelmed. Angry residents spilled out into the streets. Police were called in to quell several hot spots where young Black men sought to retaliate. It took several hours to restore order. In the days that followed, however, complaints were filed against police officers and firemen, accused of having done little or nothing to reduce tensions.

The failure of the authorities to identify the perpetrators further escalated suspicions that the city's Police and Fire Departments were full of Klan sympathizers. The mayor of Des Moines, Carl M. Garver, who had beaten a Klan-backed candidate only the year before, was among those who wanted answers.

A resolution, authored by Garver and unanimously passed by the city council on April 28, called for the dismissal of any police or fire personnel complicit in the cross-burning incident. Allegations of dereliction of duty were made against a police captain, a lieutenant, and several patrolmen. Police Chief James Cavender dismissed all of it, saying that the matter had already been investigated and that there was no wrongdoing. "Everyone knows as much about the matter as I," Cavender told the council. "Bah! Every man is doing his duty." Cavender had the support of his boss, John W. Jenny, the Des Moines public safety commissioner, who oversaw both the Police and Fire Departments. Jenny was the highest-ranking Klan-backed candidate to win in the 1924 Des Moines city election. A week later, four men confessed to putting up the burning crosses but claimed it was meant to be a joke and denied any ties to the Klan.[23]

The first big Klan rally held in Benton County, where Myrtle Cook was murdered, took place in an open pasture near the village of Mount Auburn on the night of October 16, 1923. According to the *Vinton Eagle*, the event attracted more than two hundred local residents. Rev. Ira Edwards, a Baptist minister from Cedar Rapids, led the proceedings, in which eight new members were inducted. Edwards, the *Eagle* noted, "paid his respects to the Catholics, the Jew and the Negro."[24]

Giving front-page coverage to the Klan rally might have startled some readers of the *Eagle*. The paper had been run since the 1870s by Bernard Murphy and, later, his son Edward. They were both prudent and measured in their news judgment. The tenor of the paper changed distinctly, however, with the arrival of Edwin S. Shortess, who had taken over as publisher in the fall of 1923.[25] Shortess was born and raised in Benton County but moved to Chicago after serving as an infantryman during the Spanish-American war. He was a Republican, a Coolidge man, and most certainly a Klan sympathizer, if not a member outright.[26]

The Coolidge Republicans, at least in Iowa, were a very different breed than those who had followed Abraham Lincoln two generations earlier. Coolidge began his political career as a progressive, voting for women's suffrage, the creation of a state income tax, and a minimum wage guarantee. By the time he reached the White House, however, his views had grown far more conservative. He believed in a small federal government and low taxes. He supported business over labor, noting once that "large profits mean large payrolls." He thought that Congress passed too many laws. "Men don't make laws," he once said. "They discover them."[27]

Silent Cal was also an "America first" nationalist. "Our country must cease to be regarded as a 'dumping ground,' and should only accept 'the right kind of immigrant,'" he wrote in a piece for *Good Housekeeping* in 1921. Just three years later, as president, Coolidge signed what is considered by many scholars as the most xenophobic law ever adopted in American history: the National Origins Act of 1924, which imposed immigration quotas for the first time. The defining feature of the act was the baseline used to determine how many immigrants could come and from where. By using the 1890 census as the starting point, the law deliberately created a racial hierarchy that favored white Protestant immigrants from western and northern Europe over Catholics and Jews from eastern and southern European states. Additionally, the 1890 census put a lid on all those coming from Asia.[28]

Shortess cheered the legislation, arguing that the country could no longer benefit from accepting any and all newcomers. "When we needed pioneers, farmers, laborers, tillers of the soil, we received the best Europe had to offer," he noted. "But today, good land cannot be had for the asking. The pioneer days are over. American civilization has grown complicated. It takes more than willing hands and a stout heart to succeed here now. The door must be shut, to keep out those who hurt, not help, the nation, and only put a little ajar for that thinning stream of the best kind of men and women, who are able to take advantage of the modern opportunities of modern America."[29]

Such thinking was not out of step with most Americans, and certainly not with most Iowans. The Sixty-Sixth Congress, which met from March 1919 until March 1921, considered legislation to restrict immigration eight times. People wanted action. "Those who find intolerable our laws, as provided by the majorities, will have to seek other counties where the laws are to their liking," the *Jefferson Bee* editorialized on November 12, 1919. "We are beginning to believe, in the view of events now transpiring, that we shall be forced into a position where we must declare that America is for Americans."[30]

17

Comes a Killer

When the U.S. Postal Service sent a man out to Vinton in 1850 to set up service, he found that the locals wanted to call their town Fremont in honor of the California explorer, military man, and U.S. senator, John C. Frémont. The postmaster told them there was already a berg in Iowa named Fremont. So the folks got together and agreed to rename the town Vinton, this time in honor of a congressman from Ohio.[1]

Among the earliest settlers was Anson Underwood, whose granddaughter was Myrtle Underwood Cook. Anson Underwood arrived in Vinton around 1854, just before stagecoach service from Iowa City and the first serious discussions about bringing a railroad down from Dubuque. Like many of the first pioneers in Iowa, Anson was born in America hailing from Syracuse, New York, in 1804.

The population of Benton County was nearly eighty-five hundred by 1860. The soil was rich and moldy black, comparatively easy to till and tend. Nearby, the Cedar River ran slow and steady in summer and fall. Later, the county would become internationally known for the quality of a Japanese hull-less varietal of popcorn grown there.[2] Underwood found land to his liking in the Taylor Township, which would later form the center of town. There was plenty of wood, too, with stands of oak, hickory, ash, and cottonwood. Initially, he farmed but he later earned his living in land speculation and did well enough to help his two sons establish their own families.[3]

Ensign, Myrtle's father, bought land near Garrison and raised hogs with his sons. Myrtle, the eldest child, would have worked long hours in the house with her mother. They did all the cooking, cleaning, washing, and mending. They baked bread, churned butter, canned fruits, raised chickens, and tended the garden. Water had to be drawn from a well and hauled into the house seven or eight times a day. There was ironing, sweeping, sewing, and lifting to do, hour after hour, day after day.[4]

To a young woman like Myrtle, life in town would be appealing. Vinton was a bustling commercial center by the early 1920s. Most people bought their groceries at Biel's City Market. They got their shoes at Burt McIntyre's store. The Muhl family operated the lumber mill. Jeff's Sweet Shop, the Vinton Savings Bank, Conter's Clothing, and the Lents Drug Store all lined Fourth Street. If something else was needed, trains to Cedar Rapids left twice a day.[5]

Vinton had a baseball team, and when they were called the Cinders and played at the fairgrounds, Bing Miller was the main attraction. Miller would later become an All-Star center fielder for Connie Mack's championship Philadelphia Athletics, playing alongside future Hall of Famers Mickey Cochrane, Jimmy Foxx, and Lefty Grove.[6] Vinton also bragged of an award-winning rifle club, which was organized in 1916 as part of the effort to prepare men for the war. The club was affiliated with the National Rifle Association, which, before the war, allowed its members to buy their ammo directly from the War Department. "Don't hang back because you can't shoot," the *Vinton Eagle* urged. "The purpose of the club is to teach you to shoot."[7]

Myrtle's father, Ensign Underwood, was probably not an easy man to get along with. He had taken a Christian vow at the age of sixteen, and later, as a husband and father, he insisted that everyone in his family take to reading the Bible daily. His piety only went so far, according to one of the few notices of him in the local paper. In October 1882 Ensign Underwood was arrested at the Vinton train station while in the company of a younger woman. No charges were detailed, but the report strongly suggested that the two of them were on their way to Sioux City to start a new life. The young woman was returned to her family, and Ensign Underwood apparently took the train west, having already deeded the family farm to his wife.[8] A stroke in 1911 left him partially paralyzed, and he moved south to Excelsior Springs, Missouri, where the natural waters that oozed from a deep fissure were said to cure all sickness. He died a few days short of his sixty-fifth birthday, in 1914.[9]

Her parents' break up probably had a lasting effect on Myrtle. Although she was only eight years old, the scandal may have helped fuel her fierce commitment to evangelical Christianity and her intolerance for anyone who wasn't equally inclined. She was intelligent and gifted musically, a trait that was nurtured by her mother such that she sent her to study at the Drake Conservatory of Music in Des Moines, where she was awarded a bachelor of arts degree around 1904.[10]

Her time in Des Moines was likely a welcome respite from the drudgery of life on the farm. As a young adult, Myrtle would have been among those who longed for life in town. The migration from farm to city had been trending since the end of the Civil War, becoming so noticeable by 1908 that President Theodore Roosevelt appointed a commission to study the phenomenon. There was a real fear that Jefferson's ideal of a "nation of farmers" was threatened by the exodus. The takeaway from the commission's review was that more should be done to mechanize labor on the farm, roads should be improved, rural schools should be upgraded, and efforts should be made to make farm life less isolated.[11] These enhancements would take decades to take hold, and Myrtle would not wait. Just after graduating from music college, she rented a studio in town, or perhaps living quarters, where she set up her music school.[12]

Far less is known about Clifford B. Cook, Myrtle's husband. He was born in 1883 and had at least one brother.[13] His father, Steve, appears to have worked in town, probably as a clerk or laborer.[14] There is some evidence that Clifford was a member of the Iowa National Guard. A report in the *Vinton Eagle* from September 1907 noted that Private Clifford Cook participated in a shooting contest in Independence. Only a few weeks later, Clifford Cook was again reported to be in a shooting contest, this time in Des Moines, but on this occasion, there was no mention of him being in the military.[15] Arguing against Clifford Cook's service in the military, however, is the absence of a military pension among the few public records that can be found from his life, as well as any mention of it in his obituary.[16]

There is, however, a photograph of Clifford Cook in uniform, perhaps the only one ever taken of him. He looked young, in his midtwenties, and handsome too; it was probably taken about the time he attended the shooting contests. The photo, however, became an object of criticism eighteen years later when Cook became a statewide focus of attention as the primary suspect in his wife's murder. The editor of the *Quad-City Times* (then known as the *Democrat and Leader*) in Davenport complained bitterly that the only photo of Clifford Cook was decades too old. "So we suggest that Vinton advertise for a live photographer, and that the people there move en masse upon his studio to 'get their pictures took,'" he wrote. "There's no telling how soon any of the rest of them will be involved in a shooting or scandal that might get their faces in the papers, and when the time comes, they ought not to be found putting comic illustrations into a perfectly good murder story."[17]

Before their wedding announcement ran on the front page of the *Vinton Review*, on July 27, 1910, there was no mention of the courtship between Myrtle and Clifford Cook.[18] News of their union, however, would have sparked some gossip. She was nine years older and came from a prominent farm family. Clifford's parents rented in town, and while he could read and write, he earned his living by loading and unloading a horse-drawn wagon, which was then called a dray service. Even more in contrast were their physical characteristics. Even on her wedding day, Myrtle Cook was dour and plain, while Clifford Cook cut a dashing figure in uniform. He certainly would have had other potential romantic interests, whereas Myrtle probably did not. It is likely that the groom's financial status played a role in his decision. Just a few months after the wedding, Clifford was able to swing the purchase of two vacant lots near the train station, where he built a barn and expanded his delivery service.[19] The storage barn was badly needed, opined the *Vinton Review*, after news of Clifford's plans became public: "As Mr. Cook puts it, this building will be fire, mouse, and rat proof and then our grocery men can store away flour and not have every sack perforated by mice."[20]

Myrtle gave birth to a son in March 1911, but the baby lived only a week.[21] Not too much later, the Cooks adopted a little girl named Gertrude.[22] For a while, they might have been happy. Clifford's delivery service was doing well during the war years. Myrtle's music lessons were popular, and her student recitals were often mentioned in the local papers.

To the outside world, they seemed to fit well into the community. Benton County had, by the mid-1920s, a population of twenty-five thousand. Immigrants represented about 20 percent of the residents, with the largest number coming from Germany, Ireland, and Denmark. In the town of Vinton, 80 percent of the locals were white and native born. Most people attended a Protestant church, with Methodists being the dominant congregation. Catholics were more numerous outside of town. Nearly everyone voted Republican, which, in 1925, translated into the GOP holding all but two of the Benton County offices and 30 of the 35 seats the county had in Iowa's massive 158-member general assembly.[23]

Following the end of the war in Europe, the farm economy slipped into a deep recession. Clifford's dray business failed. He either couldn't find work in town or decided he wanted to look elsewhere. Things had soured between him and his wife as well. Sometime in 1920 or 1921, Clifford and Myrtle Cook ceased living together and never would again.[24]

On the day of the murder, Myrtle Cook went looking for the sheriff early. She had seen something or someone. A known killer, perhaps. A truck filled with liquor and out-of-state license plates. Maybe a late-model car with men dressed in expensive suits and carrying weapons. Who or what she saw isn't known, but the record shows that she wanted Sheriff Levi Whitfield Ruhl to know about it. He was one of the few in town who took her reports on bootleggers seriously, and he had used her tips to make arrests.

It was September 7, 1925—Labor Day. A series of blistering heat waves had scorched the Midwest late that summer. The temperature hit 103 in nearby Cedar Rapids on Thursday, September 3, and while cooler air moved in that night, the heat and humidity returned over the weekend. Anyone who could spent the holiday in the shade of a river park or took a breezy automobile ride on the few paved highways around Benton County. The forecast suggested that rain might finally come Monday night.

In those days, it was customary for a lawman's wife to open and attend the jail while he was out on his rounds. It was likely that Myrtle Cook came to the courthouse looking for the sheriff and found Marie Ruhl. Marie would have known all about Myrtle's temperance crusade. Moreover, she would have known that Myrtle wasn't just the president of the Benton County Woman's Christian Temperance Union but an informant for the law. Marie would also have been aware that Myrtle spent hours at her parlor window, which had a clear view of the Rock Island Railroad station and the dive café next door, and that Myrtle kept good notes on the comings and goings of the bootleggers and their customers, who regularly conducted their business at the depot.

Marie Ruhl would later remember their conversation that morning. She told reporters that Myrtle Cook seemed anxious. Myrtle called herself a "marked woman" and warned of a premonition that "something might happen." Myrtle didn't tell Marie what or whom she had seen but ended the conversation with a chilling remark: "I believe this work will be the end of me."[25]

Some in town would not have taken Cook too seriously. From the snippets gleaned from news reports after the murder, Myrtle Cook projected a personality that would have been seen as haughty and pretentious. Even though she was twice elected president of the county WCTU and held leadership positions in both the woman's auxiliary of the Klan and in her church, she probably had few close friends. "Mrs. Cook was not generally liked," the editor of the *Cedar Valley Daily Times* said the day after the murder. "Many people, indeed, most emphatically disliked her. That was because she was generally regarded as being meddlesome and quarrelsome."[26]

And why should she be anything else? Hers was a life of struggle and disappointment. Her estranged husband had long since stopped even pretending to support her and their thirteen-year-old daughter. Her music classes had mostly dried up years ago. What little income she had came from boarders that she put up in their home and, most likely, an allowance from her mother.[27] Her last refuge was her conviction in faith and temperance. She believed that demon rum was the wellspring of depravity and that the vessels for its transmission were immigrants, all of them. "Our danger is not without; our danger is from within," she wrote just days before her murder in a speech that she would never deliver. "We have left our doors open too long; we now have an alarming situation in our very midst: so much foreign illiteracy, so much grasping greed and selfishness. A very grave crisis is facing American ideals today, when traitors in our midst—seeking to undermine our Constitution—are trying to make ridiculous the great flag in the world."[28]

Such views were common in the Midwest during the 1920s, and some of her neighbors might have cheered her words had she made the speech. She might not have been liked, but she was, perhaps, admired. "There was never room for doubt for where she stood," the *Cedar Valley Daily Times* said. "Mrs. Cook was not diplomatic in her work for prohibition. It was not her nature to be diplomatic. She could see no reason for diplomacy. It was a case of having to fight. And fight she did. She went to her death fighting."[29]

The most prolific bootlegger in Vinton was Wayne "Shorty" Snader.[30] His booze came from Waterloo, whose criminal underworld, like so many of their ilk, was controlled by crime lords in Chicago.[31] Snader owned a popular night spot, the Red Ball Inn, located in the otherwise dreary town of La Porte City.[32] But much of his business was conducted at the train station in Vinton or the diner adjacent to the depot called the Palace Café. The café was owned by Joe Gilchrist, who was most likely a partner in Snader's liquor operation.[33]

The back of the Cook home was just across the railroad tracks from the station, and her parlor window had an unobstructed view of the station platform and the café that was interrupted only by train traffic. In June 1925 Myrtle Cook witnessed a liquor transaction between Snader and Merlin Swartzbaugh, twenty-one, who worked at the ice plant just down from the station.[34] Ruhl arrested both men, but their arraignment was put off until the September term of the grand jury.[35]

On the night of July 4, Swartzbaugh and some of his friends had been drinking when one of them got the idea that they should do something to Myrtle Cook in retaliation for turning in Snader and Swartzbaugh. Cook was away that evening, giving an anti-liquor speech at her church. One of the boys knew where to find a pail of rotten eggs, which they used to pelt the backside of the Cook home. She returned to find a stinky mess and probably made a complaint to the sheriff, but since she couldn't identify her attackers, no arrests were made.[36]

It is unlikely that Mrs. Ruhl ever got a chance to tell her husband about the conversation she had with Cook on the morning before the murder. Although it was a holiday for the rest of the town, Sheriff Ruhl was most likely busy with the sort of small-town dramas that can fill the day of the local lawman. He probably didn't see his wife until he arrived home, probably late, for his evening meal. By then, Marie was most likely getting their four-year-old daughter, Adah, ready for a bath, or perhaps bedtime. Marie might have been ready for bed herself; she was less than a week away from giving birth to their second daughter.[37] Mrs. Ruhl had probably forgotten all about Cook by the time the sheriff got home.

Had she remembered, had she told her husband what Cook said, the sheriff might have put his dinner back in the oven and taken a drive out to the Cook home. His mere appearance might have been enough to chase off the would-be assassin.

The weather forecast called for rain Monday night, September 7, and, as promised, a sizable front moved in around dusk. The sky grew nearly black, and the air stilled. The first bolt of lightning lit up the pastures, and then the thunder rattled the windows. Violent gusts came suddenly, bending the trees and snapping some limbs. The torrent sent ribbons of water cascading off the rooftops, filling the culverts, and flooding the streams.[38]

The call came into the Ruhl home around 10:30 p.m., just as the last curtain of showers moved east. It was Dr. B. F. Wolverton, who told the sheriff simply that Myrtle Cook had been shot.[39]

Ruhl contacted A. H. Brewer, the Vinton night marshal, and Deputy Sheriff H. M. Stufflebeam, telling them both to meet him at the Cook residence. When the sheriff arrived, he found the victim's family gathered in the kitchen. Present were her mother, Martha Underwood; Myrtle's in-laws, Stephen W. Cook and his wife; Myrtle's daughter, Gertrude; and J. A. Gregory, who identified himself as a boarder. Dr. Wolverton was in the living room, where Myrtle Cook lay on the floor, unconscious and barely clinging to life.[40]

Wolverton said Mrs. Underwood had called him a half hour earlier, saying that Myrtle had fainted and remained unconscious. The doctor said he hadn't realized that Mrs. Cook had been shot until he turned her body over and found the chest wound. He showed Ruhl where Myrtle was sitting when the attack took place: her favorite chair against the parlor window, which offered the best view of the train station. The bullet had made a small hole in the windowpane without breaking it.

When his deputy and the night marshal arrived, Ruhl sent them to canvass the neighborhood. He ordered one of them to check at the train depot, recalling that the 11:10 to Chicago would be leaving soon; maybe someone saw something. Next, the sheriff went into the kitchen and spoke to the family members. Mrs. Underwood said she was upstairs in bed and didn't hear the gunshot because of the thunder. But between the blasts from the storm, she heard Myrtle making strange gasping or gurgling sounds and came down to investigate. She said she couldn't revive her daughter and immediately called the doctor. She then called Stephen Cook, who lived nearby.[41]

Myrtle Cook died at 11:35 p.m.[42]

The body was taken to Dr. Wolverton's office, where he conducted an autopsy. He removed a single .32 caliber bullet from her chest. He said it could have been fired by either a pistol or a rifle. It hit her in the right arm first before lodging in the wall of her heart. It was Dr. Wolverton's opinion that the killer fired at close range, but he couldn't be certain. He said that it was nearly a straight line between where the bullet came through the window and where it entered the victim's chest. He surmised that the shooter was either tall or standing on something.[43]

18

The Investigation

Sheriff Ruhl probably never went to bed on the night of the Cook murder, or if he did, he didn't get much sleep. He was summoned early to a meeting at the courthouse by the Benton County Attorney, J. D. Nichols, and the county coroner, L. C. Modlin.[1] Iowa law required that an inquest into any unnatural death be quickly organized and convened. By sunrise, they had assembled a witness list with sixteen names and planned to hold the first hearing that same afternoon, Tuesday, September 8, 1925.[2]

Next came the reporter inquiries and telegraph messages from concerned state officials. Thanks to the *New York Times,* the national press was scrambling to cover the story of what appeared to be a gangland killing right in the middle of the American heartland. A clamor for justice rang throughout the state. Iowa governor John Hammill issued a reward of $500 (about $8,000 today) for assistance in the capture of the killer. He also called Iowa's sheriffs and police chiefs to the capital for an emergency meeting to discuss what he called a "crime wave." In the past three months, the governor said there had been nine murders in Iowa, the Cook killing among them.

"I wish to serve warning upon the bootleggers, rumrunners, and all criminals that no quarter will be shown them," Hammill told the *Associated Press.* "Crime in Iowa is to be cut to the minimum by whatever means we are able to employ."[3]

One of the first notable outsiders to reach Vinton was celebrity prohibitionist John Brown Hammond. Hammond, a former chief of police in Des Moines and the second cousin of the infamous abolitionist John Brown, was press savvy and ambitious. He postponed a speaking engagement in Kansas City and jumped on a train to Benton County. "We will stay here a month if necessary," Hammond told reporters on his arrival. "Our theory is that she was killed by a rumrunner or bootlegger. No one else would have any reason to kill her."[4] Next to arrive was George K. Atkins, special agent from what was then called the Iowa Bureau of Criminal Investigations, sent by the governor. Atkins, a former sheriff of Harrison County, had made headlines only a few months before by arresting "Tex" Maynard, a member of the notorious "Red" Burzette gang.[5]

The hearing room of the county supervisors was used for the inquest. Coroner Modlin opened by reading into the record the autopsy report. The first round of witnesses called included members of both the Cook and Underwood families, as well as neighbors. None of them could shed any new light on the crime. A pair of gun experts testified, disagreeing on the likely murder weapon: one said the shot came from a pistol at close range; the other argued that the shot came from the second floor of an adjacent barn and that the killer most likely used a rifle.[6]

Absent from the initial list of witnesses was Clifford Cook, Myrtle's estranged husband. It is not clear why he wasn't subpoenaed right away, although it could have been because even his family members didn't have his new address in Sioux City. Also not called to testify was Wayne "Shorty" Snader, Benton County's biggest bootlegger, who was facing indictment for bootlegging because of evidence Mrs. Cook had provided the sheriff just three months before.[7]

Clifford arrived at his parents' house in Vinton on the day after the murder. Upon learning of the killing, he went quickly to the Cook home to console his daughter and his mother-in-law. A reporter with the *Vinton Eagle* was on hand, and Clifford told him that it was a coincidence that he had decided to come to visit. He had been living and working in Sioux City and was on his way back to Vinton when the murder took place. He repeatedly said that he knew nothing of the crime until he arrived home Tuesday morning.[8] Those who knew him best believed him. They said he expressed true shock and sorrow for the loss of his wife.[9]

Agent Atkins and Sheriff Ruhl, however, both took note of Clifford Cook's denial and both were skeptical of the assertion.

There is nothing in the surviving record to indicate why investigators didn't consider Snader a prime suspect. He had motive: Mrs. Cook had given evidence that led to his arrest in June, and, no doubt, she had interrupted other transactions. Snader had opportunity too. He was at the depot frequently enough to know where she sat and the times of day when she was likely to take up her vigil. It would be hard to imagine that Snader wouldn't have at least contemplated how a man with a gun could approach her parlor window without being seen.

Perhaps concerned that Snader might have sent someone else to commit the crime, Sheriff Ruhl brought Swartzbaugh, a frequent customer of the bootlegger, in for questioning. Swartzbaugh denied having anything to do with the shooting but admitted to egging Cook's home on July 4 and gave the names of the other boys, who were subsequently brought to the jail. The boys confessed to the egg attack but denied they had anything to do with the murder. All of them, except for Swartzbaugh, came from prominent families, including one whose father was a state senator. Another was Louis Gilchrist, younger brother of Joe Gilchrist, owner of the Palace Café, where bootlegging deals were often made. Despite that connection to the booze trade, Ruhl also knew George K. Gilchrist, who was the father of Louis and Joe and a prominent businessman, well known throughout Benton County.[10]

Ruhl was inclined to believe the boys had nothing to do with the murder.[11]

Early on, Ruhl appeared to also dismiss the notion that Snader could have been in on the crime. While Snader had been convicted several times of liquor violations, nothing in his record suggested he was violent. That Myrtle Cook had turned him in months earlier would not be motive enough. A conviction for bootlegging, including attorney fees and other costs, could run about $1,000 (about $16,000 today), which was a lot of money. Still, a liquor conviction was just a misdemeanor, and Snader was a businessman; he paid his fine and got back to work. Ruhl likely reasoned that whoever killed Mrs. Cook would have had far more compelling motivations—Clifford Cook, for instance.[12]

There were, however, two more immediate suspects on whom Ruhl needed to check. One was Charlie Perifield, a laborer on a bridge gang, who got drunk and was heard making general threats of violence on the day of the murder. The sheriff found another witness who said that Perifield was too intoxicated to even walk at the time of the killing.[13]

The other suspect was much more promising: Harold Ponder, who had walked away from a work detail outside the walls of Fort Madison prison just one month before the Cook murder. Ponder had been seen in Vinton on the morning after the murder. He was believed to be driving a stolen seven-passenger Buick. Ponder had been given a five-year sentence and sent to Fort Madison in 1923 for receiving stolen property. He was known to have been part of a ring of thieves and bootleggers.

The day after the murder, the Buick was found near Colfax, which was just outside Des Moines and nearly a hundred miles from Vinton. Ponder had vanished.[14]

The first to notice the remarkable visitors to Vinton on the morning of Mrs. Cook's funeral might have been Reverend C. S. Kleckner, pastor of the Christian Church, where the victim worshipped. Kleckner and his wife, Lula, were recent arrivals. He had been officially elected pastor only a week before the murder. Both he and his wife were Iowa natives; in fact, both had studied divinity at Drake University in Des Moines. They had spent the last four years in Redlands, California, ministering to the needs of another Christian Church congregation.[15]

Thursday afternoon, September 10, was selected for the funeral. Reverend Kleckner could not have known Myrtle Cook too well; however, given the shocking nature of her death and Kleckner's status as a newcomer, the minister would have been very sensitive to the needs of the Cook family as well as those of his new church members. Kleckner would have risen early that day, anxious to attend to his duties well in advance of the services.

He would have driven from his home on Fourth Street to the church, on the edge of town, to begin making preparations. It is most likely that on his way to the Cook home in the midmorning, he drove past the town square and the courthouse. There, he would have seen the growing crowd of men and women adorned in white robes, some of the men in tall, pointy hats.

The Klan.

To Kleckner, who came from Southern California, where the "invisible empire" had a swelling membership, the sight of them in Vinton would have been both startling and familiar. He would have known of the gun battle between police and Klansmen that took place in Los Angeles County in 1922. He would also have seen news coverage of robed and armed Klansmen patrolling the streets of Anaheim during the tumultuous city election just a few months before he left California in February 1925.[16]

Waiting for Kleckner at the Cook home was most certainly A. A. Wright, the minister of the Prairie Church, located just north of town. Wright would have introduced himself as being affiliated with the Ku Klux Klan, and between sharing his thoughts with Kleckner and the Cook family about hymns and scripture passages that might be used in the service that afternoon, Wright would have pointed out that the Christian Church building was far too small for the expected turnout. Wright might have already arranged to move the funeral to the much larger Methodist Church premises (where the service was eventually held). Wright would have also asked permission to lead the service, given his position as the Klan's leading pastor in Benton County and Myrtle Cook's standing as a Klan leader. It was clear that Wright had already received permission from the Cook family, and being in no position to object, Kleckner would have accepted a secondary role.[17]

All the merchants in town closed their doors at about 1:30 in the afternoon. When the time came, six Klansmen and more than a dozen of their women formed a line following the horse-drawn hearse that proceeded slowly from the funeral home to the church. Then the Klansmen carried Mrs. Cook's coffin inside. At the end of the service, the same guard brought the coffin back to the hearse, which the mourners followed on a slow fifteen-minute walk to the cemetery. A twenty-foot wood cross was erected over the gravesite, and it was ignited by a torch as more than a hundred Klansmen and women stood by in respectful silence.[18]

After the services, Kleckner returned home, probably hoping to take a nap before dinner, or at least enjoy some peace and quiet. Instead, he found his wife in near hysterics. She said that earlier in the afternoon, while the service was going on, two masked men forced their way into the home and began searching the house. She told her husband that one of the men kept demanding to know if Reverend Kleckner was a Klan member. The reverend summoned Sheriff Ruhl, who was alarmed enough to call a man in Waterloo who owned a team of bloodhounds. The sheriff had officers and volunteers cordon off the whole neighborhood. When the dogs arrived, they seemed to pick up a scent at the Kleckners' back door, but whatever it was, they lost it about two miles out of town.[19] A week later, under further scrutiny from Ruhl and Atkins, Kleckner's wife confessed to making up the entire episode. She told her husband that she was unhappy with their move back to Iowa and that she had hoped the tale of the intruders would convince him that Vinton wasn't welcoming.[20]

The same morning as the funeral, Benton County was buzzing over a story in the early edition of the *Chicago Tribune* that claimed authorities were closing in on the killer and that the murderer wasn't tied to a liquor gang: "The officials working on the case are waiting for the development of only one more angle in the affair before making the seizure of the man, who, they are confident, does not suspect that he is being watched," the *Tribune* reported. "These officials say that the case which they have worked up is so nearly perfect that the further proof is hardly needed. One thing is admitted by the county authorities. This is that they have abandoned the theory that Mrs. Cook was killed by bootleggers."[21]

The Chicago papers had been slow to recognize the Cook murder as a major story—the *Tribune* in particular. To catch up, the paper sent one of its best reporters, John Boettiger. Years later, he would be assigned to the paper's DC bureau, and he would cover the 1932 presidential campaign, Franklin Roosevelt's first. As the White House correspondent, Boettiger would meet the president's only daughter, whom he would fall in love with and marry in 1935.[22]

It was Boettiger who broke the story that investigators had given up the bootlegger theory in the murder of Mrs. Cook. His scoop threw a bucket of cold water on what was thought to be a "man bites dog" story. Now, it turned out the crime was probably nothing more than another routine murder.

The source for Boettiger's scoop was probably Atkins, who had been dubious from the beginning that the murder was a Chicago mob hit.[23] He became convinced he was right when Clifford Cook testified before the coroner's inquest. Clifford said he was in a hotel room in Grundy Center, which was only fifty miles from Vinton. He testified that the heavy thunderstorm had turned the roads muddy and impassable. Atkins didn't believe him. Even with poor road conditions, Clifford could have easily driven to Vinton, committed the murder, and returned to Grundy Center well before morning.

Clifford Cook also testified that he had spent virtually all of his time in Sioux City either working or alone in his room. He not only denied having any female companions but also claimed that he and Myrtle had been a perfectly happy married couple.[24]

Atkins and Sheriff Ruhl knew that Clifford was lying, at least about his happy marriage. One of Clifford's friends had already told the sheriff that the couple had split up and that Clifford recently asked Myrtle for a divorce, only to have her fly into a rage and refuse to even consider it.[25] Before the jury concluded its work that week, Atkins drove to Sioux City, found Clifford Cook's rooming house, interviewed the landlady, and discovered that Clifford had a lady friend named Hester Seiling.[26]

Atkins quickly located Seiling, who freely admitted to having a friendship with Clifford Cook. She said she met Clifford in the spring of 1925 while she was working for a company that Clifford serviced on his sales route. She told Atkins that they spent most Sundays together and attended morning church services, sometimes taking a drive or even seeing a ball game. More recently, she said, they dined together Sunday nights at the place where she lived. Seiling was thirty-five years old—sixteen years younger than Myrtle Cook—and the press would later delight in calling her "a pretty divorcee."[27] Atkins was sure Clifford Cook was responsible for his wife's murder.

"I am convinced that he and the woman hired a man in Sioux City to do the gun act and that Cook and possibly the woman were present when it was done," Atkins reported to his boss back at the capital on September 22. "This was a cold-blooded, well-planned, premeditated murder, and they thought they had an airtight alibi, but there is no such thing."[28]

After catching Clifford in a lie about his relationship with Seiling, Ruhl and Atkins took him behind closed doors for an extended interrogation. Under Iowa law at the time, circumstantial evidence alone was enough for a conviction in a murder case.[29] The prosecution team was no doubt confident that he would eventually break.

He never did.

"During the long ordeal and grilling, Clifford Cook had made no objection, criticism, or complaint," wrote John Tobin many years later.

Tobin, who spent sixteen years as a district judge in Benton County, briefly served as Clifford's attorney during the murder investigation. "In all their conversations, he was placid and composed, always cooperative with the officers, and even talked with them outside the official hearings," Tobin wrote.[30]

Tobin's book, a memoir called *Tobin Tales,* includes a chapter on the Cook murder. As Clifford's attorney, Tobin became convinced of his client's innocence in the murder. The fact that Clifford allowed himself to be interrogated for days on end without ever consulting an attorney spoke volumes about his honesty. "As he [Clifford] said later," Tobin wrote, "he did not need a lawyer in telling the truth."[31]

The murder case against Clifford Cook fell completely to pieces after a credible witness came forward who swore he was with Clifford in Grundy Center on the night of the murder. The witness was a traveling salesman, well known and respected throughout eastern Iowa. He told the court that he spoke to Clifford around dinnertime on September 7 and then saw him standing outside the hotel at 10:30 p.m. that same night. The next morning, the witness said Clifford's car was still parked in the same space where it had been the night before and that he later saw Clifford at breakfast.[32]

There was nothing left for the prosecution to do but charge Clifford Cook with perjury for lying about his relationship with Hester Seiling, which the grand jury did on October 12.[33] In April 1926 a Benton County judge dismissed the perjury charge against Clifford. By then, he and Hester had left Iowa for Tacoma, Washington, where they were married. He went to work for the state as a highway inspector. He died of a heart attack in September 1951 while on vacation in Salt Lake City.[34]

19

The Prime Suspects

A week after the murder, while the coroner's jury was still at work, Clifford Cook made a stunning announcement to reporters outside the hearing room. He said Myrtle Cook whispered the name of her killer with her dying breath and that his mother, Mrs. S. W. Cook, had heard the name. Clifford refused to repeat the name, but he did say the killer was a young man and a member of a "prominent" Vinton family. Mrs. S. W. Cook told reporters that she would wait until after the sheriff had had time to investigate the allegation before she would reveal the name publicly.[1]

The name of the local youth was never reported, probably because Sheriff Ruhl dismissed the accusations out of hand. He told reporters that the family mentioned was "above reproach" and that it was a waste of his time to investigate the young man. The prosecution team's sole focus was on Clifford Cook; there was no room to consider anyone else.[2]

There was, however, one young man who came from a prominent family and had connections to both Myrtle Cook and the Vinton liquor trade, Louis Gilchrist. His older brother, Joe, owned the Palace Café next to the train station and was almost certainly a partner in Wayne "Shorty" Snader's bootlegging operation.[3] Louis Gilchrist was also among the boys convicted of defacing the Cook home with rotten eggs the previous July and, therefore, probably one of Snader's customers. Louis Gilchrist was also tall—five feet ten inches—which was a suspected trait of the killer because of the angle of the fatal shot.[4]

Harold James Ponder was born into a poor farm family in Jasper County, Iowa, in 1900. Little is known about his childhood, but at age eighteen, in September 1918, he registered for the draft. It is unlikely that he ever served because just a few weeks after filling out his papers, Ponder was spending his days and nights in the Benton County jail.

This particular stretch in stir was made noteworthy by the *Cedar Rapids Gazette* when Sheriff Ruhl temporarily released Ponder from his cell so that he could marry Miss Bessie Terhoon of Vinton. The wedding was officiated by Reverend F. M. Goff. According to the *Gazette*, Ponder had been arrested the week before on undisclosed charges made by Miss Terhoon.[5]

Ponder's first prison term came in October 1919 after he was convicted of larceny in Jasper County. He was sentenced to Anamosa Prison for five years and was paroled in 1921. A second conviction came in 1923, this time for receiving stolen property, and he was sent to do a harder five-year term at Fort Madison.[6] In August 1925, one month before the Cook murder, Ponder had been assigned to a trustee work detail outside the prison walls. When the guards weren't watching, Ponder simply walked away. He was seen in Vinton on the day of the murder of Myrtle Cook. He was driving a Buick, believed to have been stolen, which he later ditched near Des Moines. After that, the trail went cold.

Despite eyewitnesses who placed Ponder in Vinton on the morning of the murder and corroborated his long association with bootleggers and the criminal underworld, Ponder was not pursued by either Sheriff Ruhl or the state agents. It wasn't until November 3, three weeks after the murder and after the case against Clifford Cook had imploded, that the investigators began to look seriously for the escaped convict.[7]

He wasn't hard to find. Benton County Attorney J. D. Nichols found friends of Ponder who said that he was using an alias, Jean Commeaux, and was working on a stock ranch in Laramie, Wyoming. Six days after Ponder was identified as a suspect in the Cook murder, he was arrested and extradited to Iowa.[8] On November 16 T. P. Hollowell, warden at Fort Madison, told the *Associated Press* that he had aggressively interrogated Ponder about the Cook murder and had come to the conclusion that he had nothing to do with it.[9]

Ponder died of pneumonia the following spring in the prison hospital.[10]

Albert Hertske, Malcolm Harbour, and Eugene Moore were once partners in a rumrunning operation that brought booze into Iowa from Illinois. All three had fought in the war and had come home to find that their military skills translated nicely into the dangerous new business of bootlegging.[11] The partnership, however, didn't last too long. In December 1923 there was a falling out between Hertske and Harbour that made them archenemies.

Harbour was on his way back to Waterloo after picking up a load of alcohol he had bought in Clinton from three members of Hertske's gang. It was around two in the morning, and Harbour, who had a growing reputation for violence, was alone on the road. Just as he got outside of town, he noticed he was being tailed, so he gunned his new Cadillac sedan to over fifty miles per hour. Then shots rang out from the pursuing car; one of the bullets pierced the gas tank of Harbour's car and eventually caused the engine to stall. The three men who had sold him the booze jumped from the other car. One of them smashed Harbour in the back of the head with the butt of a gun. When Harbour regained consciousness, his Caddie was gone and so was the liquor. The cops found Harbour dazed but believed his story enough to arrest the three highwaymen.[12]

In May 1925 Harbour was again victimized by Hertske when federal agents arrested him and another man at a remote farmhouse just outside Waterloo. The feds told reporters that they had received a tip that Harbour had whiskey and guns. They found both.[13] Harbour strongly suspected that Hertske was the source who had tipped off the feds. The practice was not uncommon and usually revolved around one bootlegger informing on his competition to benefit his own business. Indeed, years later, during a 1927 divorce trial, a former county attorney in Black Hawk County testified that Hertske worked as an "undercover man" during the mid-1920s for prohibition agents.[14]

There was bad blood between Harbour and Eugene Moore as well. A report in the *Des Moines Register* in December 1925 told of an undated incident in which Harbour robbed Moore of a carload of whiskey that Moore was bringing down from Chicago to Waterloo. "Harbour took the transfer then at the point of a gun; he told Moore to move on," the *Register* said. "That night their relations ceased."[15]

The conflict between Harbour and Hertske came to a violent and bloody end on the night of September 18, 1925—just eleven days after the murder of Myrtle Cook. Both men were in Waterloo. Hertske and an associate named Jack Corey noticed a Cadillac sedan that they thought might belong to Harbour was parked outside a downtown café.

Hertske and Corey checked out the car hoping to find booze but were disappointed. On their way back to Corey's Chevrolet, Harbour and two of his friends pulled up in another car and jumped Hertske on the street. They hit him several times with the butts of their guns, and then Harbour stuck his pistol into the side of Hertske's neck and killed him with one shot. The killers piled back into the other car and fled.

The next day, Corey told reporters the real reason Harbour killed Hertske: it was because Hertske "knew too much about the Cook murder."[16]

Almost immediately, Sheriff Ruhl rejected the notion that a gangster from Waterloo had anything to do with the Vinton crime. "The connection between the two murders was very far-fetched and exceedingly unlikely," Ruhl said.[17]

Once again, the investigators were single-mindedly focused on Clifford Cook. But even after the prosecutors dropped their case against him, there is no record of Ruhl or Atkins chasing down any links between Harbour, Hertske, and Myrtle Cook.

20

Who Killed Mrs. Cook?

Clifford Cook didn't do it.

Historically, homicide by an intimate partner is one of the leading causes of premature death among women. One of the most common motivations is that the husband wants to marry another woman.[1] Score two in favor of Clifford Cook being the killer, which was why the two investigators who knew the case best were both convinced he either did the deed himself or hired the killer. Yet, on balance, there are more reasons to believe he didn't do it. One of the strongest is the absence of any record of Clifford Cook committing a violent act during his life. For a man to use a gun to kill his wife suggests that he had done something similar before or would again at a later time. Nothing in Clifford Cook's life even remotely hints at violence. Of course, this fact doesn't exclude him thoroughly, but it does point to exoneration.

A second reason to believe in Clifford Cook's innocence is that the people who knew him best didn't believe he committed the murder. No one in Myrtle's family accused him, even as the sheriff and the state investigators all but publicly charged him. The members of the coroner's jury didn't either. Some of the jurors were men who might have known Clifford or certainly knew people who did. And after all the witnesses had testified, after the prosecution team had chased down every lead and pressed as hard as they legally could for a confession—the jury said no, releasing a statement that they could not issue a verdict against Clifford Cook.[2]

Finally, the question of motive must be examined. Clifford Cook was in an unhappy marriage, and he had found love with another woman. He didn't need to kill his wife to be with the other woman. He was already enjoying what appeared to be an intimate relationship with the younger, prettier Hester Seiling. Myrtle Cook wasn't an issue.

It could be argued that Myrtle Cook's refusal to give her husband a divorce might be motive enough for him to kill her. Perhaps. But, once again, her husband's temperament and character would come into play: Was he the sort of man who could have killed in cold blood? The record speaks against that. Besides, the far more common and more available option was simply to abandon his marriage. Desertion was one of the most common grounds for divorce during the mid-1920s. People up and left each other all the time, men especially.[3]

Thus, if Clifford Cook did not kill his wife, who did?

Louis Gilchrist didn't do it.

Ruhl was probably right not to spend time looking more closely at Louis Gilchrist. He had served honorably in the navy during the war and later had a productive, even prominent career as a chef working at some of the best hotels in the Midwest, including the Roosevelt in Cedar Rapids and the Ambassador in Milwaukee.

Louis Gilchrist spent the last twenty years of his career at the Terre Haute House in Terre Haute, Indiana. Interestingly, the hotel was located in the center of the city's red-light district and was rumored to be a favorite overnight resting place for John Dillinger. There is no record of Louis R. Gilchrist breaking the law or behaving violently.

However, there is one other piece of evidence to consider. One of the few surviving documents retained in the Cook murder file, still held by the Iowa Department of Public Safety, is a handwritten note, undated and unsigned, with a faint date stamp of the state investigative unit. The handwriting is similar to that of Agent Atkins. There are phrases and random sentences that suggest that the author was probably talking to a witness, maybe over the phone, scribbling away and trying to keep up. One clear entry reflects an attempt by the witness to link Clifford Cook with the bootleggers of the town. "Dick Gilcrest was a great friend of Clifford Cook," the author wrote. "His son Joe Gilcrest runs the lunchroom. Gilcrest is a bootlegger and a bad all-around fellow."

Another entry reads: "Mrs. Gilcrest, wife of Joe Gilcrest, was up angry at Mrs. Cook, saying that Mrs. Cook had said her husband Joe Gilcrest was bootlegging at the lunch counter."

At the bottom of the page, under all the other notes, is the name of Myrtle's youngest brother, W. R. Underwood. It's not inconceivable that Agent Atkins was interviewing William Ray Underwood, who was probably trying to make the case that someone in the Gilchrist family, probably Louis, killed Myrtle as a favor to Clifford Cook. No doubt, Agent Atkins listened to Underwood and took some notes, but that was it. There was nothing to go on.[4]

Harold Ponder didn't do it.

Although Ponder was never arrested or charged with the Cook murder, there was a widely held belief that he committed the crime. Judge Tobin, who represented Clifford Cook while he was being investigated for the murder and dedicated a chapter in his memoirs to the Cook murder, was completely convinced of Ponder's guilt. "He was regarded generally as 'one of those fellows who could easily be persuaded to commit any crime, no matter how bad,'" Tobin wrote, adding that Ponder was someone who "would be willing to commit murder for ten or fifteen dollars." Tobin called Ponder a "lamebrain," a "dingbat," and a "blabbermouth."[5]

Absent from the judge's memoir, however, was any evidence linking Ponder to the crime.

Myrtle Cook's killer was most likely an assassin hired by a mob boss or by a high-ranking member of a liquor gang. The triggering event for her murder wasn't that she had merely witnessed an illegal transaction. No one involved in the liquor trade would have cared about a misdemeanor violation—certainly no one who ran with the mobs in Waterloo and Chicago. What made it necessary to kill Myrtle Cook was *whom* she had seen.

A real gangster, someone like Malcolm Harbour, who was experienced in high-pressure gun play and in evading the law, would not have become too excited about anything that Myrtle Cook might have seen. This sort of criminal would have no fear of Sheriff Ruhl or even of the state agents. But what might give him pause is if Myrtle Cook saw something that would put him in jeopardy with other mobsters.

Myrtle Cook's role as an informant was well known to the bootleggers of Vinton. If a report she was ready to make to the authorities also placed a high-ranking gang member at a location that violated a territorial agreement with another gang, that could be a problem. Under such circumstances, the decision to silence Myrtle Cook would be mandatory, even rational.

Malcolm Harbour best fits the role of the trigger man. Two facts argue most strongly for his guilt: he was a violent killer, and he conducted his business in and around Waterloo, which, according to testimony during the Cook murder inquest, was the source of most of the illegal liquor coming into Vinton at the time of the Cook murder.

Another clue comes from Jack Corey, Hertske's lieutenant, who insisted that his friend was killed because "he knew too much" about the Cook murder. Corey lived in Benton County at one point, specifically in La Porte City.[6] This was also home to Wayne "Shorty" Snader, the bootlegger that Myrtle Cook turned in to the sheriff in June 1925. It seems unlikely that Corey and Snader, both in the illegal booze business, did not know each other, and it is very likely that Snader got some of his product from Corey.

What's more, Harbour's former colleague Eugene Moore had ties to Benton County. In March 1924 Moore was a prime suspect in the murder and robbery of a successful automobile dealer named Ethel Collicott. Collicott, curiously, was born and raised in Vinton, but at the time of his murder, he was living in Davenport.[7]

There is one additional suspect to consider—it's a long shot but too intriguing not to mention.

Lincoln Highway opened in 1913 and passed through the Benton County towns of Belle Plaine and Tama—both not far from Vinton, where the murder took place. The highway also bisected Cedar Rapids, about thirty miles southeast of Vinton.

Service stations, cafés, and hotels sprang up along the route to accommodate the traveling public. One of these establishments was the Lighthouse Supper Club, located on the outskirts of Cedar Rapids. In the 1920s the Lighthouse was known to serve booze along with steaks and fried chicken, and it offered a jazz combo for dancing on the weekends. The club was apparently a favorite among the bootleggers, including one from Chicago who was known to travel for business on the Lincoln Highway between his home and his interests in Omaha. His name? Alphonse Capone.

"I was at the Lighthouse back in '24 or '25," Theodore "Muggsy" Davis, seventy-seven, told the *Cedar Rapids Gazette* in 1981. "My girlfriend and I were eating chicken. I had some alcohol in my pocket, and this big, well-dressed guy with diamonds and a couple of big bodyguards walks in the place. I didn't know who the hell he was. Anyway, I asked him if he wanted a drink," Davis recalled. "He says sure, so I pour some drinks, and he throws a $10 bill down. I said, 'I don't want no money,' but he makes me take it, and the three of them down their drinks. After they left, somebody asked me if I knew who the guy was. He says, 'That was Al Capone.' I felt like a damn monkey. Here I was givin' a drink to Al Capone."[8]

Notes

INTRODUCTION

1. "Shenandoah Wrecked in Ohio Storm," *New York Times*, September 4, 1925; "Youth of 20 Kidnapped and Killed Girl," *New York Times*, September 4, 1925.
2. "Woman Dry Worker Murdered in Iowa," *New York Times*, September 9, 1925.
3. "Woman Dry Worker Murdered in Iowa."
4. "Woman Dry Worker Murdered in Iowa."
5. Rachel Gallegos, "Roads, Power Fall Victim to Winter Mix," *Iowa City Press Citizen*, December 2, 2008.
6. Terry McCoy, "Powerless," *Cedar Rapids Gazette*, December 13, 2007.
7. Dick Johnson, "Storm Disrupts Iowa Traffic, Causes Accidents," Associated Press, December 24, 2007.
8. "City Seeks Federal Aid for Ice Storm Expenses," *Cedar Rapids Gazette*, January 10, 2008.
9. Rob Daniel, "Here We Snow Again," *Iowa City Press Citizen*, February 5, 2008.
10. "Flooding Will Get Worse," *Cedar Rapids Gazette*, June 9, 2008.
11. Robert C. Buchmiller and David A. Eash, *Floods of May and June 2008 in Iowa* (Reston VA: U.S. Geological Survey, 2010), https://pubs.usgs.gov/of/2010/1096/pdf/OFR2010-1096.pdf.
12. Adam Belz, "Vinton Braces for Crest," *Cedar Rapids Gazette*, June 10, 2008; David Thompson interview by author, October 26, 2022.
13. David Thompson interview.

1. THE HAWKEYES FROM DIXIE

1. John C. Parish, "Robert Lucas," in *Iowa Biological Series*, ed. Benjamin F. Shampbaugh (Des Moines: Iowa State Historical Society, 1907), 151–53.
2. Parish, "Robert Lucas," 356.
3. Lord Acton Richard, "High Noon in Territorial Iowa," *Des Moines Register*, October 27, 1992; Lord Acton Richard, "We Could Be Yelling, 'Go

Hairy Nation,'" *Des Moines Register*, December 30, 1990. Rorer's choice of "Hawkeye" as the nickname for Iowans was based on the character of the same name in James Fenimore Cooper's *The Last of the Mohicans.*

4. *Journal of the Council* (Territory of Iowa, November 12, 1838).
5. *Journal of the Council.*
6. David Brodnax, "Breathing the Freedom's Air: The African-American Struggle for Equal Citizenship in Iowa, 1830–1900" (PhD diss., Northwestern University, 2007).
7. F. I. Herriott, "The Transfusion of Political Ideas and Institutions in Iowa," *Annals of Iowa* 6, no. 1 (1903): 46–54.
8. *The Statute Laws of the Territory of Iowa* (Dubuque IA: Russell & Reeves, 1839), 3.
9. Christopher P. Lehman, *Slavery in the Upper Mississippi Valley, 1787–1865* (Jefferson NC: McFarland, 2011).
10. Parish, "Robert Lucas."
11. Lehman, *Slavery in the Upper Mississippi Valley*; see also *Washington Post* database on members of Congress who owned slaves, https://www.washingtonpost.com/history/interactive/2022/congress-slaveowners-names-list/.
12. "Markets Abroad and at Home," *Keokuk Daily Gate*, May 18, 1855.
13. "Josiah Bushnell Grinnell," *The Biographical Dictionary of Iowa* (Iowa City: University of Iowa Press and the University of Iowa Libraries), http://uipress.lib.uiowa.edu/bdi/DetailsPagc.aspx?id=146.
14. "Ralph Montgomery," *The Goldfinch* 16, no. 4 (Summer 1995): 7.
15. "Mason, John," *The Biographical Dictionary of Iowa* (Iowa City: University of Iowa Press and the University of Iowa Libraries), http://uipress.lib.uiowa.edu/bdi/DetailsPage.aspx?id=253.
16. Henry Peterson, "First Decision Rendered by the Supreme Court of Iowa," *Annals of Iowa* 34 (Spring 1958): 304–7.
17. Richard, "High Noon in Territorial Iowa."
18. Peterson, "First Decision Rendered," 304–7.
19. "Iowa Supreme Court's First Case Freed a Slave," *Waterloo Courier*, February 1, 2015.
20. Robert Dykstra, "Iowa and the Politics of Race," in *Iowa History Reader*, ed. U. Bergman (Iowa City: University of Iowa Press, 1996), 129.
21. J. Sibley, "Proslavery Sentiment in Iowa, 1838–1861," *Iowa Journal of History* 55 (Winter 1957): 289–318.
22. Dykstra, "Iowa and the Politics of Race," 131; F. I. Herriott, *A Neglected Factor in the Anti-Slavery Triumph in Iowa in 1854* (London: Forgotten Books, 2018).

23. Dan Elbert Clark, "The History of Liquor Legislation in Iowa, 1846–1861," *Iowa Journal of History and Politics* 6, no. 3 (1908): 62.
24. "Cadets of Temperance," *Burlington Hawk-Eye,* January 18, 1849; "Celebration of 22nd," *Davenport Weekly Gazette,* February 17, 1848; "Rail Road Intelligence," *Weekly Miners Express,* November 6, 1850.
25. Clark, "The History of Liquor Legislation in Iowa," 70.
26. Jack S. Blocker Jr., *American Temperance Movements: Cycles of Reform* (Boston: Twayne, 1989), 55–58.
27. Clark, "The History of Liquor Legislation in Iowa," 56–83.
28. Clark, "The History of Liquor Legislation in Iowa," 56–83.
29. Clark, "The History of Liquor Legislation in Iowa," 56–83.
30. Senator George McCoy, *Iowa Official Register* (Des Moines: State Historical Society of Iowa).
31. Stow Persons, *The University of Iowa in the Twentieth Century: An Institutional History* (Iowa City: University of Iowa Press, 1990), 1.
32. Roger Acton, "The Magic of Undiscovered Effort: The Death Penalty in Early Iowa, 1838–1878," *Annals of Iowa* 7 (Winter 1991): 721–50.
33. W. I. Toussaint, "Charles Mason's Influence on Iowa Jurisprudence," *Annals of Iowa* 39, no. 5 (1968): 372–87.
34. Acton, "The Magic of Undiscovered Effort."

2. THE BRIDGE AT DAVENPORT

1. Dave Hubler, "Des Moines River Navigation; Great Expectations Unfulfilled," *Annals of Iowa* 39, no. 4 (1968): 287–306.
2. Hubler, "Des Moines River Navigation," 287–306.
3. "Commercial," *New York Evening Post,* December 29, 1848.
4. R. J. Glass, "Early Transportation and the Plank Road," *Annals of Iowa* 21, no. 7 (1939): 502–34.
5. Lewis F. Thomas, "Decline of St. Louis as Midwest Metropolis," *Economic Geography* 25, no. 2 (1949): 118–27, https://doi.org/10.2307/141215.
6. Thomas, "Decline of St. Louis as Midwest Metropolis," 118–27; William L. Downard, "William Butler Ogden and the Growth of Chicago," *Journal of the Illinois State Historical Society (1908–1984)* 75, no. 1 (1982): 47–60.
7. Roger H. Grant, *A Mighty Fine Road: A History of the Chicago, Rock Island & Pacific Railroad Company* (Bloomington: Indiana University Press, 1943), 1–55.
8. Stephen E. Ambrose, *Nothing Like It in the World* (New York: Simon & Schuster, 2001), 31–32.
9. David A. Pfeiffer, "Lincoln for the Defense: Railroads, Steamboats and the Rock Island Bridge," *Railroad History* 200 (2009): 48–55.

10. Grant, *A Mighty Fine Road,* 1–55; Ambrose, *Nothing Like It in the World,* 31.
11. Monetary value comparisons provided by measuringwealth.com/index.php.
12. "Taking the Other Side," *Nashville Republican Banner,* March 13, 1857.
13. Pfeiffer, "Lincoln for the Defense," 48–55.
14. Ambrose, *Nothing Like It in the World,* 7–31.
15. Iowa Census 1850, 1860.
16. Hildegard Binder Johnson, *German Forty-Eighters in Davenport* (Des Moines: Iowa State Historical Society, 1998).
17. Helmut Walser Smith, *Germany: A Nation in Its Time* (New York: Liveright, 2020): 219–23.
18. State of Iowa, *Settlement and Early Agriculture in the Upper Mississippi River Basin* (Iowa City: Soil Conservation District, 1970).
19. John Arkas Hawgood, *The Tragedy of German-America* (New York: G. P. Putnam's Sons, 1940), 43.
20. G. Ehrstine and L. Gibbs, "Iowa's Prohibition Plague: Joseph Eiboeck's Account of the Battle over Prohibition, 1846–1900," *Annals of Iowa* 78, no. 1 (2019): 1–74.
21. "A. F. Brown, James R. Hartsock, and James W. McDill," *Annals of Iowa* (Des Moines: State Historical Society of Iowa, 1894), 422–24.
22. "Meeting against the Maine Temperance Law," *Davenport Democratic Banner,* February 20, 1852.
23. Hawgood, *The Tragedy of German-America,* 250–55.
24. Bruce Levine, "The Vital Element of the Republican Party: Antislavery, Nativism, and Abraham Lincoln," *Journal of the Civil War Era* 1, no. 4 (2011): 481–505; Hawgood, *The Tragedy of German-America,* 250–55.
25. Louis Pelzer, "August Caesar Dodge: A Study in American Politics" (PhD diss., University of Iowa, 1909).
26. "Dodge, Augustus Caesar," *The Biographical Dictionary of Iowa* (Iowa City: University of Iowa Press and the University of Iowa Libraries), http://uipress.lib.uiowa.edu/bdi/DetailsPage.aspx?id=97.
27. "Early Iowa Senator," *Sioux City Journal,* November 24, 1883.
28. Herriott, *A Neglected Factor.*
29. Lowell J. Soike, *Necessary Courage: Iowa's Underground Railroad in the Struggle against Slavery* (Iowa City: University of Iowa Press), 78, Kindle.
30. David S. Reynolds, *John Brown, Abolitionist* (New York: Alfred A. Knopf, 2005), 207.
31. Robert R. Dykstra, *Bright Radical Star* (Ames: Iowa State University Press, 1993), 139.
32. David L. Bristow, "Lane's Army," *The Iowan,* Summer 1997, https://davidbristow.com/articles/lanes-army/.

33. Pauline Graham, "The Coppoc Boys," *The Palimpsest,* November 1928, 385–91; "War! War! War!" *Keokuk Daily Gate,* July 29, 1856; "John Brown and His Bloody Crusade," *Des Moines Register,* March 17, 1946.
34. Leland L. Sage, *A History of Iowa* (Ames: Iowa State University Press, 1974), 164.
35. "Alexander Clark," *The Biographical Dictionary of Iowa* (Iowa City: University of Iowa Press and the University of Iowa Libraries), https://uipress.lib.uiowa.edu/bdi/DetailsPage.aspx?id=62.
36. "Alexander Clark," *The Goldfinch* 16, no. 4 (Summer 1995): 6.
37. Steve J. Frese, "From Emancipation to Equality: Alexander Clark's Stand for Civil Rights in Iowa," Marshalltown High School, Senior Division Historical Paper, National History Day 2006 Competition.
38. Frese, "From Emancipation to Equality."
39. "Clark," *Biographical Dictionary of Iowa;* Earl Martin et al., "Clark v. Board of School Directors: Reflections after 150 Years," *Drake Law Review* 67, https://drakelawreview.org/wp-content/uploads/2019/06/clark-reflections-consolidated.pdf.
40. Brodnax, "Breathing the Freedom's Air."
41. "Iowa Items," *Des Moines Register,* February 10, 1874.
42. Myrtle Beinhauer, "Development of the Grange in Iowa, 1868–1930," *Annals of Iowa* 34, no. 8 (1959): 597–618.
43. John Lauritz Larson, "Iowa's Struggle for State Railroad Control," in *Iowa History Reader,* ed. Marvin Bergman (Des Moines: University of Iowa Press, 1996), 197–240; Sage, *A History of Iowa,* 190.
44. Frank H. Dixon, "State Railroad Control," in *Library of Economics and Politics,* ed. Richard T. Ely (New York: Thomas Y. Crowell, 1898), 27–30; Beinhauer, "Development of the Grange in Iowa."

3. THE WITCHES OF TEMPERANCE

1. George Westly Sieber, *Lumbermen at Clinton: Nineteenth Century Sawmill Center* (Madison: Wisconsin State University, 1971); Linda Barr, "Lumber Made Clinton Rich" *Quad-City Times* (Davenport IA), March 30, 1986.
2. David C. Mott, "Judith Ellen Foster," *Annals of Iowa* 19 (1933): 126–38.
3. "Timeline: History of the Des Moines Register," *Des Moines Register,* April 13, 2018; "Iowa Items," *Des Moines Register,* September 30, 1874.
4. "A Card," *Times Herald* (Port Huron MI), December 11, 1875.
5. "The Brattleboro Plan," *Burlington (vt) Weekly Free Press,* July 4, 1877.
6. Mott, "Judith Ellen Foster," 126–38.
7. "Iowa Items," *Sioux City Journal,* September 27, 1874.
8. Clark, "The History of Liquor Legislation in Iowa, 1878–1908," 85.

9. J. Ellen Foster, *Constitutional Amendment Manual* (New York: National Temperance Society, 1888), 37.
10. Sarah Boyle, "Creating a Union of the Union: The Woman's Christian Temperance Union 1880–1892" (PhD diss., State University of New York at Binghamton, 2005).
11. Mott, "Judith Ellen Foster," 126–38.
12. WCTU, *Proceedings of Annual Meetings* (1878).
13. Foster (b), *Constitutional Amendment Manual*, 47.
14. G. Ehrstine and L. Gibbs, "Iowa's Prohibition Plague: Joseph Eiboeck's Account of the Battle over Prohibition, 1846–1900," *Annals of Iowa* 78, no. 1 (2019): 1–74; "Clayton County Journal," *North Iowa Times*, May 12, 1858.
15. Ehrstine and Gibbs, "Iowa's Prohibition Plague," 1–74.
16. Ehrstine and Gibbs, "Iowa's Prohibition Plague," 1–74.
17. "Villainous Liar Exposed," *Des Moines Register*, August 1, 1874.
18. Ehrstine and Gibbs, "Iowa's Prohibition Plague," 1–74.
19. James Harfield Timberlake, *Prohibition and the Progressive Movement 1900–1920* (Cambridge, MA: Harvard University Press, 1966); Thomas R. Pegram, *Battling Demon Rum* (Chicago: Ivan R. Dee Publisher, 1998), 7; "General Items," *Des Moines Register*, April 28, 1874.
20. Ehrstine and Gibbs, "Iowa's Prohibition Plague," 1–74.
21. Foster (a), *Constitutional Amendment Manual*, 6.
22. "'Barber Brothers'—Notorious Outlaws of the 1880s," *Fayette County Leader*, December 25, 1975.
23. "Supposed Arrest of the Barber Brothers," *Davenport Morning Democrat*, September 15, 1882; "The Barber Brothers," *Muscatine Journal*, June 5, 1883.
24. Michael James Pfeifer, "Lynching and Criminal Justice in Regional Context: Iowa, Wyoming and Louisiana, 1878–1946" (PhD diss., University of Iowa, 1998).
25. Michael J. Pfeifer, "Law, Society, and Violence in the Antebellum Midwest: The 1857 Eastern Iowa Vigilante Movement," *Annals of Iowa* 64, no. 2 (2005): 139–66.
26. "Two Horse Thieves Hung," *St. Charles City Republican*, January 19, 1860.
27. "The Last Man Lynched," *Des Moines Register*, August 20, 1887.
28. Roger Acton, "The Magic of Undiscovered Effort: The Death Penalty in Early Iowa, 1838–1878," *Annals of Iowa* 7 (Winter 1991).
29. "Four Murders in Three Years," *Des Moines Register*, June 17, 1874.
30. "Murder Will Out," *Des Moines Register*, December 15, 1874; "Mob Law," *Des Moines Register*, December 15, 1874.
31. Acton, "The Magic of Undiscovered Effort."

32. Pfeifer, "Lynching and Criminal Justice in Regional Context."
33. "Mob or Magistrate," *Des Moines Register*, April 23, 1887.
34. State of Iowa, *Journal of the Senate of the Twelfth General Assembly*, January 13, 1868.
35. "Editorial News Items," *Waterloo Courier*, April 10, 1873.
36. "State Items," *Quad-City Times* (Davenport IA), June 13, 1873.
37. Richard Snavely and Steve Wendl, *Anamosa Penitentiary* (Mt. Pleasant SC: Arcadia Publishing Library Editions, 2010).
38. Joyce McKay, "Reforming Prisoners and Prisons: Iowa's State Prisons—The First Hundred Years," *Annals of Iowa* 60, no. 2 (Spring 2001): 139–73.
39. Snavely and Wendl, *Anamosa Penitentiary*; "She May Be Hanged," *Cedar Rapids Gazette*, June 19, 1894.
40. P. L. Bryan, "John Wesley Elkins, Boy Murderer, and His Struggle for Pardon," *Annals of Iowa* 69, no. 3 (2010): 261–307.
41. "Boy Who Killed Father Freed from 'Pen,'" *Ottumwa Semi-Weekly Courier*, April 22, 1902.
42. "Boy Who Killed Father Freed from 'Pen.'"
43. Bryan, "John Wesley Elkins, Boy Murderer."

4. SCHOOLHOUSE ON EVERY HILLTOP

1. Clark, "The History of Liquor Legislation in Iowa, 1878–1908," 508–9.
2. "Historical Tables of the Iowa Legislature, 1838–2022," State of Iowa, https://www.legis.iowa.gov/legislators/legisInfo/historicalLegislatureTables.
3. State of Iowa, *Acts and Resolutions Passed at the Regular Session of the 18th General Assembly, January 12 to March 27, 1880* (Des Moines: F. M. Mills, 1880), https://www.legis.iowa.gov/docs/publications/iactc/18.1/1880_Iowa_Acts.pdf.
4. G. Ehrstine and L. Gibbs, "Iowa's Prohibition Plague: Joseph Eiboeck's Account of the Battle over Prohibition, 1846–1900," *Annals of Iowa* 78, no. 1 (2019): 1–74.
5. "Beer Brewers," *Muscatine Weekly Journal*, April 15, 1881.
6. "A Brief Lecture for Des Moines," *Sioux City Journal*, May 20, 1881.
7. "The Amendment and Property Rights," *Muscatine Weekly Journal*, September 9, 1881.
8. J. Ellen Foster (b), *Constitutional Amendment Manual* (New York: National Temperance Society and Publishing House, 1888), 46.
9. "Nothing New about Distilleries in D. M.," *Des Moines Register*, November 19, 2006.
10. "The Proposed Amendment," *Muscatine Journal*, March 20, 1882.
11. Clark, "The History of Liquor Legislation in Iowa, 1878–1908," 517.

12. "A Rushing Plot," *Quad-City Times* (Davenport IA), January 8, 1882.
13. Clark, "The History of Liquor Legislation in Iowa, 1878–1908," 520–29
14. Trumbull White, "Does Prohibition Pay? III. The Test of a State that Recanted," *Appleton's Magazine*, 12, (July–December 1908): 343–50.
15. "A Hurricane Struck Omaha," *Sioux City Journal*, June 27, 1882.
16. "The murder of Rev. W.M. Todd," *Muscatine Weekly Journal*, March 12, 1880.
17. The amendment passed by a margin of only 30,000 votes out of the 281,113 cast. Clark, "The History of Liquor Legislation in Iowa, 1878–1908," 525.
18 Mark Twain, *Life on the Mississippi* (Boston: Osgood and Company, 1883).
19. "Par nobile fratrum," *Anthony Kansas Journal*, November 3, 1881.
20. "The Liquor Law," *Leavenworth Standard*, February 9, 1882.
21. "Another Snag," *Burlington Weekly Hawk-Eye*, March 2, 1882.
22. "The Amendment," *Davenport Democrat*, March 3, 1882.
23. "From the Best Intentions," *Davenport Democrat*, May 20, 1882.
24. "Walter I. Hayes," *Annals of Iowa* 5 (1901): 76–77.
25. "Cowardly Cur," *Muscatine Weekly Journal*, October 15, 1886.
26. Clark, "The History of Liquor Legislation in Iowa, 1878–1908," 529.
27. Leland L. Sage, *A History of Iowa* (Ames, IA: Iowa State University Press, 1974), 204.
28. "Vive La Gambrinus," *Des Moines Register*, January 28, 1883.
29. "One of the Clerks Speaks," *Des Moines Register*, January 31, 1883.
30. "The Davenport Hypocritic," *Des Moines Register*, January 30, 1883.
31. "Items in Brief," *Quad-City Times* (Davenport IA), January 26, 1883; "Keep the Flag Flying," *Des Moines Register*, January 26, 1883.
32. "About Iowa Taxes," *Weekly Davenport Democrat*, December 21, 1877.
33. "Some Improvident Town," *Des Moines Register*, January 27, 1886.

5. THE MARTYR OF SIOUX CITY

1. Clark, "The History of Liquor Legislation in Iowa, 1846–1861," 552.
2. "Tilden Will Follow Hendricks," *Sioux City Journal*, June 6, 1877; "'Gath' Says the Letting," *Quad-City Times* (Davenport IA), August 5, 1881.
3. *Journal of the Senate*, January 9, 1882 (Des Moines: State of Iowa), 34.
4. "Senate File Number One," *La Porte City Progress-Review*, January 31, 1884.
5. Clark, "The History of Liquor Legislation in Iowa, 1846–1861," 543.
6. Clark, "The History of Liquor Legislation in Iowa, 1846–1861," 540.
7. Gregg Hennigan, "Beer and Bloodshed," *Cedar Rapids Gazette*, August 10, 2014.
8. Clark, "The History of Liquor Legislation in Iowa," 550.
9. Clark, "The History of Liquor Legislation in Iowa," 541.

10. Randy Carlson, *The Breweries of Iowa* (Bemidji MN: Randy Carlson, 1985).
11. G. Ehrstine and L. Gibbs, "Iowa's Prohibition Plague: Joseph Eiboeck's Account of the Battle over Prohibition, 1846–1900," *Annals of Iowa* 78, no. 1 (2019): 55–61.
12. "A Scared Lawyer," *Sioux City Journal*, April 23, 1886.
13. Leisy v. Hardin, 1459 U.S. October 1889.
14. "Father of Sioux City Was a Man of Many and Varied Talents," *Sioux City Journal*, July 25, 1954; William Silag, "Sioux City: An Iowa Boom Town," *Annals of Iowa* 44, no. 8 (1979): 587–601.
15. "Close of an Eventful Life," *Sioux City Journal*, December 27, 1893; D. Spence Lewis, "Memories of Leaders in Early Day Realty Development Here," *Sioux City Journal*, May 7, 1939.
16. Silag, "Sioux City," 587–601.
17. Silag, "Sioux City," 587–601.
18. Iowa Census, 1890.
19. William Silag, "Gateway to the Grasslands: Sioux City and the Missouri River Frontier," *Western Historical Quarterly* 14, no. 4 (1983): 397–414; Tammie Adams, *Road to Garnet's Gold* (Denver: Bureau of Land Management, 2021), 35.
20. W. L. Hewitt, "Wicked Traffic in Girls: Prostitution and Reform in Sioux City, 1885–1910," *Annals of Iowa* 51, no. 2 (1991): 123–48; "Murder of Saloon-Fighting Pastor, City's Most Infamous Crime," *Sioux City Journal*, July 25, 1954.
21. "The Lower Depths," *Sioux City Journal*, June 29, 1888. The spelling "Soudan" was the most common usage for the central African nation now known as Sudan.
22. "In General," *Sioux City Journal*, May 11, 1886.
23. "Items from Exchanges," *Sioux City Journal*, May 20, 1886.
24. Hewitt, "Wicked Traffic in Girls," 123–48; "In General."
25. Matthew A. Max, "The Prohibition War: Murder in Sioux City," *Wild West Magazine* (Leesburg VA), October 1998, 28.
26. Frank C. Haddock, *The Life of George C. Haddock* (New York: Funk & Wagnalls Publishers, 1887); Max, "The Prohibition War," 28.
27. "The Injunction Suits," *Sioux City Journal*, August 4, 1886; Max, "The Prohibition War," 28; "A Pastor's View," *Sioux City Journal*, August 5, 1886; "Thrice-Told Tales," *Sioux City Journal*, November 19, 1887.
28. "Perjury Somewhere," *New York Times*, April 5, 1887.
29. "With Arensdorf's Revolver," *Des Moines Register*, April 19, 1888; "Was There a Murder Committed?" *Chicago Tribune*, June 9, 1888; "Trying to Avenge Arensdorf," *Chicago Tribune*, January 23, 1888.

30. George E. Roberts, *Letters Written by District and Superior Court Judges to the Governor* (Des Moines: Iowa State Printer, 1888).
31. "Lawful Tippling," *Quad-City Times* (Davenport IA), April 30, 1886; Clark, "The History of Liquor Legislation in Iowa," 520.
32. *Illustrated Souvenir of Vinton* (Vinton IA: The Booster Club, n.d.); Iowa Census, 1925.
33. "Vigilantes in Nebraska," *Chicago Tribune*, January 16, 1889.
34. "Y.P.S.E.," *Cedar Rapids Gazette*, June 20, 1890.
35. Ben Markson, "The Old Search Days," *Des Moines Register*, June 8, 1919.
36. "A Fatal Affair," *Des Moines Register*, March 8, 1887; Markson, "The Old Search Days."
37. Duke, *The Career of Frank Pierce* (New York: W. H. Kennedy, 1896).
38. "Frank Pierce Indicted," *Des Moines Register*, April 22, 1888; "Searcher Pierce and His Gun," *Cedar Rapids Gazette*, June 24, 1890; "Des Moines Excited," *Muscatine News-Tribune*, July 2, 1891; "The Pierce Pardon," *Des Moines Register*, November 27, 1896.
39. "Stormy Jordan Passes Away," *Cedar Rapids Gazette*, May 6, 1905.

6. SHARPERS AND SWINDLERS

1. "This Beats Jarndyce," *St. Louis Globe-Democrat*, January 21, 1894.
2. "Drive Wells," *Burlington Hawk-Eye*, December 7, 1878.
3. Earl W. Hayter, "The Patent System and Agrarian Discontent, 1875–1888," *Mississippi Valley Historical Review* 34, no. 1 (June 1947): 59–82.
4. "The Patent System Is a Gross Swindle," *Muscatine Weekly Journal*, December 20, 1878; Hayter, "The Patent System," 59–82.
5. "They Must Pay," *Dwight Field and Range*, July 1, 1887.
6. Frank Thone, "Nature Ramblings: Osage Orange," *Science News-Letter* 16, no. 434 (1929): 66.
7. Joseph M. McFadden, "Monopoly in Barbed Wire: The Formation of the American Steel and Wire Company," *Business History Review* 52, no. 4 (Winter 1978): 465–89.
8. "Piercing," *Quad-City Times* (Davenport IA), December 17, 1880.
9. McFadden, "Monopoly in Barbed Wire," 465–89.
10. "Barbed Wire," *Waterloo Courier*, August 2, 1882.
11. "Albert Baird Cummins," *Annals of Iowa* 15, no. 7 (1927): 552–54.
12. "Little Locals," *Des Moines Register*, January 16, 1883.
13. "Farmers Protection Association," *Des Moines Register*, April 10, 1886.
14. "We Are Still on Deck," advertisement in the *Des Moines Register*, January 29, 1886.

15. McFadden, "Monopoly in Barbed Wire," 465–89.
16. "Ruled by the Ring," *Muscatine Semi-Weekly News Tribune*, August 27, 1897; Leland L. Sage, *A History of Iowa* (Ames: Iowa State University Press, 1974), 206.
17. "Avoid the Man Who Blunders," *Des Moines Register*, October 9, 1885.
18. Sage, *A History of Iowa*, 201. "William Larrabee," *Annals of Iowa* 11, nos. 2–3 (1913): 232–33; "Journalism Extraordinary," *Des Moines Register*, October 16, 1885.
19. "Inauguration Address," *Des Moines Register*, January 15, 1886.
20. "Iowa Legislators Past and Present," State of Iowa, https://www.legis.iowa.gov/legislators/informationOnLegislators/historicalInformation.
21. Sage, *A History of Iowa*, 190.
22. John Lauritz Larson, "Iowa's Struggle for State Railroad Control," in *Iowa History Reader*, ed. Marvin Bergman (Des Moines: University of Iowa Press, 1996).
23. Larson, "Iowa's Struggle for State Railroad Control"; Sage, *A History of Iowa*, 190.
24. *Journal of the Senate of the Twenty-Second General Assembly of the State of Iowa* (Des Moines: Iowa Senate, January 10, 1888).
25. "Governor Larrabee's Messages," *Des Moines Register*, January 17, 1888.
26. Sage, *A History of Iowa*, 206.
27. L. S. Coffin, "Safety Appliances on the Railroads," *Annals of Iowa* 5, no. 8 (January 1903).
28. J. Williams-Searle, "Courting Risk, Disability, Masculinity and Liability on Iowa's Railroads, 1868–1900," *Annals of Iowa* 58, no. 1 (1999): 27–77. Charles H. Clark, "The Railroad Safety Movement in the U.S." (PhD Diss., University of Illinois, 1966).
29. "Accidents to Trainmen," *The Landmark* (White River Junction VT), March 11, 1892.
30. *Muscatine Weekly Journal*, September 9, 1890.
31. "Terrible Accident," *Waterloo Courier*, November 25, 1891.
32. Clark, "The Railroad Safety Movement in the U.S."
33. Robert Graves, "For the Railroad Men," *Atchison Daily Globe*, May 30, 1890.
34. "May Cost Millions," *De Kalb Chronicle*, July 30, 1892.
35. Clark, "The Railroad Safety Movement in the U.S."
36. Williams-Searle, "Courting Risk, Disability, Masculinity and Liability on Iowa's Railroads, 1868–1900."
37. Paul Michel Taillon, "Casey Jones, Better Watch Your Speed!" *Australasian Journal of American Studies* 30, no. 1 (2011): 20–38.

38. Coffin, "Safety Appliances on the Railroads."
39. "The Railroad Commission," *Sioux City Journal*, December 30, 1887; "A Jasper County Man," *Sioux City Journal*, March 30, 1888.
40. Coffin, "Safety Appliances on the Railroads."

7. THE MULCT LAW

1. George E. Roberts, *Letters Written by District and Superior Court Judges to the Governor* (Des Moines: Iowa State Printer, 1888).
2. "Republican Dissenters," *Des Moines Register*, August 20, 1887.
3. "A Revelation," *Cedar Rapids Gazette*, November 26, 1888.
4. "A Review of the Situation," *Cedar Rapids Gazette*, October 19, 1889.
5. "Horace Boies," *The Biographical Dictionary of Iowa* (Iowa City: University of Iowa Press and the University of Iowa Libraries, n.d.), http://uipress.lib.uiowa.edu/bdi/DetailsPage.aspx?id=39.
6. Richard Jenson, "Iowa, Wet or Dry?" in *Iowa History Reader*, ed. Marvin Bergman (Des Moines: University of Iowa Press, 1996), 285.
7. "Some Startling Figures," *Cedar Rapids Gazette*, October 22, 1891.
8. "Convictions in 1890," *Davenport Weekly Republican*, January 10, 1891.
9. Clark, "The History of Liquor Legislation in Iowa, 1878–1908," 587.
10. S. Bailey, "Election Verdict," *Des Moines Register*, November 8, 1891.
11. Clark, "The History of Liquor Legislation in Iowa, 1878–1908," 596.
12. Boyle, "Creating a Union of the Union."
13. "Iowans Walked Out," *Sioux City Journal*, November 13, 1889; "For the Nation's Good," *Sioux City Journal*, November 14, 1889.
14. David C. Mott, "Judith Ellen Foster," *Annals of Iowa* 19 (1933): 126–38.
15. Trumbull White, "Does Prohibition Pay? III. The Test of a State that Recanted," *Appleton's Magazine* 12 (July–December 1908): 343–50.
16. Dorothy Schwieder, *Iowa: The Middle Land* (Ames: Iowa State University Press, 1996), 216.
17. Clark, "The History of Liquor Legislation in Iowa, 1878–1908," 599.
18. Jerry Harrington, "Iowa's Last Liquor Battle: Governor Harold E. Hughes and the Liquor-by-the-Drink Conflict," *Annals of Iowa* 76, no. 1 (2017): 1–46; "Senate Votes for Dry Iowa; House to Follow," *Des Moines Register*, February 13, 1915.
19. "The Mulct Law: Is Vinton to Be Cursed with a Saloon?," *Vinton Eagle*, August 17, 1894.
20. Alexander D. Noyes, "The Banks and the Panic of 1893," *Political Science Quarterly* 9, no. 1 (1894): 12–30.
21. Donald L. McMurray, *Coxey's Army, a Study of the Industrial Army Movement of 1894* (Boston: Little Brown, 1929).

22. McMurray, *Coxey's Army.*
23. Jack London, "Tramping with Kelly through Iowa: A Jack London Diary," in *Palimpsest* 7, ed. John Ely Briggs, May 1926, 129–58.
24. McMurray, *Coxey's Army.*
25. "Kelley's Industrial Army," *Muscatine Journal,* April 20, 1894.
26. "A Speck of War," *Muscatine Journal,* April 14, 1894.
27. "A Silly Move," *Cedar Rapids Gazette,* April 17, 1894.
28. London, "Tramping with Kelly through Iowa," 129–58.
29. "A Frigid Mecca," *Cedar Rapids Gazette,* April 30, 1894; Charmain London, *The Book of Jack London* (New York: Century, 1921).
30. "State of Iowa," Terrace Hill, https://terracehill.iowa.gov/.
31. Ralph Mills Sayre, "Albert Baird Cummins and the Progressive Movement in Iowa" (PhD diss., Columbia University, 1958); "Gear, John," *The Biographical Dictionary of Iowa* (Iowas City: University of Iowa Press and the University of Iowa Libraries), http:// http://uipress.lib.uiowa.edu/bdi/DetailsPage.aspx?id=138.
32. David Hurwitz, *Dvorak* (Pompton Plains NJ: Amadeus, 2005); "Joseph Kovarik, Friend of Anton Dvorak, Is Dead," *Cedar Rapids Gazette,* February 28, 1951.
33. "To Those Who Have Taken," *Guardian,* October 24, 1892.
34. "The Deal that Brought Dvorak to New York," *New York Times,* August 23, 2003.
35. Hurwitz, *Dvorak.*
36. "Joseph Kovarik, Friend of Anton Dvorak, Is Dead."
37. "Honor to a Master," *Saint Paul Globe,* September 6, 1893.
38. Juanita J. Loven, *Dvorak in Spillville: 100 Days, 100 Years Ago* (Spillville IA: Spillville Historical Action Group, 1993).
39. Michael Beckerman, "Henry Krehbiel, Antonín Dvořák, and the Symphony 'From the New World,'" *Notes* 49, no. 2 (1992): 447–73, https://doi.org/10.2307/897884.
40. "Anton Dvorak," *Des Moines Register,* May 5, 1904.
41. "World's Most Haunting Tune Written in Iowa," *Des Moines Register,* February 5, 1922; "Freeman Conaway Dies Here," *Cedar Rapids Gazette,* July 27, 1923.
42. "'Humoresque' Will Lure a Salty Tear at the Criterion," *New York Daily News,* May 31, 1920.
43. "World's Most Haunting Tune Written in Iowa"; "Freeman Conaway Dies Here."
44. "Joseph Kovarik, Friend of Anton Dvorak, Is Dead"; Hurwitz, *Dvorak,* 50, 109, 110.

8. GOD HATES THE FOUR-FLUSHER

1. Jim Murray, "USC-UCLA: This Isn't a Rivalry, It's a Revolution," *Los Angeles Times*, November 23, 1986.
2. Kyle Munson, "Birthplace a Testament to His Down-Home Charm," *Des Moines Register*, September 30, 2012.
3. Mark Feeney, "Bob Feller, 92, Hall of Famer Had Blazing Fastball," *Boston Globe*, December 16, 2010.
4. "Cap Anson," Baseball Reference, https://www.baseball-reference.com/players/a/ansonca01.shtml and https://www.baseball-reference.com/managers/ansonca01.shtml.
5. David Pietrusza, Matthew Silverman, and Michael Gershman, *Baseball: The Biographical Encyclopedia* (New York: Total Sports, 2000), 29–31.
6. David Zang, "Fleet Walker's Divided Heart" (Lincoln: University of Nebraska Press, 1995).
7. Lyle W. Dorsett, "Billy Sunday," *American National Biography*, 21: 150–52.
8. Willam Ellis, *Billy Sunday, The Man and His Message* (Philadelphia: International Bible, 1914).
9. "Billy Sunday," Baseball Reference, https://www.baseball-reference.com/register/player.fcgi?id=sunday001bil.
10. Roger A. Burns, *Preacher* (New York: W. W. Norton, 1972).
11. Ellis, *Billy Sunday*.
12. Burns, *Preacher*.
13. "Billy Sunday."
14. Ellis, *Billy Sunday*.
15. "City Real Estate," *Chicago Tribune*, April 3, 1890.
16. Burns, *Preacher*.
17. Ross A. Purdy, "The Development of John Wilbur Chapman's Life and Thought" (PhD diss., University of Stirling, Scotland, July 2016).
18. Ellis, *Billy Sunday*.
19. Ellis, *Billy Sunday*.
20. Laws of the Twenty-Ninth General Assembly, Chapter 93, State of Iowa, April 1902, 58.
21. "Case of Inebriates," *Ottumwa Tri-Weekly*, November 27, 1902.
22. "Case of Inebriates."
23. "More Room Needed," *Ottumwa Daily Courier*, January 3, 1903.
24. "All Dipsos to Be Rounded Up," *Muscatine News-Tribune*, November 25, 1905.
25. Tony Leys, "This Iowa Government Building Used to Be Called the Booz-itorium," *Des Moines Register*, October 25, 2017.

26. Joyce McKay, "Reforming Prisoners and Prisons: Iowa's State Prisons—The First Hundred Years," *Annals of Iowa* 60, no. 2 (Spring 2001): 139–73.
27. P. L. Bryan, "John Wesley Elkins, Boy Murderer," *Annals of Iowa* 69, no. 3 (2010): 261–307.
28. Bryan, "John Wesley Elkins, Boy Murderer."
29. "Fight Elkins Pardon Case," *Waterloo Courier*, January 24, 1902.
30. Bryan, "John Wesley Elkins, Boy Murderer."
31. Bryan, "John Wesley Elkins, Boy Murderer."
32. "Elkins Gets His Parole," *Audubon County Journal*, April 10, 1902; "Elkins Parole," *Oskaloosa Herald*, April 24, 1902.
33. Bryan, "John Wesley Elkins, Boy Murderer."
34. Daniel J. Kevles, "The History of Eugenics," *Issues in Science and Technology* 32, no. 3 (2016): 45–50.
35. S. W. Tracy, "Contesting Habitual Drunkenness: State Medical Reform for Iowa's Inebriates, 1902–1920," *Annals of Iowa* 61, no. 3 (2002): 241–85; "Would Make Liquor Law More Definite," *Davenport Daily Times*, March 28, 1911.
36. "Dr. Harry H. Laughlin," *New York Times*, January 28, 1943; "Harry Laughlin and Eugenics," Harry H. Laughlin Papers, Truman State University, Kirksville, Missouri.

9. A KILL FEE

1. "The Rock Island News," *Rock Island Argus*, March 6, 1905.
2. Bill Wundram, "Who Was RI crime Boss John Looney?" *Quad-City Times* (Davenport IA), July 7, 2002.
3. Richard Hamer and Roger Ruthhart, *Citadel of Sin: The John Looney Story* (Moline IL: Moline Publishing, 2007).
4. Hamer and Ruthhart, *Citadel of Sin.*
5. "Rowdies and Police Break Up Convention," *Rock Island Argus*, March 21, 1904.
6. J. W. Potter, "Anarchy and Lawlessness vs. Law and Order," *Rock Island Argus*, March 22, 1904.
7. "34 Indictments against Looney for Libel, Extortion and Bribery," *Rock Island Argus*, June 18, 1907; Hamer and Ruthhart, *Citadel of Sin.*
8. "Pulls Gun When Taken to Task," *Rock Island Argus*, September 21, 1911.
9. Kerry Schmidt, "John Looney Made R.I. Roar in 20s," *Moline Dispatch*, September 24, 1978.
10. "One Dead, Nine Wounded, in Battle with the City Police," *Rock Island Argus*, March 27, 1912.

11. Clark Evan Ramser, "The Devil's Crowd: The John Looney Syndicate" (Master's these, Western Illinois University, 2016).
12. "Mayor Schriver, Cox and Pedigo Guilty; Go to Pen," *Rock Island Argus*, April 7, 1923; "Looney Guilty of Conspiracy, Gets Prison Term; Jailed for Contempt," *Rock Island Argus*, July 31, 1925; "Looney Guilty of Murder," *Rock Island Argus*, December 23, 1925; "John P. Looney Is Ready to Be Given Parole on April 8," *Belleville Daily Advocate*, March 8, 1934; Hamer and Ruthhart, *Citadel of Sin*.
13. "Negros Are Nearly Lynched by Angry Mob," *Des Moines Register*, July 17, 1906.
14. "Negro Admits That He Held Girl Up," *Des Moines Register*, June 10, 1906; "Le Mars Crowd May Lynch Negro," *Des Moines Register*, June 8, 1906; "Crowd Threatens Lynching," *Des Moines Register*, June 25, 1906; "Shoots in Crowded Car," *Cedar Falls Gazette*, July 3, 1906.
15. "Negros Are Nearly Lynched by Angry Mob."
16. "Brown Denounces Mob Demonstration," *Des Moines Register*, July 18, 1906.
17. "Samuel Brown," *The Biographical Dictionary of Iowa* (Iowa City: University of Iowa Press and the University of Iowa Libraries), http://uipress.lib.uiowa.edu/bdi/DetailsPage.aspx?id=45; "George Henry Woodson," *The Biographical Dictionary of Iowa*.
18. Leola Nelson Berman, "The Negro of Iowa," *Iowa Journal of History and Politics* (1948).
19. "S. Joe Brown," *The Goldfinch* 16, no. 4 (Summer 1995): 7; U.S. Census, 1890; W. J. Warren, "Evangelical Paternalism and Divided Workers: The Nonunion Era at John Morrell and Company in Ottumwa, 1877–1917," *Annals of Iowa* 56, no. 4 (1997): 321–48.
20. R. M. Breaux, "'We Were All Mixed Together': Race, Schooling, and the Legacy of Black Teachers in Buxton, 1900–1920," *Annals of Iowa* 65, no. 4 (2006): 301–28.
21. "S. Joe Brown," *The Goldfinch* 16, no. 4 (Summer 1995): 7.
22. "George Henry Woodson," *The Biographical Dictionary of Iowa* (Iowa City: University of Iowa Press and the University of Iowa Libraries), http://uipress.lib.uiowa.edu/bdi/DetailsPage.aspx?id=45.
23. Breaux, "'We Were All Mixed Together,'" 301–28.
24. "Negress Acquitted at Albia," *Des Moines Register*, February 18, 1906.
25. State v. Hesse, Iowa Supreme Court, October 19, 1915; State v. Watkins, Iowa Supreme Court, June 9, 1910.
26. "Humburd Given a Verdict for $50," *Des Moines Register*, May 7, 1904; "Levy on His Horse," *The Bystander*, July 15, 1904; Humburd v. Crawford et al., Iowa Supreme Court, November 15, 1905.

27. "Samuel Brown," *The Biographical Dictionary of Iowa* (Iowa City: University of Iowa Press and the University of Iowa Libraries), http://uipress.lib.uiowa.edu/bdi/DetailsPage.aspx?id=45.
28. "Sends Children to School," *Sioux City Journal*, November 11, 1906; "Effect of the Pure Food Law," *Waterloo Courier*, October 26, 1906.
29. Leland L. Sage, *A History of Iowa* (Ames: Iowa State University Press, 1974), 235.
30. Sage, *A History of Iowa*, 237.
31. John H. White, "The Railroad Pass: Perk or Plunder?" *Railroad History*, no. 182 (2000): 58–71; *Iowa Journal of the Senate* (State of Iowa, January 8, 1906).
32. "Inaugural of Gov. Cummins," *Sioux Valley News*, January 23, 1902.
33. "An Anti-primary Opinion," *Sioux City Journal*, January 17, 1906.
34. "The Message," *Des Moines Register*, January 9, 1906.
35. Grieder, "Standpatters versus Progressives" (Master's thesis, University of Nebraska at Omaha, 2017).
36. F. E. Horack, "Primary Elections in Iowa," in *Proceedings of the American Political Science Association* 7 (1910): 175–86, https://doi.org/10.2307/3038354; "Gov. Cummins for Senate," *Quad-City Times* (Davenport IA), May 29, 1907.
37. "More Prohibition Counties in Iowa," *Des Moines Register*, January 5, 1907.
38. Herman E. Bateman, "Albert B. Cummins and the Davenport 'Riots' of 1907," *Journal of the Southwest* 1 (Summer 1976): 111–24.
39. "Two Attempts to Burn Home in Burlington," *Des Moines Register*, January 14, 1907; "Marshal Bill Is Out for Passage," *Des Moines Register*, February 26, 1907; "Seeks to Enjoin 79 Saloonkeepers," *Des Moines Register*, May 1, 1907.
40. Bateman, "Albert B. Cummins and the Davenport 'Riots' of 1907," 111–24.
41. "Twenty-Seven Saloons are Threatened with Injunctions," *Davenport Democrat*, August 4, 1907; "Injunction Suits Are Filed Today," *Quad-City Time* (Davenport IA), August 13, 1907.
42. "German-Americans of Davenport Join in Monster Demonstration," *Quad-City Times* (Davenport IA), August 16, 1907.
43. Bateman, "Albert B. Cummins and the Davenport 'Riots' of 1907," 111–24.
44. "Cummins and Funk," *Sioux City Journal*, October 22, 1907.
45. Bateman, "Albert B. Cummins and the Davenport 'Riots' of 1907," 111–24.
46. Sage, *A History of Iowa*, 240–41.

10. THE SUFFRAGISTS

1. *Worship Material to Mark the Centenary of the Induction of Gertrude Von Petzhold as England's First Woman Minister*, Worship Panel of the General Assembly

of Unitarian and Free Christian Churches, 1904; "Society Events," *Des Moines Register*, December 24, 1908.

2. Laura E. Nym Mayhall, "Defining Militancy: Radical Protest, the Constitutional Idiom, and Women's Suffrage in Britain, 1908–1909," *Journal of British Studies* 39, no. 3 (2000): 340–71.
3. "Insists on Distinction," *Des Moines Register*, January 16, 1909.
4. "Senate Recedes on Graft Jobs," *Marshalltown Evening Times-Republican*, January 19, 1907.
5. "Suffragists in Great Parade," *Muscatine Journal*, October 30, 1908.
6. "House Arranges to Hear Contests," *Marshalltown Evening Times-Republican*, January 12, 1909.
7. "Rate Bills Pass Senate," *Sioux City Journal*, January 17, 1909.
8. "Women Suffrage Is Not," *Cedar Rapids Gazette*, October 28, 1908.
9. Sara Egge, *Woman Suffrage and Citizenship in the Midwest, 1870–1920* (Iowa City: University of Iowa Press, 2018).
10. Thomas G. Ryan, "Male Opponents and Supporters of Woman Suffrage: Iowa 1916," *Annals of Iowa* 45, no. 7 (1981): 537–50.
11. William L. O'Neill, "The Fight for Suffrage," *Wilson Quarterly* 10, no. 4 (1986): 99–109; Egge, *Woman Suffrage and Citizenship in the Midwest.*
12. "Suffrage Bill Killed," *Des Moines Register*, March 12, 1909.
13. "An English Woman's View," *Des Moines Register*, March 14, 1909.
14. "Women Plan War on State Senate," *Des Moines Register*, March 15, 1909.
15. "Whipple Defends Fellow Senators," *Des Moines Register*, March 22, 1909.
16. "To Debate on Suffrage," *Des Moines Tribune*, June 21, 1909.
17. "Vast Crowd Hears Debate," *Des Moines Tribune*, July 9, 1909.
18. "Here's the Real Enemy of Equal Suffrage," *Des Moines Register*, December 29, 1909; "Ezra Simpkins Will Not Debate," *Des Moines Tribune*, January 4, 1910.
19. "Women Launch Campaign," *Des Moines Register*, March 4, 1910.
20. Libby Jean Cavanaugh, "Opposition to Female Enfranchisement: The Iowa Anti-Suffrage Movement" (Master's thesis, Iowa State University, 2007), 34–57.
21. "Unknown Springs Surprise on Sex," *Des Moines Register*, March 7, 1911.
22. "M'Manus Opposes Equal Suffrage," *Keokuk Daily Gate*, March 22, 1911.
23. "Senate Opposed Equal Suffrage," *Des Moines Register*, March 22, 1911.
24. Tom Lewis, *Divided Highways* (New York: Viking, 1997).
25. "Combination Tax Passed by Senate," *Des Moines Register*, April 6, 1911; Leo Landis, *Building Better Roads: Iowa's Contribution to Highway Engineering* (Ames: Iowa State University Center for Transportation Research and Education, 1997).

26. "Treat Autoists Leniently," *Decorah Public Opinion*, July 19, 1911.
27. William Lind, "Thomas H. MacDonald: A Study of the Career of an Engineer Administrator and His Influence on Public Roads in the United States" (Master's thesis, American University, 1966), 24–30.
28. "Hard Trip to Davenport," *Des Moines Register*, June 9, 1912.
29. Lind, "Thomas H. MacDonald."
30. Tom Lewis, *Divided Highways: Building the Interstate Highways, Transforming American Life* (New York: Penguin, 1999).
31. Lind, "Thomas H. MacDonald."
32. "Thomas MacDonald," *The Biographical Dictionary of Iowa* (Iowa City: University of Iowa Press and the University of Iowa Libraries), http://uipress.lib.uiowa.edu/bdi/DetailsPage.aspx?id=241.
33. Lincoln Highway Association, https://www.lincolnhighwayassoc.org/history/.
34. Earl Swift, *The Big Roads* (New York: Houghton Mifflin Harcourt, 2011), 36. There was no drivable route from Omaha to Wyoming: "The agent led him [Joy] out of town to a wire fence and told him to take it down and drive on to the next fence and likewise after that. Soon enough the fences have given way to open prairie and Joy soon found himself surrounded by broken planks, rusty bits of iron, fossils of the previous century's wagon trains."
35. "Rival Routes Seek National Highway," *Des Moines Register*, August 10, 1913.
36. "Lincoln Highway Will Cross Iowa," *Des Moines Register*, September 14, 1913.

11. LAST CALL IN MARSHALLTOWN

1. Hazel Barnes, "Billy Sunday's Visit to Spokane Is Recalled," *Spokane Chronicle*, February 16, 1969.
2. "Letter from Ex-Convict Alarms 'Billy' Sunday," *Butte Miner*, January 1, 1909; "Sea for Sunday Party," *Los Angeles Times*, February 9, 1909.
3. "Jail, then Asylum for Bill Sunday's Foe," *Spokane Chronicle*, March 4, 1909.
4. "Saloon Nearest Neighbor to Sunday's Tabernacle," *Boston Globe*, May 3, 1916; "News of the Churches," *Wichita Eagle*, February 11, 1912; "Churchmen Break Ground on Sunday Tabernacle," *Los Angeles Express*, June 4, 1917; "20,000 Attend Sunday Tabernacle," *Baltimore Sun*, February 21, 1916.
5. William Ellis, *Billy Sunday, The Man and His Message* (Philadelphia: International Bible, 1914).
6. "Sunday Is Coming," *Marshalltown Evening Times-Republican*, November 12, 1908.

7. "Billy Sunday and Marshalltown," *Muscatine Journal,* June 15, 1909; "Tabernacle Notes," *Marshalltown Evening Times-Republican,* April 17, 1909.
8. "Sunday Opens Revival with Great Sermons," *Marshalltown Evening Times-Republican,* April 26, 1909.
9. "Interviewer," *Des Moines Register,* April 29, 1909.
10. Ellis, *Billy Sunday.*
11. "Sunday Opens Revival with Great Sermons."
12. "Volunteers at Work," *Marshalltown Evening Times-Republican,* June 14, 1909; "Suits to Close Six More Saloons," *Marshalltown Evening Times-Republican,* June 30, 1909.
13. "Anti-Saloon League Denies," *Des Moines Tribune,* July 24, 1909.
14. "Saloon Case to Higher Court," *Keokuk Daily Gate,* June 28, 1910.
15. Harvey Graeme Furbay, "The Anti-Saloon League," *North American Review* 177, no. 562 (1903): 434–39.
16. Daniel Okrent, *Last Call* (New York: Scribner, 2010), 39–40.
17. "To Enforce New Liquor Ruling," *Des Moines Tribune,* June 12, 1911; "Liquor Cases against Druggists Being Tried," *Cedar Rapids Gazette,* September 14, 1911.
18. "Only 700 Bars in Iowa," *Marshalltown Evening Times-Republican,* July 1, 1911.
19. "Dry Forces Hope to Get Amendment," *Quad-City Times* (Davenport IA), March 10, 1910; "Preparing Large Petition," *Sioux City Journal,* November 18, 1910.
20. "Debate Liquor Question," *Des Moines Register,* March 14, 1910.
21. "Prohibition the Issue of 1911," *New York Times,* July 16, 1911; "Women's Suffrage in the U.S. by State," Center for American Women and Politics, 2014, https://tag.rutgers.edu/wp-content/uploads/2014/05/suffrage-by-state.pdf.
22. "Colonel Eiboeck Sends a Message," *Quad-City Times* (Davenport IA), April 10, 1910.
23. "Iowa Senate Has Shut Out Prohibition," *Davenport Daily Times,* April 1, 1909; "Prohibition Amendment Is Defeated," *Des Moines Tribune,* March 15, 1911.
24. "Suffrage Workers Will Visit House," *Des Moines Register,* February 20, 1913.
25. "Brilliant Gallery of Suffragettes Witness Victory for Amendment," *Des Moines Register,* February 20, 1913.
26. "Suffrage Bill Wins After Fierce Battle," *Muscatine Journal,* March 8, 1913.

12. THE HYPHENATED AMERICANS

1. Josh Wilson, "The Blizzard," *Cedar Rapids Gazette,* August 7, 1913.

2. "Iowa in Billion Dollar Class by Herself in 1914," *Des Moines Register*, October 18, 1914.
3. "Farm Sold Twice," *Des Moines Register*, August 4, 1912.
4. "Sale Makes Record," *Marshalltown Evening Times-Republican*, November 7, 1913.
5. "Three Elements in Land Prices," *Denison Review*, January 28, 1914.
6. Leland L. Sage, *A History of Iowa* (Ames: Iowa State University Press, 1974), 249.
7. "Wilson No Teetotaler," *New York Times*, September 9, 1913.
8. "Four States Go Dry Out of Six Voting," *New York Times*, November 5, 1914; "Prohibition Beaten in House," *New York Times*, December 23, 1914.
9. "Demand Pledges for Amendment," *Des Moines Register*, January 30, 1914.
10. "Dry Roundup to Choose Candidate," *Des Moines Register*, August 31, 1914.
11. "Myers Will Make Active Campaign," *Des Moines Register*, September 7, 1914; "Dry Roundup to Choose Candidate," *Des Moines Register*, August 31, 1914.
12. "Convention Passes Resolutions," *Webster City Freeman*, October 13, 1914.
13. "Harding Choice Displeases Drys," *Des Moines Register*, January 20, 1915.
14. "No Secret Vote on Liquor," *Davenport Daily Times*, January 28, 1915; "Senate Votes for Dry Iowa; House to Follow," *Des Moines Register*, February 13, 1915; "Cosson Plans to Enforce the Law," *Muscatine Journal*, February 16, 1915; "Radicals Seek Stringent Law," *Cedar Rapids Gazette*, February 18, 1915; "Rumbling Beer Wagons Break Capital Sleep," *Cedar Rapids Evening Republican*, February 13, 1915.
15. "Senate Votes for Dry Iowa; House to Follow"; "Cosson Plans to Enforce the Law"; "Radicals Seek Stringent Law"; "Rumbling Beer Wagons Break Capital Sleep."
16. "Flora Dunlap Dies Wednesday in Residence," *Circleville Herald*, August 27, 1952; Louise Noun, "Carrie Chapman Catt," in *Patterns and Perspectives in Iowa History*, ed. Dorothy Schwieder (Ames: Iowa State University Press, 1973), 283–322.
17. "School of Suffrage," *Keokuk Daily Gate*, February 5, 1914.
18. "Women Confident of Their Victory," *Keokuk Daily Gate*, May 27, 1914.
19. "Cause of Suffrage Now up to Voters," *Des Moines Register*, February 24, 1915; "Stand for Mulct Law," *Marshalltown Evening Times-Republican*, July 16, 1914.
20. "Week's Exports $70 Million," *New York Times*, December 12, 1915.
21. "Brisk Trade in Munitions of War," *New York Times*, June 14, 1915.
22. Clifton J. Child, "German-American Attempts to Prevent the Exportation of Munitions of War, 1914–1915," *Mississippi Valley Historical Review* 25, no. 3 (1938): 351–68.

23. Sage, *A History of Iowa*, 253.
24. Iowa Census, 1915.
25. "Not Violation of Neutrality Is Decision," *Meriden Daily Journal*, September 3, 1914.
26. "Will See Bryan About Ammunition Shipments," *Washington Evening Star*, September 2, 1914. "House Committee Will Ask Ruling on Sale of American War Supplies," *Washington Post*, September 2, 1914.
27. Child, "German-American Attempts to Prevent the Exportation of Munitions of War," 351–68.
28. "A Gift for Germany," *Nebraska State Journal*, September 3, 1911.
29. William S. Allen, *Iowa Official Register, 1913–1914* (Des Moines: Robert Henderson, State Printer, 1913); "Congressman Pepper Dies at Clinton Hospital," *Davenport Daily Times*, December 22, 1913; "Harry E. Hull Again Candidate for Congress," *Quad-City Times* (Davenport IA), April 8, 1914.
30. "Henry Vollmer," U.S. Census, 1870; "Henry Vollmer," *Annals of Iowa* 17 no. 6 (1930): 472–73.
31. "Vollmer Will Retire," *Cedar Rapids Gazette*, April 13, 1914.
32. "Think War Would Be Disastrous," *Davenport Daily Times*, July 30, 1914.
33. "Local Germans Raise Big Fund for Red Cross," *Davenport Daily Times*, August 10, 1914; "To Raise $25,000 Relief Fund for German People," *Quad-City Times* (Davenport IA), August 10, 1914; "Claims England Is Responsible for Great War," *Quad-City Times* (Davenport IA), August 17, 1914.
34. Child, "German-American Attempts to Prevent the Exportation of Munitions of War," 351–68.
35. "Aid to Germans in Canada," *New York Times*, November 17, 1914; "Sees German Hand in Plan to Put Embargo on Arms," *New York Sun*, December 15, 1914.
36. "Maurice Leon, French Official at New York, Brings Wife to Her Native City," *San Francisco Chronicle*, August 18, 1912.
37. "Aid to Germans in Canada"; "Sees German Hand in Plan to Put Embargo on Arms."
38. "Three Give Hot Reply," *Washington Post*, December 11, 1914.
39. "Folk Rumor Hits Stone," *St. Louis Globe-Democrat*, November 7, 1912; "Letter to the Chairman of the Senate Committee on Foreign Relations (January 20, 1915)," Teaching American History, https://teachingamericanhistory.org/document/letter-to-the-chairman-of-the-senate-committee-on-foreign-relations/.
40. "This Nation Fair to All Fighters, Bryan Asserts," *New York Times*, January 25, 1915.

41. "U.S. Owes It to Self-Respect to Act, Says Roosevelt," *New York Tribune*, May 8, 1915.
42. "The President's Address," *Quad-City Times* (Davenport IA), May 11, 1915.
43. "Always Criminal," *Des Moines Register*, May 9, 1915.
44. "Words of Approval," *Des Moines Register*, May 12, 1915.
45. "Holding Up Wilson's Hands," *Sioux City Journal*, May 11, 1915.
46. "J. P. Morgan Shot by Teacher of German Who Put Dynamite Bomb in the Capitol," *New York Sun*, July 4, 1915.
47. "Enforcing Peace," *Kansas Scammon Miner*, August 20, 1915; Brigit Farley, "We the People Civics Lessons: Why Did the United States Enter World War I?," *Spokane Spokesman-Review*, April 18, 2021.
48. "'Shoot Them in the Back' Says Mr. Roosevelt," *Mt. Vernon Daily Argus*, August 26, 1915.
49. "Roosevelt Assails Pacifists, Others Who Would Refuse to Sell Supplies to Help Revenge Belgium," *Muncie Morning Star*, September 25, 1915.
50. "German Arms Plot Seen by Roosevelt," *New York Times*, September 23, 1915.
51. "The Hyphen," *Des Moines Register*, November 12, 1915.
52. Richard Striner, *Woodrow Wilson and World War I* (Lanham MD: Rowman & Littlefield, 2014).
53. "Wilson's New Front," *Des Moines Register*, November 6, 1915.
54. "Uncle Joe Is Right," *Des Moines Tribune*, December 9, 1915.

13. WET TO DRY AGAIN

1. "Great Production Seen at Palace," *Muscatine Journal*, February 15, 1915; Christopher Beach, *A Hidden History of Film Style* (Berkeley: University of California Press, 2015), 37.
2. John Hope Franklin, "'Birth of a Nation': Propaganda as History," *Massachusetts Review* 20, no. 3 (1979): 417–34.
3. David Rylance, "Breech Birth: The Reception to D. W. Griffith's 'The Birth of a Nation,'" *Australasian Journal of American Studies* 24, no. 2 (2005): 1–20.
4. "Wilson's Daughters Give 'Movie' Show," *San Francisco Examiner*, February 19, 1915.
5. "The Clansman," *Des Moines Register*, February 17, 1906.
6. "The Color of Villains," *Quad-City Times* (Davenport IA), June 7, 1915.
7. "Vicious Picture Film Condemned by Censors," *New York Age*, March 4, 1915.
8. "Hurls Eggs at Film," *Newport News Daily Press*, April 18, 1915.
9. "Good Authority," *Des Moines Register*, April 22, 1915.

10. "Rock Island, Ill.," *Iowa Bystander*, June 18, 1915.
11. "The World's Mightiest Spectacle," *Sioux City Journal*, November 14, 1915.
12. "The World's Mightiest Spectacle"; "The Birth of a Nation," *Sioux City Journal*, November 22, 1915.
13. "Photo Play Will Stand," *Sioux City Journal*, November 23, 1915.
14. "The Birth of a Nation," *Bystander*, January 28, 1916.
15. "Thompson, John Lay," *Biographical Dictionary of Iowa* (Iowa City: University of Iowa Press), http://uipress.lib.uiowa.edu/bdi/DetailsPage.aspx?id=377.
16. "The Birth of a Nation," *Iowa Bystander*, February 11, 1916.
17. "Want State Board of Movie Censors," *Des Moines Register*, March 11, 1916.
18. "Council Bars Film Show by Four to One," *Des Moines Tribune*, April 21, 1916.
19. "Prohibited Film to Be Exhibited," *Des Moines Register*, April 23, 1916.
20. "Police Arrest 3 Men," *Des Moines Register*, May 1, 1916.
21. "Five Men Condemn Nation Photoplay," *Des Moines Register*, May 5, 1916; "Too Much of Dixie in Nation Movie," *Des Moines Register*, May 6, 1916; "Nugent Indorses 'Birth of Nation,'" *Des Moines Register*, May 9, 1916.
22. "Meyer Gives Screen Show a Clean Bill," *Des Moines Tribune*, May 11, 1916.
23. "Came Back, Got Drunk," *Cedar Rapids Gazette*, July 31, 1906.
24. "Wants to Take the Cure," *Cedar Rapids Gazette*, April 11, 1911.
25. "Fined Extra for Making Protest," *Cedar Rapids Gazette*, November 5, 1913.
26. "The Day's Grist in Police Mill," *Cedar Rapids Gazette*, January 3, 1916.
27. "Debaucher Gets 20 Years," *Sioux City Journal*, May 2, 1915.
28. "Gay 'Masher' Lands in Jail," *Cedar Rapids Gazette*, December 9, 1910.
29. "Beer in Iowa Breweries," *Sioux City Journal*, January 2, 1916.
30. "Drunks Sentenced to Jail," *Des Moines Register*, December 27, 1915.
31. "Test of Liquor Law at Keokuk," *Quad-City Times* (Davenport IA), December 24, 1915.
32. "Repeal of Mulct Law Valid," *Keokuk Daily Gate*, June 30, 1916.
33. Carl Anthony, "Twentieth Century First Ladies and Liquor in the White House," National First Ladies Library, https://tinyurl.com/29vkv9ym.
34. Milton Cooper Jr., *Woodrow Wilson* (New York: Vintage, 2009), 308.
35. "Wilson to Tour U.S. on Defense," *Muncie Star Press*, January 20, 1916.
36. "Will Wilson Visit Us?," *Iowa City Press-Citizen*, January 22, 1916.
37. "Fix Details for Wilson's Visit to City," *Des Moines Tribune*, January 22, 1916.
38. "Many Calling for Plates at Wilson Dinner," *Des Moines Tribune*, January 24, 1916.
39. "Helen Keller, Here for Lecture Series," *Des Moines Tribune*, January 24, 1916.

40. "All Social Plans Defeated by Final Word from Wilson," *Des Moines Register*, January 26, 1916.
41. "How about Reception?" *Des Moines Register*, January 26, 1916.
42. "Biggest Torpedo that Can Spit at Warships," *Ottawa Journal*, January 5, 1916.
43. "Ice Over Des Moines; It Will Get Colder," *Des Moines Tribune*, January 29, 1916.
44. "President Leaves Chicago," *Marshalltown Evening Times-Republican*, February 1, 1916; "Four Additional Platform Talks Made," *Iowa City Press Citizen*, February 1, 1916.
45. "President Wilson Spends a Day Amid Peace Loving Iowans," *Des Moines Register*, February 2, 1916.
46. "Yes, One Person Saw President and Bride Dine at Chamberlain," *Des Moines Register*, February 2, 1916.
47. "Met by Immense Crowds," *Des Moines Register*, February 2, 1916.
48. "The Seeds Bears Fruit," *Muscatine Journal*, February 3, 1916.
49. "Just Where Suffrage Stands in the United States Today," *Boston Globe*, November 13, 1915.
50. "Increased Activity in Suffrage Case," *Des Moines Register*, January 23, 1916.
51. "Suffragists to Raise $25,000," *Iowa City Press-Citizen*, February 23, 1916.
52. "Former Iowan Will Talk in Opera House," *Ottumwa Tri-Weekly Courier*, May 23, 1916.
53. "Lack Muscle to Enforce Laws," *Ottumwa Semi-Weekly Courier*, May 25, 1916.
54. "Suffs Claim State by Good Majority," *Des Moines Register*, June 6, 1916; "Equal Suffrage Is Defeated in Iowa," *Des Moines Register*, June 7, 1916.
55. "Suffrage Forces in New Campaign," *Des Moines Register*, June 11, 1916.

14. THE HANGINGS AT CAMP DODGE

1. "Iowa Training Camps," *Marshalltown Evening Times-Republican*, March 29, 1917.
2. "Alien Enemies Must Go," *Des Moines Register*, April 25, 1917.
3. "Found Cache of Guns and Ammunition," *Quad-City Times* (Davenport IA), May 16, 1917.
4. Bernard Harris, "Chipping Away at the Bedrock of Racial Intolerance: Fort Des Moines and Black Officer Training, 1917–1918," *Annals of Iowa* 77, no. 3 (2018): 231–62.
5. Milton Cooper Jr., *Woodrow Wilson* (New York: Vintage, 2009), 408.
6. Harris, "Chipping Away at the Bedrock of Racial Intolerance," 231–62.
7. "At Fort Des Moines," *Des Moines Tribune*, June 1, 1917.

8. "Glad They Aren't at North Pole," *Quad-City Times* (Davenport IA), November 5, 1917; Matthew Lindaman, "Home Away from Home: The Camp Dodger Newspaper and the Promotion of Troop Morale, 1917–1919," *Annals of Iowa* 76, no. 4 (2017): 381–405.
9. "Opportunity and Responsibility," *Des Moines Register,* October 12, 1917.
10. Harris, "Chipping Away at the Bedrock of Racial Intolerance," 251.
11. "5 Negroes Assault White Girl," *Des Moines Tribune,* May 27, 1918.
12. "5 Negroes Assault White Girl."
13. "Negroes Are to Be Hung for Assault," *Des Moines Register,* July 5, 1918.
14. "Hang the Negro Rapist," *Marshalltown Evening Times-Republican,* May 28, 1918.
15. "Whole Army Division Sees Negroes Hanged," *New York Times,* July 6, 1918.
16. Petra DeWitt, "'Clear and Present Danger': The Legacy of the 1917 Espionage Act in the United States," *Historical Reflections/Réflexions Historiques* 42, no. 2 (2016): 115–133.
17. "Federal Authorities Arrest Daniel Wallace," *Quad-City Times* (Davenport IA), July 27, 1917.
18. "U.S. Grand Jury Holds Red Heart League Head and Other for Trial," *Davenport Daily Times,* August 2, 1917.
19. "Seize 8 in Raid," *Chicago Tribune,* June 15, 1917.
20. "Wallace's Speech Is Reviewed," *Quad-City Times* (Davenport IA), October 4, 1918.
21. "A Disgraceful Meeting," *Quad-City Times* (Davenport IA), July 26, 1917.
22. "Retake Six Prisoners," *Davenport Daily Times,* January 22, 1919.
23. "Retake Six Prisoners," *Davenport Daily Times.*
24. "Wallace's Speech Is Reviewed," *Quad-City Times* (Davenport IA), October 4, 1918.
25. "Dr. Matthey Is Granted Stay," *Davenport Daily Times,* November 29, 1921; "Dr. Matthey Is Granted Clemency," *Davenport Daily Times,* April 6, 1922.
26. "Good for Sutherland!" *Sioux City Journal,* January 11, 1918.
27. "Board to Drop German in the Grade Schools," *Davenport Daily Times,* February 12, 1918; "An Intellectual By-product of the War," *Boston Globe,* April 3, 1918.
28. "Iowa Newspapers," *Evening Times-Republican,* May 6, 1918; "German Language Gets Death Blow," *Muscatine News-Tribune,* May 25, 1918.
29. "Iowa State News," *Audubon County Journal,* June 27, 1918.
30. Ralph Mills Sayre, "Albert Baird Cummins and the Progressive Movement in Iowa" (PhD diss., Columbia University, 1958).
31. "Senator Cummins Finally for War," *Davenport Daily Times,* April 5, 1917.

32. "Iowa and the War," *Des Moines Register*, April 11, 1917.
33. "Big Parade to Precede Patriotic Meeting," *Davenport Daily Times*, April 11, 1917.
34. "Hall, James Norman," *Biographical Dictionary of Iowa* (Iowa City: University of Iowa Press), http://uipress.lib.uiowa.edu/bdi/DetailsPage.aspx?id=150.
35. Martin Gilbert, *The First World War* (New York: Henry Holt, 1994), 421.
36. George C. Herring, "'Glad I Was in It': An Iowa Doughboy in the Great War, 1918–1919," *Army History* 103 (2017): 6–23.
37. "Deaths," *Cedar Rapids Gazette*, November 27, 1978.
38. "Benton Sheriff as Klansman to Seek Place in Assembly," *Cedar Rapids Gazette*, February 6, 1926.
39. "Vietnam Veterans' Fears Still Surfacing," *Des Moines Register*, May 27, 1984.

15. SHOOTOUT AT THE CARBARN CAFÉ

1. "Eight Slain in Home While They Sleep," *New York Times*, June 11, 1912.
2. "Urges a State Police Force," *Waterloo Courier*, November 2, 1912.
3. "State Police Bill," *Sioux City Journal*, February 25, 1915.
4. "Minister Insists 'Let's Go' Motto Wrecking Homes," *Waterloo Courier*, September 16, 1925.
5. Douglas M. Wertsch, "Resisting the Wave: Rural Iowa's War against Crime, 1920–1941" (PhD diss., Iowa State University, 1992).
6. "Law Enforcers to Meet at Bluffs," *Des Moines Register*, July 15, 1921; "Organized to Protect Banks from Robbers," *Davenport Times*, August 5, 1920.
7. "What Happened to Them," *Des Moines Tribune*, January 19, 1959.
8. "James E. Risden, 87, Dies in D. M.," *Cedar Rapids Gazette*, April 7, 1961.
9. "May Face Murder Charge," *Sioux City Journal*, July 24, 1919.
10. Matthew Leimkuehler, "What to Know about Buddy Holly and 'The Day the Music Died' in Iowa," *Des Moines Register*, January 24, 2019.
11. Willis F. Forbes, "Mason City Tragedy Recalls Red Burzette's Reign of Terror," *Des Moines Register*, May 9, 1926.
12. "Sioux City Man Murdered," *Sioux City Journal*, March 30, 1919; "Burzette in $8,000 Raid," *Sioux City Journal*, July 24, 1919.
13. "Detective Killed," *Sioux City Journal*, July 23, 1939.
14. "Bank Is Robbed," *Marshalltown Evening Times-Republican*, October 22, 1919.
15. "Bank Robbers Shoot Way Out of Jail," *Sioux City Journal*, November 15, 1919.
16. "Bandits Are Caught Near Maurice, IA," *Sioux City Journal*, November 18, 1919.

17. "Get Off Light, Says Mann," *Sioux City Journal,* November 21, 1919.
18. "Bank Robbers Escape from Penitentiary," *Sioux City Journal,* December 26, 1920.
19. "Think Escaped Convicts Here; City Is Combed," *Des Moines Register,* January 1, 1921; "Two of Escaping Convicts Caught," *Des Moines Register,* April 23, 1921; "Bullet of Pal Kills O'Keefe, Iowa Bad Man," *Des Moines Register,* May 28, 1921; "Bank Bandit Is Captured," *Sioux City Journal,* October 9, 1921.
20. "Everett Burzette, Convicted Slayer, Escapes from Prison," *Mason City Globe-Gazette,* September 19, 1947; Everett Burzette, Iowa Register of Convicts, February 11, 1955.
21. "Pal of Tommy O'Connor Tells of Tierney Killing," *Chicago Tribune,* April 7, 1920; "Easy for Gangsters," *Chicago Tribune,* October 25, 1920.
22. "Slayer Suspect Kills Detective O'Neill," *Chicago Tribune,* March 24, 1921.
23. "Police Killed O'Neill, O'Connor Alibi in St. Paul," *Chicago Tribune,* July 29, 1921; "Tommy O'Connor Flees Jail," *Chicago Tribune,* December 12, 1921.
24. "Sheriffs Pick Up O'Connor Suspect Near Camp Dodge," *Des Moines Register,* February 16, 1922; "O'Connor Was in Des Moines," *Davenport Daily Times,* April 19, 1922; "Smiling Iowa Gunman in Eating House Here," *Des Moines Tribune,* November 22, 1922.
25. "Suicide of Farmer Due to Money Grief," *Des Moines Tribune,* June 15, 1921; "Father of Twelve Commits Suicide," Daily Nonpareil, Council Bluffs, August 28,1921; "Engages Room to Hang Self," *Des Moines Register,* March 1, 1923.
26. Leland L. Sage, "Rural Iowa in the 1920s and 1930s," *Annals of Iowa* 47, no. 2 (1983): 91–103; "Rail Rates Go Up Billion and Half," *Des Moines Register,* August 1, 1920.
27. "1920 Corn Crop to Be Largest Ever Produced," *Des Moines Register,* October 9, 1920.
28. "Expert Tells Why Iowa Needs Money," *Marshalltown Evening Times-Republican,* November 20, 1920.
29. Sarah Churchwell, *Behold America* (New York: Basic, 2018), 107.
30. "Dry Edicts Aids Public Health, Figure Shows," *Des Moines Register,* May 27, 1924; "Lindsey Declares Society Is Rocking Matrimonial Ship," *Waterloo Courier,* January 3, 1923.
31. "Wallace Advises Some Farmers to Burn Their Corn," *Waterloo Courier,* November 14, 1921.

16. AMERICA IS FOR AMERICANS

1. Thomas R. Pegram, *One Hundred Percent American: The Rebirth and Decline of the Ku Klux Klan in the 1920s* (Lanham MD: Rowman & Littlefield, 2011),

9–10; Dorothy Schwieder, "A Farmer and the Ku Klux Klan in Northern Iowa," *Annals of Iowa* 61 (Summer 2002): 298.

2. Pegram, *One Hundred Percent American.*
3. W. A. White, "Annihilate the Klan," *Emporia Gazette,* January 1, 1925.
4. Schwieder, "A Farmer and the Ku Klux Klan in Northwest Iowa," 286–320.
5. Linda Gordon, *The Second Coming of the kkk* (New York: Liveright, 2017), 226.
6. Gordon, *The Second Coming of the kkk.*
7. "Bogus Nun Helen Jackson," *Catholic Home,* December 22, 1923; "Helen Jackson Never Was a Nun," *Logansport Pharos Tribune,* November 3, 1924.
8. Pegram, *One Hundred Percent American.*
9. "Drys and Ku Klux Combine in Texas," *New York Times,* August 5, 1922. "Klan Nominee Wins by Overwhelming Majority in Texas," *Arkansas Democrat,* November 8, 1922.
10. "Young Arrested, Told to Stay out of Booze Raids," *Cedar Rapids Gazette,* January 10, 1924; Gordon, *The Second Coming of the kkk.*
11. Charles C. Alexander, *The Ku Klux Klan in the Southwest* (Lexington: University of Kentucky Press, 2016), 52; Pegram, *One Hundred Percent American,* 66; "Texarkana Negro Kidnaped by Mob," *Daily Arkansas Gazette,* January 9, 1922.
12. "(Bulletin)," *Munster Times,* November 7, 1922.
13. "Warning Posted by Ku-Klux-Klan," *Des Moines Tribune,* November 1, 1922; "That Big Billboard," *Des Moines Register,* November 7, 1922.
14. "How Ku Klux Klan in Five Years Grew to 500,000," *St. Louis Post-Dispatch,* September 6, 1921.
15. "Shadow of the Ku Klux Klan Grows in Congress and Nation," *New York Times,* December 10, 1922; "Klan Shadow Falls on Nation's Politics," *New York Times,* November 18, 1923.
16. "Sight Astonishes Capital," *New York Times,* August 9, 1925.
17. "Thousands Attend District Kloncave of Klan Here," *Dubuque Telegraph,* August 30, 1925.
18. Schwieder, "A Farmer and the Ku Klux Klan in Northwest Iowa," 298–99.
19. "Preacher Here Tells Why He Is a Ku-Kluxer," *Des Moines Register,* February 26, 1923.
20. "Klan Cross Blazes Near City Hall," *Des Moines Register,* February 9, 1924.
21. "Jenny and Garver Elected," *Des Moines Register,* April 1, 1924.
22. "Elliott Quits Pulpit after Row with Klan," *Des Moines Register,* September 26, 1925.
23. "Klan Initiates Big Class South of City," *Des Moines Register,* August 22, 1923; "Fiery Cross Stirs Near Riot," *Des Moines Register,* April 23, 1925. "Jenny to

Stand by His Officers," *Des Moines Register,* April 28, 1925; "Chief Will Not Make a Report," *Des Moines Register,* May 1, 1925; "Confesses to Building Fiery Cross," *Des Moines Register,* May 3, 1925.

24. "Klan Ceremony at Mt. Auburn," *Vinton Eagle,* October 26, 1923.
25. Edwin S. Shortess, "We Change Pilots," *Vinton Eagle,* November 6, 1923.
26. U.S. Census, 1880; Edwin S. Shortess, "The Eagle and the Klan," *Vinton Eagle,* August 5, 1924; "The Coolidge Platform," *Vinton Eagle,* August 8, 1924; "Someone Is Seeing Ghosts," *Vinton Eagle,* September 26, 1924. The August 5 report came with Shortless's byline and with a denial that the Klan had bought the paper or controlled it. He made a point, however, of calling the Klan a "great organization" and noted the "millions of hard working, thinking people" who had become members. The September article is an unsigned editorial that would have been approved, if not written by, Shortess. The piece came in response to an attack on a member of the Benton County Klan by the county's larger daily paper, the *Cedar Valley Times,* which was also considered to be a champion of the Democratic Party and anti-temperance policies, as opposed to the *Eagle*'s position as both Republican and decidedly "dry." Beyond the author's vigor in defending the Klan, it is important to note the reiteration of the Klan's widely disputed claim to not "cultivate or deal in hatred or divisions between races and religions."
27. Amity Shlaes, *Coolidge* (New York: Harper Collins, 2013), 114–24.
28. Churchwell, *Behold America,* 112, 143–46.
29. Edwin S. Shortess, "Restricted Immigration," *Vinton Eagle,* January 4, 1924.
30. Morain, "To Whom Much Is Given," in *Iowa History Reader,* ed. Marvin Bergman (Iowa City: University of Iowa Press, 1996), 299

17. COMES A KILLER

1. "First White Settlers Came to Benton Co. in 1837," *Waterloo Courier,* June 2, 1946.
2. Dick Woods, "Meet Vinton Industry No. 7: The Vinton Popcorn Company," *Cedar Valley Daily Times,* September 20, 1963.
3. *History of Benton County* (Chicago: Western Historical, 1878); "Real Estate Transfers," *Vinton Eagle,* September 7, 1870.
4. Morain, "To Whom Much Is Given," in *Iowa History Reader,* ed. Marvin Bergman (Iowa City: University of Iowa Press, 1996).
5. *Illustrated Souvenir of Vinton* (Vinton IA: The Booster Club, n.d.); Iowa Census, 1925.
6. Charlie Gehard, "Line Fence Lingo," *Cedar Valley Times,* March 1, 1974.
7. "Gun Club to Be Formed in Vinton," *Vinton Eagle,* February 2, 1916.

8. “Mortuary: Ensign Underwood,” *Vinton Review,* January 22, 1914.
9. “Nipped In the Bud,” *Vinton Semi-Weekly Eagle,* October 3, 1882.
10. “Miss Myrtle E. Underwood,” *Vinton Eagle,* March 4, 1904.
11. Leland L. Sage, “Rural Iowa in the 1920s and 1930s,” *Annals of Iowa* 47, no. 2 (1983): 328–29.
12. “Miss Myrtle E. Underwood.”
13. “Elson-Cook,” *Vinton Eagle,* February 7, 1906.
14. “Steve Cook,” U.S. Census, 1910.
15. “The City,” *Vinton Eagle,* September 10, 1907; “Brief Local,” *Vinton Eagle,* October 9, 1907.
16. “Man Dies in Salt Lake City,” *Tacoma Columbian,* September 14, 1951.
17. “Vinton Needs a Photographer,” *Quad-City Times* (Davenport IA), October 4, 1925.
18. “Vinton Young People Married,” *Vinton Review,* July 27, 1910.
19. “Sebern Bros. Sell Dray Line,” *Vinton Review,* February 22, 1911.
20. “Sebern Bros. Sell Dray Line.”
21. “Cook,” *Iowa, Deaths and Burials, 1850–1990,* no. 1871333.
22. “Clifford Cook,” U.S. Census, 1920.
23. U. S. Census, Iowa, 1920; *Vinton City Directory,* 1923; *Iowa Official Legislative Registry, 1921–1922;* Historic Tables of the Iowa Legislature, Party Affiliation of Legislators, 1838–2022.
24. “Call Husband, Slain Woman before Jury,” *Cedar Rapids Gazette,* September 11, 1925.
25. “Husband of Slain Vinton Woman Called before Coroner’s Inquest,” *Waterloo Courier,* September 11, 1925.
26. “Rum Must Go,” *Cedar Valley Times,* September 9, 1925.
27. “Call Husband, Slain Woman before Jury,” *Waterloo Courier;* State of Iowa v. C. B. Cook, no. 1585 (Vinton IA), September 30, 1925. This case, the prosecution of Clifford Cook for perjury, was the only criminal proceeding to come out of the Cook murder. John W. Tobin, *Tobin Tales* (Iowa City IA: Penfield, 1986), 98–99.
28. “Mrs. C. B. Cook Is Assassinated,” *Vinton Eagle,* September 9, 1925.
29. “Rum Must Go.”
30. Tobin, *Tobin Tales,* 94; State of Iowa v. Shorty Snader, no. 1573 (Vinton, IA), September Term 1925; State of Iowa v. Wayne “Shorty” Snader, no. 1574 (Vinton IA), September Term, 1925.
31. “Cook Murder Mystery Deepens,” *Cedar Rapids Gazette,* September 12, 1925; “Murder Linked with Vinton Crime,” *Waterloo Courier,* September 18, 1925; “Waterloo Knows Something of Rule of Gang and Gun,” *Waterloo Courier,* February 19, 1929.

32. "Much Building in La Porte City but Few Big Projects," *Waterloo Courier*, December 31, 1925.
33. "Business Locals," *Vinton Eagle*, September 6, 1921; Tobin, *Tobin Tales*, 94.
34. Tobin, *Tobin Tales*, 94.
35. State of Iowa v. Wayne K. Snader, no. 1574 (Vinton IA), September Term 1925.
36. "Arrest 7 in Effort to Solve Mystery of Mrs. Cook's Murder," *Des Moines Tribune*, September 10, 1925.
37. U.S. Census, 1930.
38. "Heat Records for September Broken, Mercury at 103," *Cedar Rapids Gazette*, September 3, 1925.
39. "Mrs. Clifford Cook Is Assassinated," *Vinton Eagle*, September 10, 1925; Tobin, *Tobin Tales*, 96; "Mrs. Clifford Cook, Arch Enemy of Bootleggers, Is Assassinated in Vinton Home Monday Night," *Des Moines Register*, September 8, 1925.
40. "Mrs. Clifford Cook Is Assassinated," *Vinton Eagle*, September 10, 1925; Tobin, *Tobin Tales*, 96; "Mrs. Clifford Cook, Arch Enemy of Bootleggers," *Des Moines Register*, September 7, 1925.
41. Tobin, *Tobin Tales*, 94–95; "Mrs. Clifford Cook Is Assassinated."
42. Myrtle Cook Certificate of Death, Iowa Department of Vital Statistics, September 10, 1925.
43. "Woman Dry Worker Murdered in Iowa," *New York Times*, September 9, 1925.

18. THE INVESTIGATION

1. J. D. Nichols's formal title was county attorney, but in Iowa that office prosecutes criminal cases.
2. "Mrs. Clifford Cook, Arch Enemy of Bootleggers, Is Assassinated in Vinton Home Monday Night," *Des Moines Register*, September 8, 1925.
3. "Iowa To Curb Crime Wave—Hammill," *Davenport Daily Times*, September 9, 1925.
4. "Hammond, Liquor Foe, Dies," *Des Moines Register*, July 21, 1940; Tobin, *Tobin Tales*, 97.
5. "Order Re-arrest of 'Tex' Maynard in Shooting at DeWitt," *Davenport Daily Times*, June 26, 1925.
6. "Woman Dry Worker Murdered in Iowa," September 9, 1925, *New York Times*.
7. Tobin, *Tobin Tales*, 94. State of Iowa v. Wayne K. Snader, no. 1573 (Vinton IA), October 12, 1925.
8. "Mrs. C. B. Cook Is Assassinated," *Vinton Eagle*, September 10, 1925.

9. Tobin, *Tobin Tales*, 98.
10. "Arrest 7 in Effort to Solve Mystery of Mrs. Cook's Murder," *Des Moines Tribune*, September 10, 1925; "G. K. Gilchrist Dies at Portland," *Cedar Valley Daily Times*, June 12, 1929.
11. "Arrest 7 in Effort to Solve Mystery of Mrs. Cook's Murder."
12. State of Iowa v. Wayne K. Snader, no. 1574 (Vinton IA), September Term 1925.
13. "Arrest 7 in Effort to Solve Mystery of Mrs. Cook's Murder"; "Adjourn Cook Murder Inquest," *Des Moines Tribune*, September 10, 1925.
14. "Adjourn Cook Murder Inquest," *Cedar Rapids Gazette*, September 15, 1925.
15. "New Christian Pastor Elected," *Vinton Eagle*, September 3, 1925.
16. "Round-Up of Klansmen Planned Following Confession at Inquest," *Los Angeles Times*, April 26, 1922; "Tense Night in Anaheim," *Los Angeles Times*, February 3, 1925.
17. Ralph Clements, "Masked Klansmen Bear Cook Casket," *Cedar Rapids Gazette*, September 10, 1925.
18. "Mrs. C. B. Cook Is Assassinated"; "To Question Husband of Slain Woman," *Iowa City Press-Citizen*, September 11, 1925.
19. "Vinton Woman in Confession," *Cedar Rapids Gazette*, September 23, 1925.
20. "Vinton Minister's Wife Admits Klan Query Authorship," *Waterloo Courier*, September 23, 1925.
21. John Boettiger, "Arrest Is Near to Solve Death of Dry Leader," *Chicago Tribune*, September 10, 1925.
22. Sandy Banisky, "Of Love and Sorrow in the Shadow of FDR," *Baltimore Sun*, December 9, 1978.
23. George Atkins to J. R. Risden, September 7, 1925, Iowa Department of Public Safety, Division of Criminal Investigation, "Cook Murder File, 1925."
24. "Husband of Slain Vinton Woman Called before Coroner's Inquest," *Cedar Rapids Courier*, September 11, 1925.
25. "Call Husband, Slain Woman before Jury," *Cedar Rapids Gazette*, September 11, 1925; State of Iowa v. C. B. Cook, no. 1585 (Vinton IA), September 30, 1925. This case, the prosecution of Clifford Cook for perjury, was the only criminal proceeding to come out of the Cook murder (Tobin, *Tobin Tales*, 98–99).
26. George Atkins to J. R. Risden, September 7, 1925.
27. "Arrest Cook upon Charge of Perjury," *Neenah, Wisconsin News-Record*, September 29, 1925.

28. George Atkins to J. R. Risden, September 22, 1925. Iowa Department of Public Safety, Division of Criminal Investigation, "Cook Murder File, 1925."
29. Tobin, *Tobin Tales*, 100.
30. Tobin, *Tobin Tales.*
31. Tobin, *Tobin Tales.*
32. "Husband Again Heard in Mrs. Cook's Killing," *New York Times*, September 15, 1925.
33. State of Iowa v. C. B. Cook, no. 1585 (Vinton IA), September 30, 1925.
34. "Judge Frees C. B. Cook in Perjury Case," *Des Moines Register*, April 12, 1926; "Man Dies in Salt Lake City," *Tacoma Columbian*, September 14, 1951.

19. THE PRIME SUSPECTS

1. "Whispered Name May Give Trace of Cook Slayer," *Muscatine Journal*, September 14, 1925.
2. "Adjourn Cook Murder Inquest," *Cedar Rapids Gazette*, September 15, 1925
3. "G. K. Gilchrist," U.S. Census, 1910; "Leases Commercial Café," *Vinton Eagle*, September 6, 1921.
4. "Arrest 7 In Effort to Solve Mystery of Mrs. Cook's Murder," *Des Moines Tribune*, September 10, 1925; U.S. World War II Draft Cards, 1940–1947, National Archives and Records Administration.
5. "Young Man Released from Prison to Wed Girl in Case," *Cedar Rapids Gazette*, November 7, 1918.
6. State of Iowa v. Harold Ponder, Jasper County District Court, October 17, 1919; "Harold Ponder," *Iowa, U.S. Consecutive Registers of Convicts, 1867–1970*, https://history.iowa.gov/content/consecutive-registers-0.
7. J. D. Nichols, Benton County Attorney, to James Risden, Chief of Iowa Bureau of Investigation, November 3, 1925. Iowa Department of Public Safety, Division of Criminal Investigation, "Cook Murder File, 1925."
8. J. D. Nichols, Benton County Attorney to J. D. Risden, Chief of Iowa Bureau of Investigation, November 9, 1925. Iowa Department of Public Safety, Division of Criminal Investigation. "Cook Murder File, 1925."
9. "Failed to Get Ponder in Cook Death Net," *Waterloo Courier*, November 16, 1925.
10. Harold Ponder, Standard Certificate of Death, March 3, 1926. *Iowa, U.S. Consecutive Registers of Convicts, 1867–1970*, https://history.iowa.gov/content/consecutive-registers-0.
11. U.S. World War I Draft Registration Cards: Eugene Moore, Andrew Malcom Harbour; Albert Hertske, U.S. Army Transport Service Record, June 1919, St. Nazaire, France.

12. "'High Binders' Beat Man at Clinton and Steal Car and Alcohol Worth $1500," *Quad-City Times* (Davenport IA), December 3, 1923.
13. "Booze Runner Claims Home in Sterling," *Sterling Daily Gazette*, May 19, 1925.
14. "Haffa Was Prohibition Agent, Says Cook," *Waterloo Courier*, March 16, 1927.
15. "Arrest Eugene Moore as Member of Clinton Auto Theft Gang," *Des Moines Register*, December 23, 1925.
16. "Waterloo Murder Linked with Vinton Crime," *Waterloo Courier*, September 18, 1925.
17. "Vinton Doubts Hertske Crime Is Cook Echo," *Quad-City Times* (Davenport IA), September 20, 1925.

20. WHO KILLED MRS. COOK?

1. Cynthia Grant Bowman and Ben Altman, "Wife Murder in Chicago: 1910–1930," *Journal of Criminal Law and Criminology (1973–)* 92, no. 3–4 (2002): 739–90.
2. Tobin, *Tobin Tales*, 102.
3. Tomas Cvrcek, "When Harry Left Sally: A New Estimate of Marital Disruption in the U.S., 1886–1948," *Demographic Research* 21 (2009): 719–58.
4. Unsigned note, Iowa Department of Public Safety, Division of Criminal Investigation, "Cook Murder File, 1925."
5. Tobin, *Tobin Tales*, 94–95
6. "Mrs. Corey Says Prosecution Has Ruined Chicagoan," *Waterloo Courier*, July 19, 1926.
7. "Collicott Worth $125,000 Reported," *Cedar Rapids Gazette*, March 24, 1924; "Local Fugitive Kills Policeman at Clinton," *Waterloo Courier*, August 4, 1926.
8. "Prohibition: A Wild Time," *Cedar Rapids Gazette*, January 16, 1981.

Index

www.ingramcontent.com/pod-product-compliance
Lightning Source LLC
Chambersburg PA
CBHW021528120125
19971CB00007B/3
9781496235848